SIX CONVERSATIONS WE'RE SCARED TO HAVE

Also by Deborah Frances-White

The Guilty Feminist

SIX CONVERSATIONS WE'RE SCARED TO HAVE

Deborah Frances-White

virago

VIRAGO

First published in Great Britain in 2025 by Virago Press

1 3 5 7 9 10 8 6 4 2

A CIP catalogue record for this book is available from the British Library.

Hardback ISBN 978-0-349-01581-1
Trade paperback ISBN 978-0-349-01582-8

Typeset in Garamond by M Rules
Printed and bound in Great Britain by
Clays Ltd, Elcograf S.p.A.

Virago Press
An imprint of
Little, Brown Book Group
Carmelite House
50 Victoria Embankment
London EC4Y 0DZ

The authorised representative
in the EEA is
Hachette Ireland
8 Castlecourt Centre
Dublin 15, D15 XTP3, Ireland
(email: info@hbgi.ie)

An Hachette UK Company
www.hachette.co.uk

www.littlebrown.co.uk

For Steve, who is made of the same ancient star as me, and with whom I am having the most fervent, fearless, fathomless conversation of my life.

For Wesley, a dear friend and trusted colleague with whom I have learned to argue well and honestly – and who was an immense support with this book.

And for our darling Cal, who we tragically and unexpectedly lost while I was writing this book. A world-class conversationalist and wordsmith, glorious friend and trusted confidante who did everything she could to leave this world better than she found it – with empathy, intention, joy and play. We discussed the ideas in this book while we toured together and she constantly encouraged me to write with honesty and courage. I miss her so.

Contents

Introduction

In October 2016, one month before Hillary Clinton was sure to be elected President of the United States, I was hanging around in an airport in Washington DC when I saw a TV news report that made me spit my coffee out. Footage had been discovered of presidential candidate Donald Trump engaged in what he called 'locker-room talk', boasting that he could 'grab women by the pussy' because of his fame. Lyrics from the musical *Hamilton* went through my head: 'He's never gonna be president now.' In truth I had never once believed he was capable of winning anyway, but this horror show of a recording in which he had forgotten the cardinal rule – every mic is a live mic – put the lid firmly on his chances. One month later, back home in London, I was weeping hysterically in front of my television at 4 a.m. The man had won. I was confounded. It wasn't just that my community and I had not noticed the way the wind was blowing – apparently we had our own wind machine entirely.

Almost a year earlier I had started *The Guilty Feminist* podcast, a comedy activism show that had somehow sliced the zeitgeist. It blew up as people looked for somewhere to put their feelings about Trump moving into the White House. We announced an Emergency US Election Special on social media and filled a theatre less than forty-eight hours after the news came in. There was great hope, passion and the promise of action. In January 2017, women marched around the world in protest against Trump's rhetoric and policies.

In November 2024, Trump won his second presidential election. This time I felt more of a quiet dread. When we put this recent Emergency US Election Special on social media hardly anyone could see it, due to a practice called shadow banning in which the app's algorithm filters out 'political content'. I tried to pay to 'boost the post' (a service that barely existed in 2016) so that my followers could see it. This was blocked and the reason given was that the message was 'too political', because it mentioned the word 'election'. Meanwhile, my feed seems to be full of men's rights activists spouting misogyny. Quotes from Jordan Peterson I've scrolled past recently include, 'I don't believe men can control crazy women' and 'What you don't understand is that if you don't have a family and children by the time you are 40, you are one lost soul'. I see plenty of 'trad wives' making videos about obeying their husbands who they describe as 'kings', while making a series of pies in attractive aprons and recommending this 'lifestyle' as aspirational to young impressionable girls. The social media apps deem these posts 'apolitical'.

The whole political and digital landscape is so different from 2016 as to be wholly unrecognisable. Then, Twitter featured some bickering but it was largely seen as a place for conversation, discussion and connection. In 2024, people are leaving the app (now known as X) in droves because it is overrun with alt right rhetoric and skewed algorithms.

These conversations are pushed and blocked online, but offline they are fracturing families, friendships, communities and workplaces. Studies and polls indicate there is a trend for young men to lean right and young women to lean left. This is the first generation that is polarising on gender lines.[1]

It is not that we didn't know which way the wind was blowing when Trump was elected this time. It is not just that we have our own wind machine. We are now in our own weather system entirely.

The far right has been getting organised and is reaching its goals. It has detailed and active plans to change our world. Meanwhile, some of the best efforts of progressive people and organisations are being consistently scuppered by other progressive people who actually have a similar vision for the world but different ideas of how to get there. We are tripping over our own feet because we are untying our own shoelaces.

We need to be much more skilled at talking to people on the right who will engage in the good faith and to those who are undecided or disengaged. More than that, we need to be far, far better at talking to people on the same side of the political divide.

There are conversations I believe we need to have if we are to truly unite and organise in ways that are important and constructive. In fact, it has come to the point where I can no longer do the kind of public work I have been doing as host of *The Guilty Feminist* podcast, engaging in various progressive projects and causes, without coming out about the ways I believe our communities are being left behind and how we are hamstringing ourselves and each other. For quite a while I have felt like I am going along with ways of communicating that I do not believe are healthy or productive – and it has started to feel dishonest and cowardly not to stand up and say something.

Let me go back to the beginning so I can explain what I believe has occurred and how. *The Guilty Feminist* podcast was always intended as a place for me to learn about feminism alongside my listeners. When it took off, my life changed in a number of exciting ways – and some scary ones. I understood that having 'feminist' in the title meant I was a target for criticism and scrutiny. I expected a few men to call me a man-hating bitch. I figured: I don't like the patriarchal status quo, so I'd better brace myself for backlash from those who don't want me re-arranging the furniture.

The criticism I hadn't fully anticipated was from other feminists. They wrote to me, often on public forums, telling me that I wasn't being intersectional* or inclusive enough, that I didn't have enough representation from particular minority groups, that I was misusing language – or that, in some cases, I was perpetuating ideas that marginalised or stereotyped. At first, as most human beings do when criticised, I baulked and defended myself. After all, I'd called it *The Guilty Feminist* for a reason! But after some soul searching, I realised I wanted the show to be a space that drew people in, not left people out in the cold. I also saw this was an excellent opportunity for me to learn. Public disagreements on social media often escalated quickly so I took to messaging people in private to investigate what was really bothering them. This was my first foray into difficult conversations of the type I'm exploring here.

Contentious issues, the kind that are associated with cancel culture (including attitudes about marginalised groups, demands for changes in language, freedom of speech and cancel culture itself!) are a hallmark of modern life – so much so that some people avoid them, for fear of provoking combustible conversations. I imagine you sometimes find them daunting too but also really feel you need to have them, as you've decided to read this book.

I soon came to see that the subtext of what most people were

* Intersectionality is a way of understanding power relations and how they shape inequalities. It unpacks intersecting systems of oppression and how these play out in individuals' lives (for example: racism, sexism, ableism, classism and heteronormativity). The term was coined by American legal scholar and civil rights advocate Professor Kimberlé Crenshaw.

saying when they complained was this: 'I was listening to your show and felt like part of your family and then you made a joke or used a turn of phrase that, for a moment, made me feel like I was not a part of that family at all. Often, I feel like a second-class citizen, mockable or even vulnerable to structural or physical violence in the wider world. Please remember that I'm here and note that these are words which reinforce power structures that hurt me. I know that isn't your intention and that's why I'm trusting you with this information. I feel like if you knew this, you'd change. That's a compliment to you.' Sometimes I had to read the extremely small (almost invisible!) print that sat between the angry lines to understand that.

When I looked at it from this point of view, it became easier to make many of the changes that some listeners were requesting because I understood the valid reasons behind them. Allowing the community of listeners to help shape the values of *The Guilty Feminist* has taken it from a podcast to something of a movement. I started the show to focus on the doors closed to me, and then began to understand how many were actually open to me but were locked and even guarded for others. I realised that the way I sometimes felt in rooms full of men, other women sometimes felt in rooms full of *women like me* (white, femme,* middle class etc). I learned about assumptions I'd made and heard people when they told me their life experience was, at times, fundamentally harder than mine because they seemed less like the dominant group in some way. I understood far more deeply and viscerally that 'feminism' wasn't one thing because 'being female' wasn't one experience any more than 'being male' was.

People often use the umbrella term of 'privilege' to describe the experience of being a member of the dominant group, but

---

* Femme = having feminine gender expression.

that's a word I rarely use any more because I notice it tends to put people's defences up at precisely the moment I'm trying to get them to see another point of view. Language is important when you're trying to have a conversation rather than explain to someone else why they're wrong. I find 'access' a useful word. What do you have access to that someone else might be denied? Sometimes our access is invisible to us. We tend to notice the doors that are locked, not the doors that have always been open to us.

In the early days of recording *The Guilty Feminist*, we were doing an episode about make-up. I thought it would be a pretty light topic: 'Why do many women feel we have to wear it?' etc., etc. My co-host was the actor Susan Wokoma. She told a horrifying story about appearing on one of her first ever TV studio sitcoms, when she was young and too scared to push back on anything. The broadcaster insisted the make-up artist paint her skin a lighter shade of black in order to make lighting her, alongside white actors, easier for the technicians. She called the consequent long and tedious skin painting a 'reverse minstrel'. It struck me that night how much of my media intake consisted of Black women being asked about things perceived as 'Black issues' such as racism, Black history and stereotyping, while white women were being asked about pay gaps, thigh gaps, generation gaps, childbirth, abortion, fashion and yes – make-up – as if white women could speak for all women on these issues, when clearly Black women often had very different experiences. (There is, of course, an abundance of analysis and literature on this, especially from feminist journalists and academics of colour.[2]) The more I listened to criticism from listeners and changed, the more I realised there is nothing tokenistic about requests for a variety of voices.

One reason we are finding difficult conversations to be a hallmark of modern life is that many who have been denied access in the past are challenging it now. Access to what? Influence, money, social capital, education, ambitions that can be reasonably reached, seeing people who look like us and will speak for us in public life, quality stable housing, secure employment, a good food supply, the opportunity to be heard when we have a need, reasonable support structures in a crisis, healthcare, the assumption of innocence, living without fear of harassment or violence, structures that facilitate our physical mobility and even lighting that means we can be seen on screen without our skin colour having to be painted a different shade.

There are many more things that you no doubt recognise you do or do not have access to. You may be surprised by how many of these things you have access to – or could get access to if you wanted – because you have access, in turn, to people who can help you get what you want or to where you're going. There are some things on this list that you may never have questioned having access to, the way you probably rarely turn the tap on and think about all the people around the world who do not have hot and cold running water. If so, perhaps you've not really considered what it would be like to lose those things or have been born without them or have no expectation of getting them. You may feel you have reliable and straightforward access to very few things on this list. Many of the difficult, polarising conversations begin when some people want to improve their access and others feel they don't have enough access themselves, so there is no more to share. Sometimes people with a great deal of easy access feel they are entitled to it (because it is all they've known) and that any change to the status quo threatens their favoured position in society, even if they'd never admit that – even to themselves. Our world needs major rethinking and restructuring in so many ways.

However, it is not my position that all demands for change be addressed without critical thinking. I worry when I see individuals quickly placating others, so as not to 'get into trouble'. I am concerned when I see insults and condemnation flying around or 'them v. us' tactics employed to manipulate intellectual compliance. I listen to all the criticism I receive and sometimes decide it is not valid or right for my platform. I maintain that discussion, debate and disagreement are important for human beings to be happy, relationships to be authentic, and social progress movements to flourish. However, the ability to argue well and find enough agreement to take action isn't just a 'nice to have'.

'Culture wars', which is how the media now refer to contentious disagreements that pull apart groups in society (many of which share a value set!), are being started and escalated to tie us in knots and distract us from how we are governed and how money and power are distributed. There is clear evidence that at times we are arguing with bot farms and that algorithms are actively pushing us to fight with each other. We are falling for it, sometimes at the expense of the humanity of ourselves and others. We need a way out and forward.

In private, people frequently confide in me that they're frightened to ask questions, to fail, or to learn in public, on social media or in their working life. Over the years, quite a few people with a public profile have phoned me to talk something through. They almost always begin, 'I couldn't ask this online, but . . .' to which I've replied, 'Well, I wouldn't say this on the podcast, but . . .'

Sometimes people say they're scared to even talk something through with close friends. I often see eyes look down when people feel they're on dangerous ground. Once a friend described being asked about a contentious issue in a press interview as being 'given a live hand grenade'. If this conversational landscape sounds familiar to you, you'll understand why I've titled the book *Six Conversations We're Scared to Have*. If you're not nervous, you're in the minority. I'll get into the six I've chosen soon, but I'm leaving room for you to think about times you've experienced this yourself and which topics might have been contentious in your social circles. I'm sure there'll be lots of crossover!

I'm wading in, adrenaline a little elevated, because I think the reason people confide their fears in me is because *The Guilty Feminist* is about being a force for meaningful change without being perfect. The guilt is in the title, and I've done my learning in public since it began. There are some pundits who would include me in those they charmingly refer to as 'The Woke Brigade' because I value progress for marginalised groups – those of which I'm a member and those of which I'm not. However, I have genuine concerns (which I will break down as we go on) about what is sometimes referred to as 'purity politics': a trend of progressive people, understandably wanting progress to, y'know … progress, but trying to achieve this by demanding others behave in specific ways that they judge to be flawless and exemplary, and further demanding that they 'take accountability' if they are seen to have failed. As Alexis Shotwell says in her book *Against Purity: Living Ethically in Compromised Times*:

> Aiming to stand aside from the mess can produce a seemingly satisfying self-righteousness in the scant moments we achieve it, but since it is ultimately impossible, individual purity will always disappoint. Might it be better to understand complexity and, indeed, our own complicity in much of what we think of as bad, as fundamental to our lives?[3]

I'm not claiming that I'm somehow superior to others here. That would be ironic. My attitudes on purity politics stem from my time in a religious cult which spanned from my early teen years until well into my twenties. Because of this, I am extremely attuned to cult-like behaviours. Sometimes cults are called 'high control groups' because of the intellectual, verbal and, in some cases, physical control they have over their members.[4] Over the last eight years I have seen an increase in high control group tactics used in both progressive and conservative communities to (often successfully) enforce language and behaviours and to attempt to impose thoughts and beliefs.

High control groups like to make simple ideas simpler. As Margaret Thaler Singer points out in *Cults in Our Midst*, 'cults are far from marginal, and those who join them are no different from you or me ... Not all cults are religious, as some people think. Their reasons for existing may concern religion, lifestyle, politics, or assorted philosophies.'[5] Mirroring high control group tactics, an entire election or referendum might be won or lost based on what a voter can read on a hat or a bus: 'Make America Great Again' or 'We send the EU £350 million a week, let's fund our NHS instead'.[6] Elections have always featured slogans and soundbites, but the well-documented increasing polarisation of our society has thrived on reductive, emotive catchphrases which remind me very much of the rhetoric of my time in a cult.[7] There is evidence that polarisation benefits, supports and reinforces right-wing political views. This is one reason the alt right is getting ahead.[8]

All this is to say, I recognise in my body, soul and intellect the patterns emerging around me from a traumatic and damaging years-long experience which was extremely difficult to escape and even harder to deprogram myself from. I viscerally know the consequences of these patterns, so it feels vital that I speak about these parallels even when – or especially when – I share many values and political aims with those using them.

To be very clear, I'm talking tactics, not intentions or content. I am talking about procedures not goals!

The world is at a time of great social change and our discourse seems to be, at best, stilted and, at worst, frozen. Conversations about controversial topics feel combustible, even dangerous, and like they can seriously threaten our position in a group we might want or even need to be part of.

From my vantage point, this new age of troubled, polarised conversation has four root causes:

- People are losing community and feeling isolated.
- People are fundamentally resistant to change.
- Human beings have never before experienced change at this speed.
- Polarisation isn't simply diminishing our empathy. It is in fact demanding that we feel more empathy for some people and none at all for others.

If we are to make real change in our society, we need to have difficult, scary conversations and become skilled at reasoning, listening and even, sometimes, compromising and taking on interim measures, when they are in service to greater progress and societal change. We also need to get better at making demands and knowing when compromises are just lies to fob off any hope of actual progress. And we need to recognise when to change our own minds.

In this book, I'm going to explore six conversations that are difficult, even daunting, to have. Conversations that currently quickly turn into point-scoring, screaming matches online. Conversations that divide families and friendship groups. We need to be able to get our heads together and nut out why we disagree. We need to come with an attitude of curiosity as to how someone we like and respect has drawn such a different conclusion from us, and spend time learning how to explain our feelings and reasoning. We also need to accept that we will never agree on everything, and do not need to in order to move forward.

The first conversation in this book explores why we are finding it harder and harder to hold space for dialogue and disagreement, and the ways in which current social structures model the way cults operate. We'll examine why those with differing viewpoints end up in flame wars so often and so rapidly and why this is dangerous and damaging for social progress.

In the second conversation we'll look at our relationship with the past. Why are we taking the names of historical figures off buildings and is it helping us move forward? As individuals from the past cannot measure up to contemporary values and we live with their legacies (both good and bad!) how do we reconcile our relationship with history? Can we analyse the way we are making history now, and consider what those yet to be born might judge us for?

The third conversation is about gender nonconformity: what the newspapers call 'the transgender debate'. This is one of the most flammable conversations of the twenty-first century so far and certainly the most likely to cause fury. I have looked at this topic through the lens of similar fights for inclusion in the past and one, in particular, may surprise you. I'm aware that some readers will go to this conversation first. The conversations build and flow, so it's better if you don't, but if you do, please at least read the Toolkit first, before jumping ahead. Also can I ask that you try to read this conversation with a spirit of curiosity and openness? It's only a chapter in a book about ideas. It's not definitive or conclusive and it is neither the first nor last word on this subject. Please remember – I'm not writing a gospel. I'm having a difficult conversation.

Conversation four is about freedom of speech in comedy. I

do not have the scope in this book to look at freedom of speech in its entirety but, as a comedian, I think it's a particularly interesting lens with which to examine this issue. Comedy is both a type of play and an art form, so should it be constrained in any way? Where does comedy hold power and what responsibility, if any, do comedians have when they wield it? Are progressive people effectively arguing for censorship now?

Conversation five is about cancel culture. Some say it doesn't exist. Others point to their lost jobs or their diminishing social circle and say that mob mentality has robbed them of everything. Does shaming and shunning work and, more than that, is it ethical? What's the alternative?

Conversation six is about what we can do next. Are there better ways to get where we say we want to go? How can we change what's not working to create the social progress we say we want? Can we deconstruct how empathy works and employ it to build the kind of world we want to live in? Can we make a practice of critical thinking and constantly work on our skills of reasoning and connection? Can we be at least as interested in persuasion as capitalists trying to sell soft drinks and smartphones as we attempt to introduce our most important world-changing ideas?

You may have thought or talked deeply about some or all of these conversations already and, if so, I hope this allows you to analyse them differently or more closely. Not all my readers will have engaged with every conversation in the book to the same extent, but I believe they're all topics worth considering because they all relate to the so-called culture wars that are being used to manipulate and divide us.

In all likelihood, you're not going to agree with everything I have to say. I hope you don't. I hope some of what I argue makes you debate with me in your head as you read. I hope other arguments I make will allow you to find new frameworks for ideas you've already been thinking through. Perhaps some of my ideas will compel you to discuss these topics with your friends, family and colleagues and, sometimes, what I've written might persuade you to rethink your position. Or you might decide you're even more convinced your point of view is superior to mine or that I'm way off base. Perhaps you'll meet me in the middle and it'll help you understand how better to productively debate with someone else down the line. There's value in all these things.

Ultimately, I believe most of us are desperately trying to ask with our woefully inadequate tool of language: 'Is your experience of being human anything like my experience of being human?' And we are desperately hoping for some kind of connection. It is easy for people to retreat and retaliate when we do not find it.

We are understandably scared to have some of these conversations, but I'm even more scared of *not* having them. Are you with me? Then let's turn the page.

Toolkit

Things You Need to Know to Read This Book Well

Everybody needs good neighbours

During the Covid-19 lockdowns, I started to feel like Tom Hanks in *Cast Away,* who turned a volleyball into a friend so as not to hallucinate and lose touch with reality. I once had a meltdown over a broken Zoom link and wept, saying 'I'm not good with technology, I'm good with people – and people are gone!' You may have heard about skin hunger, which occurs when we don't have affectionate physical touch from other human beings. Those who isolated completely alone were encouraged to stroke themselves and use weighted blankets if they didn't have pets, because skin hunger can damage your health.[1] Skin hunger can't be sated by the diagnostic touch of a doctor, but can be with a pat on the arm by a neighbour. Yes, remarkably, our skin knows the intention of a touch (and even cuddling or coddling yourself is better than nothing). Without other people, we can lose our sense of self and, because of this, the UN has declared solitary confinement for longer than two weeks to be psychological torture.[2] In other words, annoyingly, I need you and you need me for mental survival.[3]

We often don't like to admit that we need others, though, because it makes us feel vulnerable. But human beings crave – more than just protection and affection – connection. We have never been less self-sufficient and those we rely on to make our world go round have never been more anonymous to us. Most of us will never meet the family who grows our wheat, the father of four who bakes our bread, the woman who runs the machine that slices it, the teenager who stacks it – or the programmer coding the app that brings the sliced, bagged multigrain loaf to our door. All of those people have names, faces, hopes and heartbreaks. Our global village is full of faceless providers for whom we are invited to feel no empathy.

Fast, accessible travel and the consequences of capitalism (including that our working life often takes priority over community) means it is no longer obligatory or often even practical to live in family groups. Our childhood friends scatter. We check-in on Facebook as 'safe' during a crisis because no one is going to see us at the town hall or in the town square (and even if we turned up, hardly anyone else would be there). Urban and suburban dwellers, which is between 80 per cent and 92 per cent of us – and rising – in most Western countries,[4] are trained to be independent beings who pay for childcare, dog-care and even someone to rub our shoulders when we're in pain – assuming we can afford such luxuries.[5] The roles that used to be kith and kin are now often replaced by staff or tech. So where do we find our people? The ones who would back us in a fight or protect us from predators? The ones who might really understand our way of experiencing what it is to be human?

Belonging to a club that would have you as a member …

The word most often used to describe these people is 'tribe', but to many people this word carries negative implications, due to its imposition by Western anthropologists onto Indigenous people. Personally, I think the word is a little underwhelming anyway. The root is 'tri' as in 'three' because ancient Romans divided themselves into three territories,[6] which doesn't give us any of the rich vim and texture we need from this concept.

I prefer the German word *Stamm* (pronounced 'shtamm'). The origin of *Stamm* is the ancient Indo-European root 'sta', which means standing or being firm. It's one of the largest roots in the world, responsible for many words including 'stand' itself but also 'system', 'staff' and 'institute' – all words that carry ideas of standing firm and coming together for a common purpose.

Stamm means trunk (as in the stem of a tree) but it also means your team members or regular workforce. *Der Stamm* is the biblical word for tribe in German. If you add a prefix, it can mean your people: *Volksstamm*. *Stammbaum* is your family tree. *Stammtisch* is your Central Perk/your Joey, Chandler, Ross, Rachel, Monica and Phoebe/your hang. *Stammkunden* is how a pub owner describes the regulars in their bar. In fact, many *Stamm* compound words have the warm connotation of your bartender asking, 'The usual?' It's a word you use when *you wanna be where everybody knows your name*.[7] It has the sense of the nod you give on the street to a stranger wearing your favourite indie band T-shirt or football colours.

I'm repurposing this word because I think it evokes warmth and a sense of fellow feeling, as well as shared roots.* To me

---

* Several German speakers, in my crowd sourcing, have said that the word has many warm and interesting connotations. A German-speaking academic who

it carries the sense of 'standing together' or 'standing strong'. Above all, the word *Stamm* implies stability and the kind of connection that comes with not just being included – but belonging. With the permission, or at least the forgiveness, of my *Deutscher Stammbaum* (my maternal grandfather's family are German), I'm borrowing this word and playing with it a little (stamm, stamming, stammed, stammal. I'm modifying it as I would the word 'tribe' in English and not capitalising it for the same reason) because I think it's one the world needs.

If we no longer feel a sense of stamm with those who feed and clothe us, and don't have a village or extended family who feels responsible for us, how do we sate this deeply human need to belong? How do we stamm, as we spend more and more of our week on screens? If we are no longer sharing resources, what are we sharing? The answer is – usually – values. We stamm with those who like what we like and feel the same way about the world as we do. In different pockets of the internet, at one-on-one meet-ups and live events, we stamm with others who play the same video games as us; those who like our TikTok videos; those who cheer for the same football team; those who share our sexual kinks, our love of stand-up comedy, roller disco, memorabilia, cult TV shows or word games. Some of the ways we can stamm now are truly wonderful. We can find our people in our town or across the globe while lonely members of previous generations had to live and die wondering if they were the only ones to feel their specific passions, sexual orientation, doubts or intellectual curiosity.

These kind of stamms are joyful and all about like-minds

---

consulted on this book said that the word also had colonial impositions that we should be aware of. I'm sure every version of this word round the globe carries that tragic legacy in some way or another due to history but I feel stamm is much better than 'tribe', which really only has one meaning and isn't the root/compound of so many other interesting and useful words.

and libidos finding each other. They are rarely proselytising. In fact, some stamms do not want too many members because if everyone joins, it makes the stamm less special. We see this effect when indie bands go mainstream and gatekeeping hipsters 'preferred their earlier work'. If everyone's into it, it devalues the stammal-appeal.

But, when stamms are based on a political or ideological value set, growing the stamm is crucial to its success. The more people take on the ideas as important or even the only way of operating, the more likely the ideas will be enacted. The less you feel you have stamm in your government – people who share your values in seats of power and rooms of influence – the more you may feel driven to create that representation. If you are a queer teen, for example, misunderstood or even cast out by your family, then your LGBTQ+ stamm and their politics may replace your family entirely. In fact 'stammily' is the word I now use for 'chosen family'. This is an especially useful compound word for those with non-normative family backgrounds or those who need a second family who understand their specific experience such as queerness, displacement or neuro-diversity.*

If you feel your stamms are treated like second-class citizens, demoralised and criminalised, you are more likely to identify your counter-stamms and challenge them or even target them. If you feel your counter-stamms are stealing and hoarding resources or mistreating the most vulnerable members of your stamm, you may understandably want to be loud and visible and do what it takes to get that changed.

However, sometimes we lose sight of why we're pushing

* Thank you to Lucy Rycroft-Smith who worked on the book and pointed this out! She also noted that sweetly and coincidentally 'stamm' contains hidden within it 'am' which is the Latin root that is found in 'amigo' as in friend and 'amare' as in love. They're not related but it's an accidental Easter egg.

back. Sometimes being a valued, publicly endorsed member of our stamm, and aggravating members of our counter-stamm, becomes more important than making the changes in the wider world our whole stamm desperately needs. There's safety in numbers and sometimes we feel we're better off demonstrating how much we hate the enemy, even when more advancement could be made by building bridges. A group sustains itself both by stating and restating what all its members have in common, and by identifying what it stands in opposition to. But recognising an enemy and coming up with imaginative insults for them does not do anything more than make those participating feel vindicated. It may, in fact, end up weakening the group as the standards set by the loudest voices become impossible for anyone to live up to, meaning that the group turns on its own members and, again, demands purity. It may also motivate those in your counter-stamm to be louder and even more active, creating a vicious circle of stamm and counter-stamm which serves no purpose other than to eat itself.

Online: a uniting/dividing force

Most of us do not know how to have conversations with people whose world-view is so different from ours and sometimes we can feel targeted, exposed and even in physical danger. The online world, which is wonderful for finding stamm, can also demand conformity and convergent thinking as proof of membership. When we can't see faces, read tone and build trust, our only way of demonstrating we share an identity might be toeing the party line in every respect. Marginalised people often say to others who ask them to speak for their whole community, 'We're not a monolith' – meaning, 'We don't all think the same just because we're an underrepresented group'. But then members of that stamm, in the same breath, can demand monolithic behaviours and attitudes from their membership. Stamms based on identity or ideas can quickly demand convergent thinking.

The online world – which, given the time we spend on screens, can quickly bleed into the 3D world – is also a fast and furious place to try to win over counter-stamms. It's much easier to burn a bridge than build one if you only have 280 characters or sixty seconds. Also, being seen talking empathetically to a counter-stamm member might cause members of our stamm to doubt our loyalty: *better to show our stammal colours and maintain our solidarity and systems of protection – even if the price we pay is the progress we're fighting for in the first place.*

Social media, dating apps and other common ways of stamming fast are between twelve and seventeen years old – and yet to many, they're ubiquitous obsessions. They're not things we use daily – but hourly, or even every two to five minutes. Given all of this, we're doing pretty well, gang. We are in the adolescence of a new age, and like all teenagers we oscillate between depression, wonder, anger, excitement and curiosity – and we're always freaking out a bit and worried we're not getting it right. That's okay. Like all teenagers, we have to learn, to evolve, to grow. We don't want to still be here when we're twenty or twenty-five. We need to take stock. Slow down. Figure out what we're doing and why we're doing it and how to do it better.

If we agree that the world is not as we'd wish it to be, we need to have many conversations about how to change it. A conversation is an exchange of ideas and by both necessity and probability those ideas must at times be at odds. Even when we agree about *what* should be changed, creative human beings with different experiences, personalities, educations, tastes and neural pathways firing will disagree about *how* they should be changed. And more than that, we *should* disagree; we must. All progress is a consequence of someone saying, 'This isn't good enough – I've got a new idea!' and of someone else listening and arguing and mulling and changing their mind. Human progress is the story of conversations turning into actions and consequences provoking more conversations. It is also the story of people who disagree, mildly or wildly, working in tandem to create a complicated tapestry of change over time.

Everything we value about our lives and our rights has required conversation, debate and compromise from those who've come before us. It's also involved resistance, fury and revolution, but anger cannot be the only tool in our box. We must converse. Critical thinking is, in essence, having a conversation in your own head: holding two or more conflicting ideas and letting yourself debate them. If human beings had not learned to argue well with ourselves and each other and find enough common ground to agree on a course of action, we'd have died out long ago. Conversation is human. Conversation is life. Let's have our first one.

Conversation One

The Conversation about Why We Can't Have Conversations Any More

Why are birds of a feather such dicks?

I crave being part of a group. A medium-sized, fun gang of friends who look out for each other and are working together on something cool. They demand I come out to the pub no matter what, because it won't be the same without me. They want us to get matching tattoos, because we go together like *rama lama lama ka dinga da dinga dong*.[1] In this imaginary group, I am not unconditionally loved, you understand. I am loved because I am such an important member of the gang and I'm a tent pole of the non-stop fun and super-cool action.

There are certainly people out there who follow me on social media who assume my life is just like that. To the casual observer, perhaps it looks like I'm at the throbbing heart of some ever-widening circle of movers and shakers who beg me to come and have important, hilarious, world-changing conversations in a series of glamorous locations.

It's not true. The high-profile people standing next to me in photos are generally too busy cultivating, creating and changing the world to be kicking it in Central Perk with me. I've never really felt like I was part of a space I didn't invent. Deep down inside, in the place I don't visit much, I'm aware I instigate activity because I don't just want to be included – I want to belong. I almost always create collaborative projects.

Before I started *The Guilty Feminist*, I ran comedy improv groups. I found that people will talk endlessly about wanting to start something but never commit. However, if you book a theatre and make a poster, FOMO will motivate them. Everyone wants to be on a metaphorical train that's leaving the station. Most people don't even need to know where it's going, they just want to be moving with other passengers. Hot tip for unwilling loners: the hardest space to be excluded from is one you host. I mean, it's not impossible – Steve Jobs was fired from Apple. But it's much harder to be evicted if you're the landlord, as it requires a revolution and, frankly, most people just don't have the get-up-and-go.

My therapist thinks my feelings of rootlessness and lack of belonging began at birth. My birth mother was in labour with me for three days behind a sheet so she couldn't see who she was giving birth to. Traumatic for both of us, as I never got to pop through that curtain and meet her – and I wonder why I'm in show business? I was ten days alone in the hospital with only nurses on a rota to feed and change me before my loving parents were invited to come and collect me. Adoption bureaucracy doesn't care about cuddles. I once worked with a film director who guessed I was adopted and said, 'That is why you like attention and that is why you like food.' Rude! But possibly accurate. I guess if you don't have a mother fussing over you, you learn pretty quickly, when the milk and attention comes, you'd better drink it all up.

However, I think my real sense of being an outsider comes from being a time traveller, and that is why I believe I am uniquely placed to understand why communication between people who disagree is so difficult right now. Of course, I don't really have my own TARDIS, but I genuinely do feel like a time traveller, because of my time as part of a mind-controlling cult. I believe my experience in a high control group is extremely relevant to our divided world now. I'll unpack this more later, but for now I'm going to tell you about my experience.

Sometimes people ask me what kind of person is likely to join a cult. I think a better question to ask is 'at what time of your life are you most susceptible to joining a cult?' My family started studying with the Jehovah's Witnesses when I was fourteen, and I was slowly and then quickly indoctrinated.* Your brain is very plastic as a teenager[2] and it's seeking new stamm† so that you are more likely to dilute the gene pool when you're ready to procreate. That is why you start finding your parents annoying and become obsessed with your friends. You are much more likely, as a teen, to seek out new circles and new modes of self-expression, and reject the old ones.[3] You often do that by finding a bonding activity. It's an ideal time to get into heavy metal or ketamine or Jesus.

In an effort to create new stamm, I should have found high school plays and first kisses to put between me and my parents. Instead, I found peer approval and pressure in this new, hyper-controlling religion, which meant I didn't leave the family nest. I lost what school friends I had, and started socialising with much older, devout people. I hung out with some teens my own

* Jehovah's Witnesses are members of a Christian-based religious movement probably best known for their going from house to house, offering Bible literature and recruiting and converting people before the end of the world, and their refusal of blood transfusions.

† My alternative word for 'tribe'. See Toolkit, page 15, for more details.

age who were 'born-ins', and who weren't like the studious kids I'd befriended at school. Some of them had never read a book except the regulation Watchtower Society ones.* Homework was not a priority for Jehovah's Witness kids. Late night, mid-week meetings and weekend door-knocking were everything.

It still makes me a little shaky and heart-racy to think about my early teenage self, entering a high control group.† I was made of putty and the possible. The day after I graduated from high school, I gave up my place at university because two local Jehovah's Witness elders came to my home, stood on my parents' driveway and strong-armed me into it. I was informed that the best (only) future for me was to go and knock on doors full time, telling people Armageddon was coming. I agonised over this decision, but it was made clear that I needed to leave the decision in 'Jehovah's hands', as He knew what was best for me. Right out of high school, I started working on a zero-hours contract (before we knew to call them that) as a hotel concierge to pay the bills. I felt deeply isolated and trapped, but I couldn't see any way out. I'd been brainwashed into thinking that this was what my god wanted.

Leaving a busy, full life of opportunity and education and entering into the Jehovah's Witnesses was much like stepping out of a TARDIS into the 1800s. The transition from twentieth-century teenager to young Victorian woman didn't take long. If you thought you'd never get through lockdown at the start of the pandemic and later found yourself a happy

---

* The Watchtower Society is the official organisation of the Jehovah's Witnesses. Their self-reported 2023 figures claim that each issue of the flagship *Watchtower* magazine has a 24.4 million circulation and is available in 413 languages. https://www.jw.org/en/library/magazines/watchtower-no1-2023/

† To date in the UK, 'there is either no or very limited oversight and assurance of child protection in religious organisations'. https://www.iicsa.org.uk/reports-recommendations/publications/investigation/cp-religious-organisations-settings/part-h-conclusions-and-recommendations/h1-conclusions.html

hermit who had to be coaxed back out into the world, you'll know that human beings are spectacularly adaptable. It is one reason why we are the most 'successful' species on the planet.

In my pre-cult world, women and girls were listened to and could be, if not anything, many things we wanted to be. There were plenty of glass ceilings to break and there still are, but stimulation, creativity, opportunity and adventure were on the agenda. A patriarchal cult is a very different paradigm because men are in charge of everything. A woman has never made a decision in the history of the Jehovah's Witnesses. Not even domestic issues (like who cleans the Kingdom Halls – their local meeting places) are handled by women. Women cannot take on administrative or secretarial roles in congregations as they are not allowed to be privy to any information. Men have headship. Women are in subjection.[4]

All of the 'spiritual food' – the thoughts we were obliged to think as Jehovah's Witnesses – came from eight old men who lived and worked in 'Bethel', their HQ, in Brooklyn, New York. (They've since sold that prime real estate to Jared Kushner for $345 million and have moved upstate![5]) These men were collectively known as the Governing Body. The correct thoughts and beliefs were delivered to us in the form of the *Watchtower* magazine and other publications, and sometimes as directives given to the local 'body of elders'. There were usually about six elders in each congregation – local men who appointed each other without formal training or qualifications – who were in charge of making sure we said, did and thought what the Governing Body directed. The elders police the eight million plus Jehovah's Witnesses around the world, divided into about 120,000 congregations. These men are unpaid volunteers and most of them have jobs that require few to no qualifications in the real world, and the organisation does not provide its own equivalent training in meaningful pastoral care or even theology. The elders are automatically given respect, authority and real power over people's lives within their local congregations. Human beings with this kind of power, over people who have little or no recourse to object, often enjoy it and frequently abuse it. Jehovah's Witness elders are no exception to this.

If someone were disobeying or seen to be portraying attitudes, activities or hemlines that contravened the letter or spirit of the law, the elders would be informed by the rank-and-file Jehovah's Witnesses and a visit would be paid. Sometimes a meeting would be called. The elders would attempt to correct the attitude, thought or behaviour to get that sister or brother back in line with the directives of the Governing Body.[6] Pressure would be brought to bear. We were all expected to participate in this Stasi-like arrangement to look after the 'spiritual health' of each other. Both my flatmate and I reported each other to the elders when we were worried. It wasn't meant to be vindictive, but it was, of course, disturbing and invasive.

I remember an older sister called Pamela joining our congregation. She was a little eccentric but very nice. One of our weekly meetings was called the *Watchtower* Study. A brother would read out an article written by the Governing Body and then the elder leading the meeting would ask the assigned question after each paragraph. Anyone in the congregation could raise their hand and a microphone on a broom handle would be brought to them so they could recite or summarise what 'we had just learned' in the article.

One Sunday morning, Sister Pamela did something unthinkable. The article being discussed was about a very specific interpretation of a prophecy from the inscrutable book of Revelation full of 'wild beasts' and 'whores of Babylon'. Their definitive interpretation of these mystical metaphors was *absolutely unquestionable*, like everything else they declared. Not to

Sister Pamela. The mic on the long stick hovered in front of her and she pulled it towards her and said these words, which will forever be burned on my brain: 'Just to look at this scripture through another framework . . . '

Another framework!? There is no other framework! What is Sister Pamela daring to say? A titillating hush fell over the hall. And on she went with her own theological interpretation of the prophecy. We sat and listened with our jaws dropped. Sister Pamela was questioning the *Watchtower*. We'd have been less in awe if she'd questioned the Bible itself. We spoke of nothing else for days.

Sister Pamela was counselled by the elders and publicly 'marked', which meant we were no longer allowed to socialise with her and she could no longer knock on doors. She definitely couldn't speak into the broom handle mic any more. Nevertheless, she persisted. She defied those elders by raising her hand for every single question. One day an elder forgot he wasn't meant to call on her and the startled young brother carrying the mic panicked and gave it to her. Pamela disagreed mildly but surely with the *Watchtower* again. Everyone gasped. We knew that was curtains and we were correct.

It was publicly announced that Sister Pamela was disfellowshipped from our congregation and could no longer call herself one of Jehovah's Witnesses. If we saw her in the street, we had to pretend she was invisible. If we acknowledged her, we'd be shunned too. Now I think Pamela was a hero, but at the time I could not believe her audacity. What astounds me most in retrospect is how innocent her ideas were. Many religions would welcome that kind of engaged discussion and theological debate. I do not know why she did it. I imagine it was a combination of defiance and integrity that burst out of her after she had acquiesced for longer than she could stand. Sometimes older women just explode after a lifetime of conformity. I think sometimes when patriarchy writes women off as irrelevant because they're no longer fertile, the relief of not trying to be hot the whole time manifests in all sorts of mini-riots.

The irony was that the *Watchtower* changed interpretations and doctrines all the time. This practice was presented as 'New Light' (Proverbs 4: 18)* being shed on scriptural interpretation by Jehovah God to us via the Governing Body through the *Watchtower* publications. If such a new thought was dispensed it had to be accepted there and then. No discussion. No time to digest. No questions. One of the elders told us that years ago he knew a brother who had argued with a doctrine and been disfellowshipped for it. A few months later, the official stance from the top changed ('New Light' Alert!) and it turned out that brother 'was right' but he wasn't reinstated because the key issue was obedience.

A high control group relies on an absence of critical thought from its members. During my time in one, I said and did things I didn't believe in, because the consequences of asking questions, engaging in a debate or being honest about my doubts or feelings were too drastic. There was no time to get on board emotionally with new ideas – even if they were the opposite of the old ideas. One 'truth' was replaced with another, and you had to obediently think the new thoughts and suppress the old ones. There were whole public talks (sermons) on how to squelch your doubts by replacing rogue thoughts with *Watchtower* readings and fervent prayer: Satan puts doubts in your head, so any conversation you have with yourself that invites a counterpoint is actually a conversation with the voice of the devil.

---

* Proverbs 4: 18: 'But the path of the righteous is like the bright morning light that grows brighter and brighter until full daylight.'

Believe it or not, the missionary school we were encouraged to aspire to attend was actually called Gilead, the same name Margaret Atwood gave to the oppressive patriarchal regime she created in her dystopian novel *The Handmaid's Tale*.* The similarities between my world and Atwood's are apparent – although while my experience in the cult felt psychologically and emotionally abusive, I was not subjected to physical violence.

As The Royal Commission in Australia exposed in 2015,[7] some children and women within the Jehovah's Witnesses have been physically and sexually abused. Many people from other cults, institutions and colonised lands – especially Black, brown and Indigenous women – have been subjected to terrifying prolonged abuse and trauma, and I understand the gap between my situation and theirs.[8] Trauma comparisons are often not useful for individuals in therapy, but they need to be acknowledged in the wider world, so if you're reading this and you carry deep institutionalised or inherited scars of abuse, I see you and acknowledge you.

I never got to know myself as a teenager because all my potential was gutted like a fish. After I graduated from high school, I worked full time for the Watchtower Society for many years, unpaid. I had to work two days a week in a minimum wage job to survive, often couldn't afford groceries and sometimes had my electricity cut off. I've always lied about the length of time I was in a high control group. I'm ashamed of how long it took me to wake up and get out, which is ridiculous because I don't judge anyone else for it.

In hindsight, I feel foolish for not walking away at the first opportunity. But I didn't because I couldn't. The indoctrination and emotional manipulation of a high control group

---

* In the Bible, Gilead is a place name that means 'hill of testimony'.

meant I was compelled to stay. When I finally broke away, got to university and read George Eliot's *The Mill on the Floss*, I was the only one in my study group who understood why its hero, Maggie, didn't run off with the man she loved, after having spent a chaste night with him and being shunned as a 'fallen woman'. In her mind, she deserved to be ostracised – a life of loveless loneliness followed by an untimely death was God's will for her disobedience. I went to university in the late twentieth century, trying to rid myself of the values and life experience of a heroine from a novel published in the late nineteenth century.

Because of my experience as a time traveller, I knew I could revolutionise my views. But because of my mind being taken over by the Watchtower Society, I was determined never again to abandon critical thinking. I also know, from exiting a cult and landing in the wider world, what it is like to be uninformed and how this can make you feel insecure. To reiterate and underline in bold, I am *not* saying that social movements fighting for progress (or even those trying to turn the clock back) are all cults. I'm saying that many of them are definitely employing cult tactics.

When leaving the tight community of a cult, you start completely from scratch with no friends, support network or life skills. When I left, I knew no one who'd speak to me in London – and I didn't want to tell new people that I had been a Jehovah's Witness because I didn't want to be defined that way. Someone who knew me at that time told me years later, 'I knew there was something odd about you. I thought you had been sexually assaulted – the way you were when men came into the room.' That's how deeply the prolonged psychological abuse had manifested itself in my body. I was disassociated from my physical self and although I am greatly healed, I still sometimes struggle with that to this day, as I have suffered some arrested development.

I am not asking you to feel sorry for me. It is a curve ball in my life that in some ways has made me who I am and given me the skills I have. The road less travelled is a really tough climb – but the views can be spectacular.

But it means that deep in my soul, I get why losing community can feel like a life-or-death situation, and what you might be tempted to do or say to stay within it. I know what it means to be shunned. It is a truly traumatic experience because we are social animals who have evolved to need community for physical and mental survival. The reason your hand hurts so badly if you cut it is so you attend to it quickly. Pain is your body prioritising something potentially fatal. Being ostracised can feel like a prolonged, intense, deep physical pain inside the body, because our ancestors needed to survive in an environment full of predators, where being left alone could essentially mean a death sentence.[9]

I am in a number of online support groups for former Jehovah's Witnesses, and every day I read the pain of those who reach out to their families and close friends and who are ignored or rebuffed even when in extreme situations. It doesn't matter if their child has been rushed to intensive care or they themselves have had a serious diagnosis, their families will refuse kindness or even contact. This can be as damaging for those doing the shunning as it is for the ones being shunned. A friend of mine was told as a child to imagine that her much-loved older brother and sister had been killed in a car accident – when really they had just chosen a different path in their late teens. Another woman I know was told as a child that if she even turned around to look at her shunned sister (who was sitting up the back of the Kingdom Hall trying to look repentant every Sunday) she was looking back like Lot's wife fleeing the city of Sodom as God destroyed it – and therefore she too was in danger of God's 'pillar of salt'-style wrath.*

Causing this kind of pain is strategic on behalf of the Watchtower Society. Their official website says on this subject: 'Losing precious fellowship with loved ones may help [the disfellowshipped one] to come "to his senses", see the seriousness of his wrong, and take steps to return to Jehovah.'[10] As well as 'keeping the congregation clean' of your sinful ideas or actions, they're denying you familial love – that would normally be unconditional – to bribe you back into conformity, even if you have to hide your true beliefs to get it. In 2021, Norway withdrew state support from the Jehovah's Witnesses because of these practices[11] – and academics in other countries are positioning shunning as coercive control akin to domestic abuse.[12] In March 2024 the Watchtower Society announced some 'New Light' which allows minimal contact with disfellowshipped ones, such as greetings and invitations to come into the fold, with the caveat that no further conversations should take place. Apostates, meaning people who've spoken out against the religion, will still experience being fully shunned. This loophole might improve their legal standing but, if anything, it could make the emotional impact worse. If someone greets you and you burst into tears, they cannot ask you why you are crying or give you a hug.

The formalised, structurally violent ostracism endured by those ousted from the Jehovah's Witnesses is an extreme and calculated version of something we all fear: social isolation. We've all experienced that pang of anxiety when it looks like nobody is going to remember our birthday, turn up to the party

---

* The Bible tells the story that Lot's wife is the only one of the escaping family to disobey the warning not to look behind when escaping from Sodom and Gomorrah. Lot's wife looks back, and because she disobeys the warning, she becomes 'a pillar of salt' (Gen. 19: 26).

we're throwing or like our Instagram post when we're feeling down. Even if that pang is short-lived, we internalise it. We learn to go along with what the group is doing or saying so as not to be ostracised.

You cannot have a cult without a 'them' to your 'us'. There must be an enemy. When I was a Jehovah's Witness we were encouraged to feel for each other but to see 'worldly people' (non-Witnesses) as dangerous. Witnesses were referred to as 'sheep' or 'sheep-like ones' (yes – being 'sheeple' was a good thing ...) and worldly people were referred to as 'goats'.* 1 Corinthians 15: 33 was quoted to ensure we had as little contact with them as possible: 'Bad association spoils useful habits.' When an area was ravaged by a natural disaster, the organisation would bring supplies only to Jehovah's Witnesses and rarely shared them with others. A total lack of empathy was shown to anyone who left the organisation whether willingly or unwillingly. You must be empathetic to Sister Pamela while she toes the line. You must limit your empathy when she is shamed. You must show no empathy to Sister Pamela the day they announce she's out. In a cult, your access to empathy from your stamm is determined by your willingness to show no empathy to outsiders.

When I left the Jehovah's Witnesses, I found a great freedom from these high control group tactics that had made my life so restrictive and interfered with my own mental, emotional and physical development. In the last eight years or so I have started to feel many of these methods are being employed by stamms I am a member of, as well as stamms that I have no desire to join. I recognise the techniques employed and you may have

---

* Matthew 25: 31–33: 'But when the Son of Man comes in his glory ... he will separate the people as a shepherd separates the sheep from the goats. He will place the sheep at his right hand and the goats at his left.'

noticed the parallels to some areas of modern life. You may have become concerned that there is a 'them and us' attitude in political discussions in your country and even within your own family. There are some issues you probably do not speak about in certain contexts, if at all.

Shaming and threats of shunning, direct attacks and person-to-person strong-arming on ideological grounds are currently being used in various strengths and forms online and off in an attempt to reshape society.

I will unpack the ways in which this is happening in more detail later – but first, why are people behaving like this now?

Is it all social media's fault?

It is often assumed that the internet in general, and social media in particular, is making us less empathetic: keyboard warriors and trolls writing ghastly things to each other because they can't see each other's faces. A study of American college students published in *Personality and Social Psychology Review* suggested that empathy has decreased over time; that successive cohorts from 1979 to 2009 had an overall decrease in empathy of 48 per cent.[13] This has since been quoted widely in the media as a demonstration that human beings in general are losing empathy.[14] In fact, if you've ever read an article claiming we're all less empathetic now, I am willing to bet it referenced this study. The study speculates that an increase in online interactions may be a factor, and as so often happens, many news outlets have interpreted this as definite causation.

In fact, on closer examination, many of the inferences drawn seem to be dubious. First, all the data is self-reported, and second, there is no standard, agreed-upon definition of empathy used in the research. One example of the study's argument is that college students donate less money to churches than they did in the past. This may only demonstrate that students have less disposable income and less faith in organised religion. College students confessing that they are more competitive and self-focused than previous generations declared themselves to be is suggested to be evidence of a lack of empathy, but it might point to a lack of resources and a fear of the future. The study was concluded the year after the financial crash of 2008, during the worst economic downturn in the US since the Great Depression. Those students may have felt that they could not afford to be as generous to their peers as those coming into the job market in better times. It could also be that this younger generation is more self-aware or more openly self-deprecating, having been raised in a culture of therapy and self-help. However, there did seem to be some indication that this sample of American college students felt, or at least admitted to feeling, less empathy than college students of previous generations.

A second study some years later, referencing the one above, investigated whether social media is a cause of this perceived lowering of empathy. It focused on children in the Netherlands aged between ten and fourteen.[15] Both studies differentiated between:

a) **cognitive empathy** – the ability to recognise and understand another's mental state, and
b) **affective empathy** – feeling another's emotions with them.

Here's a useful way to differentiate these two. Autistic people are often accused of not being empathetic. It is true that many autistic people struggle with cognitive empathy – reading facial cues or understanding why a remark or action would upset a neurotypical person. However, autistic people tend to be very high in affective empathy.[16] This means autistic people also often have a deep sense of feeling for societal injustices.[17]

Psychopaths are also called unempathetic, but they often score very high on cognitive empathy. In other words, a psychopath knows exactly how to upset you and when to twist the knife. They usually have no affective empathy at all – they can torture you for fun because they feel nothing for you.

Both autistic people and psychopathic people are neurodivergent but in opposite ways. When reading this, your cognitive empathy may have gone up for both groups as you came to understand them, but your affective empathy probably only went up for autistic people. You might have thought, 'I must correct people when they say autistic people lack empathy! That's so unfair.' However, your blood might have run cold when reading about someone who could deliberately toy with you and feel nothing for you. Consequently, you possibly felt nothing for them except fascination or trepidation.

Back to our study of Dutch children. One might expect that children having access to information about how other people live, outside their own small world, might raise their cognitive empathy. However, the study demonstrated that it also raised their affective (or emotional) empathy. Perhaps this is because social media like TikTok and Instagram demands video content which reveals the users' emotional cues in a way that written status updates and blogs of 2009 did not. Perhaps it is because, as the study suggests, 'development in one component of empathy benefits the other component as well'. Interestingly, the study found no significant correlation between social media use and sympathy in the children. In other words, they feel *with*, not just *for* others more when they spend time on TikTok and Instagram.

What is the reason for these different results in these studies? Perhaps children and young teens are more likely to be talking to people online who they know in the real world and already feel some empathy for. Perhaps it is because they have not yet got to college or university where financial worries, strong political differences with their peers and talking to strangers outside their stamm have caused greater divisions in their life, all of which might lead to a reduction in empathy. Maybe empathy is on the decline for young people, but social media is not the cause.

I believe there is some truth in both studies, and empathy is both declining and increasing. How can both things be true? Well, because social structures are encouraging us into cult-like groups. I believe we are all being encouraged to empathise *more, but with fewer people*. Before the internet and the twenty-four-hour news cycle, our understanding of a crisis or cause was limited to radio and television news which was aired two or three times a day, and daily newspapers and weekly magazines which were limited in their column inches. Media directed at children and teens was usually light entertainment or 'fun education' with a 'society approved' point of view. University students had to find time to meet up and talk about the information they had access to and organise marches and sit-ins by passing out flyers.

Now children and college students have 24/7 access to information, points of view and first-hand accounts of the experiences of others. This 'news' is often a potent cocktail of fact, opinion and indignancy catalyst. Algorithms often show you information that reinforces your beliefs. Social media platforms will show you material that may or may not be well researched and accurate but that your stamm will approve of. It will also show you posts from extremists in your opposing stamm threatening violence or even behaving violently. Your stamm encourages you to disregard information or videos that contradict your views as 'fake news' and immediately dismiss them before you engage with them.

Much like the Jehovah's Witnesses, stamms feeding off

the internet often see their team as 'good sheep' deserving of cognitive and affective empathy, and those with opposing views as 'bad goats', deserving of neither. If someone publicly admits online or in the pub that they can 'see where someone is coming from' even if they don't feel for them, they may well be scolded by multiple members of their stamm. If this happens to you, you are being discouraged from practising cognitive empathy, and analysing or imagining how that human being might have ended up voting for a party or supporting a cause or point of view due to their upbringing, life experience, education, power structures or fear of being evicted from their own stamm. You don't have to feel for someone in a way that compromises you, to understand them. Understanding them helps you engage with the reasons for their conclusions and very likely gives you information about the structural inequalities and systems you want to dismantle.

The other scary thing about this trend of selective empathy is that our brains are plastic. Neuroplasticity is the ability of neural networks in the brain to change through growth and reorganisation.[18] Repetition is part of the way that brains adapt to change. Empathy is a key part of being human – even if we express and experience it in different ways.[19] If you're a member of a stamm that teaches you it is wrong to empathise with those you disagree with, you are literally training your brain to dehumanise others.[20] If you make a practice of this, you are eroding your own humanity. This doesn't mean we have to connect with or make excuses for those who are structurally and physically violent. It means we are able to make a choice whether or not we are going to mirror their lack of empathy and become just like them.

How can you possibly believe that, darling?!

When I was at university (between 1997 and 2000), it was quite commonplace to be friends with people we agreed and disagreed with. One of the points of going to university was to stay up late into the night with a bottle of wine (and sometimes a joint) disagreeing, sometimes with passion, sometimes as a mental exercise, and even at times being shifted from your position. Being persuaded to see things from other points of view is something that often happens around this age – whether your first years out of school are spent in another bigger school, or in the world of work, or living in a shared house or commune.

Especially in universities, this kind of interaction has long been formally encouraged and it helps you learn to empathise while you intellectualise. However, this should come with the caveat that there's an institutionalised bias to those conversations. For many generations, only one sort of person was allowed into seats of higher learning. Men who were white, straight and wealthy (or at least well connected) learned to empathise with each other. The gay men and gender-nonconforming people among them generally had no opportunity to safely explain their position, because they were obliged to hide their queerness in spaces where debates might take place – so no empathy was able to be built for them, only by them.

Most men of colour and white working-class men were, of course, not allowed in at all – women were specifically banned. Consequently, many people who have had no access to shaping conversations that lead to policy, laws and the blueprints of the world are sick of being on the periphery – done with being left out, tired of being trampled down. Compared to the historically rarefied, exclusionary world of universities, the modern platforms of social media are accessible to all – so for some voices, the advent of Facebook, Twitter, Instagram and their ilk represented their very first chance of seriously being heard. I relate to this as a woman in comedy whose success has come from building my own platform online. Some may understandably feel that people like them have always been left out of all the conversations where leadership decided who was to benefit from societal empathy and that they were not heard when they asked nicely or even directly and loudly. Some may feel people not of the dominant group are left with only one sort of power – to name, shame and shun, to demand conformity and reduce stammal empathy. I get it but my concern is that this means that we are very limited through no fault of our own. We are limited because we only have patriarchy's more brutal processes modelled for us, and we don't feel we have the time and luxury for intellectual doodling when our communities are suffering. However, these are not the only two models available. We are entitled and able to design and build new frameworks for our stamms. As a cult survivor, let me assure you, it is impossible to create the compassionate, humanising world we are demanding, with the dehumanising, punitive, conformist tactics of patriarchy. When time and resources are scarce, blunt instruments are sometimes used for expediency. Some of our communities have been left gasping for breath and so change feels urgent but that means strategies can be heavy handed and counterproductive. Yes, we need immediate change but we also need long-term, structural, lasting change with strong foundations and that takes time, skill and collaboration to craft well.

Whereas late-night debate in student common rooms can give you access to subtlety and complexity, online interactions tend to be staccato and unable to acknowledge that there can be some truth in two ideas which contradict each other. This is one reason why they usually only help you build greater empathy for those you already agree with, and the more you limit your circle, the more you need that circle to survive and dare not contravene its rules for fear of total abandonment. It's not like all of our conversations live there. We also interact in the real world. But most of the reductive policy by social groups, or at least what the Watchtower Society would call 'the spiritual food', does seem to be disseminated online.

Where are the empathetic, thoughtful opportunities for discussion offline with people who disagree even lightly with the received wisdom of your stamm? And when is it okay to ask someone to explain something to you? When an individual is newly trying to engage and understand, someone will frequently snap – 'Google it! I don't have to educate you!' Emma Dabiri points out in her excellent book *What White People Can Do Next* that 'googling it' isn't always what people need: 'The internet has often facilitated dissemination of information rather than knowledge; as such even in cases that aren't quite "fake news", online commentary skews to the reductive. It tells you what to think, rather than teaching you how to think!'[21] Apart from anything else, we can search until we find the answer that confirms our bias, so sharing a thoughtful reading list, if we have the bandwidth, can be much more productive. We also have the option of saying nothing rather than discouraging someone who may have asked in good faith.

Some of the ideas we're being asked to adopt at such short notice feel to me like the 'New Light' of the Watchtower Society. Many thoughts are delivered like the cult's 'spiritual food,' and those issuing them expect others to treat them as fact. If you do not agree with these ideas or if you want time and space to debate, discuss them or think them through, you might be disciplined and shunned by others who fear they'll be shunned by aligning themselves with you. You may be able to think of times where you were publicly scolded for reasons you did not fully understand and you either complied and apologised or argued and then disappeared. These things have certainly happened to me and everyone I know well, but I do not wish to get lost in the detail of individual examples because we might well disagree about what is perfectly progressive and reasonable, and what is draconian and unreasonable. The point is not the individual example but the way we are managing progress.

Will you 'unlike' or be disliked?

One common practice that worries me is individuals publicly contacting others on social media and demanding they unfollow someone who has 'liked' or acknowledged a post from a person who is considered to be outside an assumed shared stamm. One of my listeners wrote to me about a post I'd made quoting Gloria Steinem. She told me Steinem was known to sometimes have lunch with another feminist of her generation who was publishing stuff that was widely thought to be pretty unpleasant across all the feminist communities (even ones that disagree pretty vehemently). I replied that (while I have no evidence either way) she probably does have lunch with her. These two well-known women were at the forefront of feminism together in the 1970s. Steinem's entitled to have lunch with whoever she likes and most likely challenges this provocative former colleague on her ideas. (Or perhaps they just discuss old times and their love lives.) What is the alternative? That someone who's missed the turn-off (even dramatically) finds herself a complete social pariah in an empathy vacuum?

We will explore how isolation can exacerbate extremism later, but the listener who wanted me to cut off Gloria Steinem gave me chills, because this approach is fundamental to a high control group. If someone has an idea that we find repugnant, we don't automatically catch it by talking to them. The elders always told us that was a real danger. They called it 'keeping the congregation clean'. Goats were contagious and if you allowed yourself exposure, you too could wake up with an attack of the goats.

This doesn't mean you have to engage with people who you feel are undermining your humanity or identity, or accept the status quo. It does mean that creating an environment where members of your stamm are looking over their shoulder for fear of being seen as a collaborator with anyone who disagrees with the party line (in large or small ways) is highly draconian on a human level and is going to immobilise your movement by fragmenting it.

Who is my enemy's enemy?

People fighting for social change have always had disagreements and sometimes, so much so, they've divided. Emmeline Pankhurst set up the Women's Social and Political Union because she thought the tactics of the suffragists were too compliant and peaceful to win the vote for women.[22] The suffragists campaigned using peaceful methods such as lobbying, and Pankhurst's suffragettes were determined to win the right to vote for women by any means, including civil disobedience. The suffragettes thought the suffragists were politely waiting for the patriarchy to have manners while they were kept busy filling out paperwork. The suffragists thought the suffragettes were doing more harm than good and losing the good will of the public with civil disobedience and by destroying private and public property.[23]

However, at the 1911 coronation procession, a demonstration of an estimated 60,000 suffragists and suffragettes protested side by side. These groups fundamentally disagreed and sometimes publicly apologised for each other (embarrassing and infuriating each other) but when it was expedient, they knew how to work together.[24] Emmeline Pankhurst's post-procession speech included the triumphant pronouncement: 'We have proved that we can combine; we have proved that we can put aside all personal beliefs and all personal doubts for a common end'[25] while the leader of the suffragists, Millicent Fawcett, was reported to have said, 'I never was surer of anything in my life than that it was the right policy for the cause ... to cooperate in it.'[26]

They fundamentally disagreed about how to get the vote. However, no one would've been outraged to see Millicent Fawcett retweeting Emmeline Pankhurst's call to come to a protest. It wasn't a betrayal for a suffragette to socialise with or work with a suffragist. How do we know this? Well, it is hard to know how many women were suffragettes and suffragists at the time, because 1911 was the same year women refused to participate in the census by way of protest ('If women don't count, we will not be counted'[27]) but 60,000 is a substantial number to put aside their differences and protest a coronation at a time when there was far more reverence for monarchy.[28]

This was not the only time the two factions teamed up. In fact, Emmeline wrote to Millicent when they were on the home stretch in 1917 and asked to meet so they could come together and strategically get it over the finish line.[29]

This kind of collective action between those who fundamentally share a fight but heavily disagree on tactics is, on the left, far less likely to happen today. The speed at which ideas can travel and the instant reductive conformity that can be demanded on the internet and permeate offline is what's new. Please don't misinterpret this as me saying 'Cancel culture has gone mad!' Marginalised groups (including ones I'm in!) have benefited greatly from online and street movements like #MeToo, Time's Up, Repeal the 8th and Black Lives Matter.

Without online campaigning, Harvey Weinstein would still be pressuring twenty-one-year-old actresses to see him in his hotel room and blacklisting them if they didn't comply with his heinous demands. Derek Chauvin, George Floyd's uniformed murderer, would still be on the beat – intimidating, physically abusing and probably even killing other Black citizens. The recent wins for feminism born of online activism have made my life immeasurably better. I am grateful that power is shifting. But we need more progress, and we have to examine closely whether the strategy of dividing ourselves is allowing the powers that be to conquer our aims.

Is surround-sound power any better?

We tend to be most comfortable with top-down power structures, even if we despise them, because we are used to them. By contrast, surround-sound influence is how I refer to change-making authority held by members of the community around us. This phenomenon feels scary because we have the sensation that it is new, although boycotts and voting with feet and wallets has long been a practice. There are certainly some new forms of surround-sound influence being used. Mostly it diffuses power and is therefore less open to abuse. Less. But it is still open to it. Every tool known to humankind can be used as a weapon. I believe we need new forms of surround-sound influence to begin to mature. We don't want our collective power to escalate in the way a coup sometimes brings in a different sort of dictatorship and not the longed-for justice or equality the people were hoping for. In other words, if we don't want to throw the baby out with the bath-water, we will have to let it grow up.

Let's look at an example of how stamms that broadly share values and are overall working for the same aims divide themselves. If your shared community value set included *making the world a fairer place*, you would probably think fast fashion is harmful and sweatshops must be closed down. If another one of your values was *helping others in a crisis*, you might also be willing to ship a hundred waterproof coats (yes, perhaps they were made in a sweatshop, but they are now just sitting in a warehouse) to a homeless shelter because temperatures have dropped below zero and they're on sale for a fiver. You might ask others in your community to join you in sharing their resources this way.

Someone in your community may respond that *making the world a fairer place* is of paramount importance and will never happen if we compromise when we need to *help others in a crisis*. You may respond that you have no time to debate this because *there's a crisis right now*. Wasting the sweatshop-made coats will not help those working in appalling conditions who have already made these garments. If you were freezing on the street, your top value would be *not dying of exposure*, which is too personal and immediate a value to give you time or interest in debating needs higher up Maslow's Hierarchy.*

Someone else may argue that closing sweatshops without providing other better, more ethical workplaces is counterproductive to those who live in a work-or-starve economy. If we put the sweatshops out of business to salve our own well-fed Western consciences and leave the people who have too little with absolutely nothing, we will be ironically sending the coats from the warehouse back to the very people who made them, to protect them from the elements.

These discussions can feel frustrating, exhausting and even

---

* Devised by Abraham Maslow in his 1943 paper *A Theory of Human Motivation*, this begins with basic needs such as food and shelter, progresses through psychological needs such as emotional security and culminates in 'self-actualisation'.

literally nauseating at times. More than that, they can feel dangerous. Sometimes, people are harassed and threatened. Coming off social media doesn't help if that's where the reductive policy is being made and where many of the influential directives are happening. If we express ideas out of step with our stamm, often we feel our best or only strategy is to quickly apologise. Sometimes we are scolded for expressing our intention because impact > intention and we may be accused of centring ourselves or our feelings if we explain ourselves. This is very much the Watchtower's model. All you can do to save yourself is repent and be small and quiet or you will be labelled rebellious. There are occasions when the apologies are genuine, and other times they're just made to bring an interaction to a swift end. We may whisper to a confidante that we think we were right, or that we felt bullied into complying.

Some people believe they can eradicate what they perceive to be objectionable or potentially harmful points of view on the internet, as if they're killing weeds. They act as if when you shame someone into being quiet or apologetic, the offending thought or action is dead. Can I tell you – as a cult survivor who was constantly forced to apologise and say things I didn't believe – it is not. It is just swallowed and often strengthened.

Again, I'm not discussing substance here. Just method. Your point of view may be as progressive and empathetic as the views of religious cults can be regressive and dictatorial. It may be one that humanises marginalised and oppressed people! But if there is no empathy and humanity in your approach, then you'll likely burn a bridge when you need to be building one. If the oppression is your own, you may feel too angry and exhausted to build a bridge, but the definition of an ally is one who comes to another's aid in a time of need. If you meet someone exhibiting racist views, online or off, and you're a white person, it's important that you leave that person *at least no more racist than you found them.* If you whip that person up into a frenzy by cursing at them and insulting them online and then they head off onto public transport, you're conceivably making the world actively worse for people of colour who might be on the receiving end of their behaviour, while getting a heroic feeling of being right.

The question is, what is your aim in trying to shame someone who feels pride in their ideology if your opprobrium serves as evidence to them that they're on the right team? Is it enough to show your rejection of their world view because someone in a civilised society should publicly name prejudice when they see it? If so, can you name it and walk away – or will you allow it to escalate in a way that reads to others like two irrational sides of the same coin? In our final conversation we will examine further strategies to make genuine change, and not just get things off our chest, but for now let's think about arguing with people in our own stamm.

Much of the internet weed-killing is done by progressive people asking or even demanding that other liberal people accept new language or ideas, or give up old ways of thinking that are thought to be harmful. In this case there is a real and powerful weapon that can be used to control others – they can be shamed and threatened with ejection from your stamm.

The practical risk of enthusiastically weeding your side of the garden, ridding it of all its visible wrongness, is that you may push someone who was in your stamm or could have been, to another stamm – where they'll be expected to take on values that are far removed from your own. They may go to a stamm where they feel they can live up to community guidelines more easily. Bridges could have been built, but the social media norms meant they were burned instead. Now the world has one more person in a stamm that you feel is making the world worse – and your stamm is one person down. Maybe many more who've witnessed this public event back slowly away, silently drawing no attention to themselves.

There are risks to weeding your side of the garden – the possibility that it might become a fearful place where people are hiding their thoughts and feelings for fear of punishment, and the risk that, over time, members will train each other to become people who are not independent, active, vibrant critical thinkers, but people who become very good at being told what to think and do. And people like that rarely change the world. When we think about leaders and members of historical and contemporary civil rights movements who we admire, compliance and fear of stepping out of line are not characteristics that come to mind, so we cannot shape our movements using those qualities.

If people are thinking critically, it is unlikely they'll agree with you about everything and that is more than okay; it's desirable. Human beings are individual, multifaceted and fallible and so the solutions to our problems cannot and should not be simplistic, one-size-fits-all and mandated. There are no perfect solutions to imperfect problems. There is no right way to fix all the wrongs of the world. There are no easy answers to complicated, historical power abuses. All change will have costs as well as benefits.

If we outsource our sense of right and wrong and our decision-making, who do we put in charge? I often think the appeal of a cult is that you make the one really scary decision to join and then from that time, all further decisions are made for you. If we are to be happy and have a shot at making a real impact in the world, we cannot absolve ourselves from intellectual participation in social change and nor should we want to. If we do, what looks like surround-sound influence may really be top-down power. Someone dispenses wisdom that becomes ideology we all must follow. That operates on the model of rank-and-file religious cult members, policing each other in a Stasi-like way.

Can't something be done about all this progress?

The speed of change is a significant factor in all of this – and it is brand new. When I was a child, it would have been unthinkable for an out gay man to be on television at all, let alone be the most popular chat show host in the entire country, as Graham Norton is today in Britain. In many countries, in the space of a few decades, homosexuality has gone from being considered a shameful secret to being a mainstream, celebrated part of life. (That doesn't mean homophobia has disappeared – it means the most influential channels and voices normalise gay people's identities and create space for pride.) In the late twentieth century, that progress was considered fast – the way some horses and buggies were considered fast before the car was invented.

In reality, this has happened very slowly – far too slowly for those affected by it. Why? Because people are generally resistant to change, and then we had to rely on the platforms gifted by those in power, who were nervous about what advertisers and viewers would accept. The status quo can feel safe, even if it makes the world a dangerous place for some of us.

Most people view the progress that happened in the past – especially the progress that benefited them – as vital, important and overdue. Many people also view the progress that is happening now – even sometimes the progress that will resource their stamm – as hurried, unnecessary and too much of a good thing. Or even an undesirable thing. Any inclusion that happened before you were born is, on the other hand, not progress but normality. Even hardcore men's rights activists and incels don't tend to argue for the vote to be taken away from women, because it's all they've ever known.

We will look at our relationship with the past in our next conversation, but even if you went back just ten years in a time machine, you'd probably be surprised by some of the language you and your friends were using. It would likely seem lazy and hurtful to you now. Even if you sometimes roll your eyes at the ways you feel language is overly policed, this is still probably true for you. We all change. Sometimes so slowly, we don't even notice it. Generation Z are shocked by some millennials' favourite episodes of *Friends* and *Sex and the City*, and we all have to admit – even if they were in some ways breaking barriers with primetime lesbian weddings and Rampant Rabbit female sexual empowerment – they haven't aged well with their gay and bi panic and fatphobia.

It didn't seem odd to most network television viewers in 2002 that a well-educated, metropolitan character like Doctor Ross Geller from *Friends* would declare a male nanny to be 'weird' and to ask him during a job interview whether he was gay – and when told no, to come back with, 'You must at least be bi!' But while it was always horrible and exclusionary for those on the sharp end of that behaviour, and the writers were parodying the ridiculousness of Ross's attitude, it didn't land as absurd or outrageous because we knew that the plot of *The One with the Male Nanny* was easily something that could have happened in real life. It would be extremely odd if a thirty-something academic living in the Village now expressed that view, and his contemporaries would be shocked. More than that, if we could have a coffee with Ross now, of course he'd realise he'd behaved like a dinosaur in retrospect.* I also think, as an old-school Gen X, he'd judge his Gen Z students to be

* All dinosaur/palaeontologist puns intended.

draconian and extreme. Almost everyone changes very slowly all of the time, even if they outwardly resist change.

This is one reason why social change is usually gradual. Sometimes glacial. We can look back on riots, revolutions and iconic moments, but shifting attitudes in the wider population usually needs at least a decade. It takes a generation (and often longer) for the radical idea to become received wisdom. That is not to say activists haven't fought for immediate change, but they usually knew they were playing a long game. Today we expect everything to be fast. If you want a new ironing board, in a couple of clicks, Jeffrey Bezos will arrange to have it delivered to your door in a matter of hours. Want a one-night stand? You are probably just a few right swipes away from one, if you're not too fussy about who it's with.

We feel we don't have time to wait around any more, and therefore social change doesn't either – it piggybacks on the speed of the internet.[30] A new idea can catch fire and become gospel within hours, but our brains don't have time to digest it. That's one reason why social weed-killing doesn't work. Change takes time and, like empathy, has both cognitive and emotional aspects. My feelings didn't go away because the elders told them to. They festered. More than that, the fact that I wasn't allowed to express my doubts was in itself a reason to doubt. You can't just tell people to think something new and have them do that. It's not how thinking works. It's how people-pleasing and faking it works. That doesn't mean we have to shrug and say, 'Give it a decade'. It means we need to factor into our urgent activism that brains can't be double-clicked or swiped right on. They don't work that way, and would we want to flick a switch in someone else's brain even if we could? That feels like turning a computer off and on again to reset it, not like the process of a wholly evolved human developing empathy.[31] This is not a plea to slow down progress for marginalised groups, including my own. It is a plea to understand that speeding it up will require a more complex approach than the ones being employed most often today.

How can we expand our 'circle of empathy'?

We can't just tell people what to feel, we have to engage with the complex process of how feelings are developed. Sociobiologists talk about society's collective 'circle of empathy', by which they mean who we care about and include.[32] This has observably been getting larger for generations.[33] Every time there is social progress in the form of an identity group winning freedoms, representation or legislation, it is a sign that more people understand the needs of the group and/or feel with them and, because of that, those who make decisions have seen the benefit of including them. The powerful will rarely be ahead of the population in creating rights for under-represented people in case doing so loses them power. We need our populations to have empathy to create meaningful, integrated social change. You can frighten people into behaving in certain ways, but you can't scare them into seeing things from a different perspective or feeling with you or others. That takes conversation, work, allyship and time.

In the summer of 2020, I watched some white people shouting at other white people to 'educate themselves' about Black Lives Matter, forgetting that they themselves had learned these things just a few years before (or even more recently), probably from Black women who had taken time to discuss it with them. If someone took that time with you, isn't there some responsibility on your part to give someone else the opportunity to see things through a new lens?* And not just give them

* To reiterate, if you don't have time or bandwidth, you can point others in the direction of resources or just leave them to it and say nothing.

bumper stickers and tell them that's their new doctrine, but to think around and through the subject. To see that even a small shift in their thinking is worth having and not labelling people as all-in or all-out, insisting they buy every detail of your world-view.

Also, when trying to convince someone of something else, it's important to remember that the received wisdom of your stamm is always changing, so something you present dogmatically today, you may think differently about tomorrow. That's a good thing as long as you analyse it personally, read widely and genuinely agree with it. It is not 'doing the work' to listen to the loudest voice on your social media feed, especially if that voice is not addressing the complexity of a given topic. Of course we need to listen to people's life experience. I don't like it when men say, 'I've never noticed that, so it's not real' or try to intellectually argue that my experiences with sexism aren't valid. In turn, I have no desire to do that to others. However, true social change cannot be based on military-like obedience. Your community is evolving, and we cannot present models for thinking about inequality or justice as a doctrine that can only be changed with someone else's permission. If you're not sure how to go about this, I think you need to find a quorum of trusted voices on a topic: thinkers, writers and academics, ideally some (or even most) who also have expertise born from their experience of living with marginalised identities, who can develop your cognitive and affective empathy. Read around and find recommendations from those you trust. These thinkers will no doubt disagree in some ways about how exactly to proceed. It's important they do because it highlights to us that there is no one easy answer or doctrine and we need to develop our own ideas and 'do the work' of complex thinking and not just 'loud repeating'.

When I was a Jehovah's Witness we had to refer to our way of life and world-view as 'the truth': 'How long have you been in the truth?' 'When did you come into the truth?' 'I hear he left the truth.' This is emotive language designed to brainwash you into believing that critical thinking is engaging with lies, and conversations in which you contemplate other points of view are only to be had with liars. Some of the language around identity politics is presented now as absolute truth that must not be thought through or questioned. Of course, academics, thought-leaders, public intellectuals and many other people from marginalised groups are constantly questioning, discussing and debating those ideas and not treating them as 'the truth' but often, I notice, they are not attacked for this because they hide their ideas in books and academic publications. Their complex arguments won't fit on Instagram so they do not 'get into trouble'. Find these people and put them on your quorum. Sometimes those same complex arguments are discovered by individual social justice campaigners and reduced, turned into 'the truth' and enforced. When a contrasting theory or study provides an evolution or even contradiction of the last reduction, it is often introduced online like the Watchtower's 'New Light'.

Let me unpack an example of this. About seven years ago I was introduced to the idea of trigger warnings.* People online frequently told me that my podcast should use them all the time whether we were discussing eating disorders, violence, suicide or a number of other topics. I could see some value in occasionally flagging that we would be discussing some things, but I didn't make a practice of it because I could not understand how saying 'violent assault' in a free-standing, startling way at the top was less likely to cause a traumatic response in the body than introducing it in a sensitive nuanced way within a conversation. You can always turn the podcast off the first

* Trigger warnings are alerts to upcoming sensitive material likely to trigger trauma responses in those listening, reading or watching.

time it's mentioned, whether that's at the opening in an isolated way or later when it's introduced in context. If anything, I think hearing, 'We are going to be discussing this list of bleak things!' may deter the very people who'd find valuable healing in someone else sensitively sharing expertise or artistically relaying an experience.

Personally, sometimes I seek out cult content (which I might describe as my 'trigger') and other times I am feeling a little raw and it can ignite some mild traumatic vibrations – but if that happens, I turn it off or, better still, I breathe through it and use it as an opportunity to work something out. I see it as trapped trauma escaping the body at a safe moment because it couldn't get out when I was in survival mode and had to 'freeze and friend'. I get value from exfoliating the bad stuff when I'm not in direct danger and in fact, the more I do it, the more my body releases it. When I first stood on a stage and said I was an 'apostate' (someone who's turned against their religion and speaks out about it), I shook quite violently, because to teenage me that was the worst thing I could be. I performed my stand-up show about it for a month at the Edinburgh Festival and I shook a little less every time, until day twenty-four, when I didn't shake at all. After that I could say it with some ease. I let go of it by looking at it head on. Of course, that was on my own terms, in my own way. I am lucky to have access to that outlet because of my make-up which allows me to be a storyteller who enjoys writing and performing and living in a country with (much) freedom of speech – and I didn't do it until I was ready.

When thinking through all of this, I found evidence that certain things trigger PTSD – such as the well-known example of helicopters and Vietnam war veterans[34] – but I couldn't find any evidence that words in isolation ignited trauma, just that it had become a practice on university campuses.[35] So I used my own judgement and mostly I did not use trigger warnings.

However, on the rare occasions I shared a video on Instagram depicting actual disturbing footage, I always posted a slide before it warning viewers so they could opt out – because jumping from a video of a kitten to witnessing a war crime without preparing mentally is obviously shocking (and if it's not, I fear the viewer has become desensitised). These were the conversations I had with myself and my colleagues after doing the thinking and the reading. Some people still wrote to me telling me that what I was doing was wrong, and I always explained my reasoning. Sometimes they furiously told me I was heretical, and I should just do as I was asked. Other times people thanked me for talking through my thinking.

About a year ago, I started to see social media posts explaining that trigger warnings were not useful – in fact that they stopped survivors building resilience – and insisting that everyone had to stop using them. It seemed to me to be presented as 'New Light'. One day somebody messaged me out of the blue and told me I was to stop using them. They must've heard a rare episode where I'd added a warning about something specific. The person who sent me the message stated it as a fact: warnings were of no use and, in fact, could be detrimental. It was presented as if I should have known. No one seems to ask each other what they think or whether they'd found trigger warnings useful or send each other links to studies or invite each other to think critically about it. There's almost always a slightly superior or scolding tone. It almost always seems to be presented as 'what you must do because the thought [or the truth!] has changed'.

I found a study that discovered that groups who were warned that traumatising content was coming had no significant difference in their response to it than those who were not.[36] Moreover, warning people seems to make their trauma a bigger part of their identity than it otherwise would be. Trigger warnings may also get in the way of building a resilience to their traumatic experiences in the manner that I had been able to by referring to myself as an apostate.[37] I thought critically about this study, which tracked with my instinct all along.

My feeling is that if I'm going to platform an activist who's going to be speaking about something truly shocking or violent, I should introduce it right before that part comes up. Someone might be listening with a child in the car or while on their commute on a crowded train carriage. It's polite to let people know so they can pause it and save it or skip it altogether. In short, I feel the way I did seven years ago. Warn people sometimes. For some topics. In some contexts. Mine is a comedy podcast that changes gears (sometimes dramatically) in the second half of the show. It's not appropriate to say unpleasant words in a list and then do jokes immediately afterwards. Using your own judgement throughout this kind of process can mean critical thinking will stop you from conforming to the received wisdom, but not always. In our third conversation I'll examine a situation in which I thought through another 'new directive' and came to the conclusion that it had merit and adopted it into my life. Just because an idea has been presented to you as 'New Light' doesn't mean it has no merit. We can also lack critical thinking by throwing away a gift because we don't like the wrapping. The important thing is that we stop to smell the analysis and know why we are changing, if we are changing.

Just because we need to be open to discussion doesn't mean anyone is entitled to our time, energy or platform. Sometimes people say they want to debate and it quickly becomes apparent that they are not well intentioned or open. I have learned not to spend all afternoon online with someone I'd move pubs to avoid. I now also refuse to debate extremists on radio or television who broadcasters assure me are there 'for balance'. I will debate people who are politically far removed from me but not conspiracy theorists or climate change deniers. I am not interested in engaging in gladiatorial spectacle. I am interested in talking to people who want to learn and from whom I can learn. I want to have debates with people who are open to change and want a better world but aren't sure of the right way to get there.

I am interested in creating and belonging to spaces where we can all learn together. I am keen to develop a stamm full of interconnecting bridges with people who see the world through different lenses and share without needing to indoctrinate. I want to work with people who value both cognitive and affective empathy and want to build it in themselves and others. I want to be more like Sister Pamela and say what I think, not what I think you want to hear. I never want to be that compliant 'sister' again. I want to help create a kinder, fairer world and that requires one-on-one conversation and time – not threats and dogma.

You may have felt horrified by Sister Pamela being shunned for asking us to consider things through a different framework, by men who had no right to dictate the thought processes of others. Now ask yourself if these same mandates are acceptable coming from thought-leaders on social media you've never met, even if you agree whole-heartedly with their agenda or message. I believe we need to reconsider how we make new models for creating progressive coalitions.

Even if you think the ends justify the means, the means cannot create the beginning of the more compassionate, humanitarian society progressive people are aiming for.

What if we don't?

Employing our empathy and learning how to have difficult conversations well isn't just a 'nice to have' to create a better world. There is a far more urgent driver demanding that we take stock right now before the world we have gets much worse. In 2018, a research report from independent non-profit the Data & Society Research Institute revealed that YouTube was a breeding ground for far-right radicalisation. It identified the 'Alternative Influence Network' and found that its members 'cast themselves as an alternative media system by 1) establishing an alternative sense of credibility based on relatability, authenticity, and accountability and 2) cultivating an alternative social identity using the image of a social underdog, and countercultural appeal.' It also stated that 'Members of the Alternative Influence Network use the same proven engagement techniques of brand influencers to spread ideological content.'[38] What is the real-world consequence of this?

In 2020 the *New York Times* released a podcast called *Rabbit Hole* which follows the radicalisation of a young man called Caleb Cain who started out watching YouTube self-help videos at a low point in his life and quickly fell down a 'rabbit hole', driven by algorithms designed to get the watcher to engage for long hours on the platform. Caleb Cain has since woken up and taken stock and, on the podcast, he deconstructs his own radicalisation by alt-right broadcasters who talk for hours at a time. He explains how he began to see far-right commentators and their movements as the new punk counterculture. More than that, he saw the battle lines drawn against feminists and progressives as 'less of a culture war and more of an actual war'.[39] That war has casualties.

In 2020, after a spate of shootings directly connected to this kind of YouTube radicalisation of young men, the then CEO of YouTube, Susan Wojcicki, announced that the platform was taking steps to mitigate its own worst excesses, but a multidisciplinary research team in communication and computer science at the University of California performed a comprehensive audit of YouTube's video recommendations in 2021 and 2022 – after this supposed clean-up.[40] They created 100,000 sock puppet accounts and found that if you start looking for right-wing content it is still enormously likely that you'll be pushed further and further right – and quickly. 'YouTube's algorithm doesn't shield people from content from across the political spectrum,' said Magdalena Wojcieszak, author of the study and a University of California professor. 'However, it does recommend videos that mostly match a user's ideology, and for right-leaning users those videos often come from channels that promote extremism, conspiracy theories and other types of problematic content.' Not so for left-wing sock puppets, who were offered significantly fewer left-wing options. Perhaps this is because the left has not quite organised itself in this way to form an 'Alternative Influence Network'. It is possible this is because we allow what are often small disagreements to stop us forming coalitions and focusing on what is important.

You may already know that YouTube is the most popular video-sharing platform. Its official 'penetration' stats say it's used by 81 per cent of the US population, 82 per cent of Europeans and 90.9 per cent of the UK population, with a steadily growing user base.[41] Astoundingly, over 70 per cent of the content we watch on YouTube is not what we choose, but what is shown to us by its algorithm. We might think regulation is the answer, but further tightening of YouTube rules will not put this genie back in its lamp. When radical 'alpha male and manosphere* influencer' Andrew Tate was banned from YouTube, he set up shop on Rumble – known as an 'anything goes'-type platform – which reports 78 million monthly

* The manosphere is a complex collection of sometimes interconnected online forums and web media promoting masculinity, misogyny and even opposition to feminism.

users,[42] having seen a significant spike since Tate moved there. QAnon, the conspiracy theory and political movement that tends to radicalise older users, was banned from YouTube at the end of 2020 – but the links between QAnon and the storming of the US Capitol building in early 2021 are well documented and much QAnon content is now to be found on Rumble and other online spaces.[43]

Other apps include the extremely popular TikTok platform that you might associate with teens, memes and dance videos. A 2021 report called 'Hatescape: An In-Depth Analysis of Extremism and Hate Speech on TikTok' outlines how this newer platform is used to 'promote white supremacist conspiracy theories, produce weapons manufacturing advice, glorify extremists, terrorists, fascists and dictators, direct targeted harassment against minorities and produce content that denies that violent events like genocides ever happened.'[44] The report found of the random sample of 1,030 videos they analysed, a staggering 30 per cent of the content promoted white supremacy and 24 per cent featured support for an extremist or terrorist. TikTok now has more than one billion users, which means almost 25 per cent of internet users are there and almost half of those users are under thirty, so this is really serious stuff.[45]

The closing remarks of the *Rabbit Hole* podcast from *New York Times* reporter Kevin Roose are these:

> First we know that the internet is largely being run by these sophisticated Artificial Intelligences that have tapped into our base impulses, our deepest desires . . . and they've used that information to show us an image of reality that is hyperbolic and polarising and entertaining and essentially distorted . . . We are giving them exactly what they are programmed to want, which is more of our attention . . .

> The AIs keep showing us this distorted reality and then we keep paying attention to that and in doing so we are telling them we'd like to see more of this distorted reality . . . and essentially we are living inside of this loop . . . showing us a world that is getting more and more distorted.[46]

The more we participate, the more the real world reflects this distortion.

This sounds disturbing, of course, but why does it matter so deeply? Well, because what the AIs are doing (much like the alt-right commentators who exploit them) is making a science of cognitive empathy. However, because their intelligence is artificial, they are figuring out exactly what makes us tick without being able to feel anything for us. Remember, that is what many psychopaths do. They figure out what we want and how we work so they can twist the knife. An algorithm has cognitive empathy no human can hope to have and no affective empathy at all. But scarily, it can fake it very convincingly. It's a psychopath that can't even feel for itself. Furthermore, even if we avoid the internet entirely except for train tickets and sporting match times, AI programs are shaping the minds of those we catch trains with and sit next to at sporting matches.

A useful definition of radicalisation is a process in which a person who feels like no one has empathy for them in an overwhelming world is told by someone, 'We understand you, and we feel for you, and we want to spend a lot of time with you'. During that time, that person is asked to heighten their empathy for a few and eradicate it for many. What happens next depends on the type of person they are. Radicalisation is one way that nature can be nurtured. Radicalisation will brook no dissent and so the radicalised will sometimes go to extreme and irreversible lengths, dehumanising themselves and their victims in the process.

Harnessing our cognitive empathy is to learn and truly understand what will make other people listen, feel and change. The alt-right are becoming masters at it, and this is beginning to have real-world consequences. Surely the left, which is a movement all about feeling with and acting on behalf of others, cannot dial back our empathy now to demand conformity. Using empathy and compassion as tools for justice and fairness is the bedrock of progressive thinking. We cannot let the far right manipulate those tools to create an exclusionary and hateful agenda. We are not just talking about rogue radicals encouraging each other to random acts of violence on the internet. We are also looking at calculated attempts to influence legislators to remove our hard-won rights.

You will know that in the US, Roe v. Wade, the ruling that guaranteed the right to an abortion, was overturned in 2022, which means that in many states abortion access is now limited and in some illegal.[47] What you may not know is that the religious far-right have been getting organised and strategic and using the very tools we've been analysing here with the mission of diminishing and eventually eradicating abortion rights elsewhere. They have been specifically and directly targeting Europe.

I interviewed Neil Datta, the Executive Director of the European Parliamentary Forum for Sexual and Reproductive Rights, a pan-European network which brings together legislators from all democratic parties to advance sexual and reproductive health and rights. The Forum focuses on access to contraception, abortion rights, reducing maternal deaths, improving cervical cancer treatment and prevention. Because of this work, Neil has done research into religious extremists who are working to undermine women's rights to healthcare. He explained that there were well-known 'pro-life' groups who started out picketing abortion clinics. Then in 2013, they 'rebranded' and expanded their remit.

Neil explained:

> They really invested time in hiring lawyers and political scientists so that they understand how power works. And we saw them gradually, between 2013 and 2018, really develop that skill so that they were able to write draft laws and bills, they were able to initiate proceedings in front of national and European-level courts, they were able to start petitions, which then provoke a certain reaction from public authorities, such as a referendum . . . They style themselves as NGOs (non-governmental organisations), think tanks, in some cases, political parties. In Europe, they have the specificity of usually masking their religious ties. But when you scratch beneath the surface, you see religious connections in almost all of them . . . We also have a number of organisations coming from the United States, from the US Christian right, and setting up permanent offices in different European countries and specifically certain cities, such as Brussels, Geneva, Strasbourg, Vienna, and London. These are all the centres of decision-making power.

They decided to organise, get pragmatic and, crucially, harness the tools of influencing empathy to get what they want. And what they want is your rights.

These organisations make up what is known as the 'anti-gender movement'. Gender here is shorthand for 'women's issues'. Neil continued: 'With gender, we needn't overthink it. You simply put the word "gender" somewhere, and that can provoke an allergic reaction by these anti-gender actors. This can be gender studies, gender-based violence, gender mainstreaming, gender quotas etc.'

This movement is also against LGBTQ+ rights, including equal marriage. There are numerous academic studies and symposiums on the anti-gender movement and reports show the groups within it have spent $78 million (US), that we know of, in the last decade. They have decided to get what they *can* now, with the aim of getting what they *want* eventually.

Are their efforts working? Shockingly, yes. A report from the BBC in February 2024 says: 'An unprecedented number of women are being investigated by police on suspicion of illegally ending a pregnancy . . . Abortion provider MSI says it knows of up to sixty criminal inquiries in England and Wales since 2018, compared with almost zero before.'[48]

Between 1861 and November 2022, three women in Great Britain were convicted of an illegal abortion. Since December 2022 (at the time of writing), one woman has been convicted and six women are awaiting trial.[49] Also, at the time of writing, there are three new bills in the House of Lords that would potentially restrict women's ability to have legal abortions in the UK.[50] By comparison, the last anti-abortion bill presented to the Commons was in 1990.[51]

Dr Jonathan Lord, co-chair of the British Society of Abortion Care Providers, has warned that police are seizing women's phones, searching for period apps and combing through their internet history. Health care providers are also reporting that police are also testing distressed women, who have suffered miscarriages, for abortion drugs.[52] Some have called an ambulance for late-stage pregnancy loss and the police have arrived first. Those anti-abortion campaigners who were using anger have learned to use seemingly rational and empathetic techniques – some more sophisticated than those found on YouTube – to influence our policymakers and those working in our communities

If all this sounds to you like a flashback scene in *The Handmaid's Tale*, then you'll be as worried as I am about how organised and well-funded this 'anti-gender' far-right religious movement is. Some of the groups organise what are called influence factories, composed of think tanks, foundations and media enterprises which arrange events. We need to get organised to properly decriminalise abortion in the UK, the way France has responded to the anti-gender movement by enshrining the right to abortion into the constitution.[53]

If we continue to expel people from our stamm for not thinking exactly as we do, if we will not cognitively empathise with those on the other side of the political divide to understand how they think and to influence rather than just shout or ignore, then we are opening ourselves up to a sinister future – one run by people who are prepared to work with anyone who will help them get what they want and who will activate their cognitive empathy to understand how to win others over. They will organise. They will galvanise. And we will end up living in their world.

We have to get savvy and get sorted and that will mean compromise. Remember, ten years ago, the people now changing the conversation about our right to choose were shouting outside abortion clinics with homemade signs. They've made a decision (ironically their right to choose!) to become influential by having conversations they didn't want to have and work with people they don't agree with – and they're getting things done. Things we need undone as soon as possible. If we do not organise, strategise, upskill, rethink and make connections with people we don't wholly agree with, we may find ourselves – and our human rights – hurtling back into the past.

And that brings us to our second conversation, which is about the past and our relationship to it. How did we get here? What are our fiercest judgements of those who came before us? What is the value of being honest about figures from history that we have put on literal marble pedestals? And what happens when the present, a place where we often seem so certain of our modern moral high ground, becomes history? Our next conversation is this – does history have a right side?

Conversation Two

Does History Have a Right Side?

Are we standing on the shoulders of problematic giants?

In 2020, students at the Royal Academy of Dramatic Art (RADA) petitioned the administration to change the name of the George Bernard Shaw Theatre.[1] The theatre is named after the playwright largely because a third of his plays' royalties have historically gone to RADA. His most famous play (which has probably been the most lucrative for the Academy) is *Pygmalion*, the story of Eliza Doolittle, a young woman selling flowers on the street, who agrees to be 'trained' in accent and deportment by Henry Higgins, a linguistics academic. Henry teaches Eliza how to speak and act like an aristocrat so he can win a bet. First performed four years before women had the vote, it makes a strong argument for women's suffrage and the abolition of the British class system. Ellen Dolgin, a renowned Shaw academic, remarked that he was trying to prove that 'what [they thought] of as absolutely innate – social placement – is not. It can be learned – and it can be fudged.'[2]

As Eliza herself says in the play, 'The difference between

a lady and a flower girl is not how she behaves, but how she is treated.' Shaw fought furiously against the twee romcom ending of Eliza and Higgins getting together when producers altered it to get bums on seats. While that ending is now firmly in the public psyche (mostly due to the musical adaptation, *My Fair Lady*) the point, for Shaw, was that Eliza was emancipated in the end: 'If I can't have kindness, I'll have independence.'

His plays were so socialist and feminist they were often banned by the Lord Chamberlain, who at that time had to read and red-pen everything that was performed on the British stage (so much so that improvising in a theatre was illegal until 1968).[3] *Mrs Warren's Profession*, Shaw's play which argued the case for the rights and dignity of sex workers, was banned for twenty-two years. Shaw said he wrote it 'to draw attention to the truth that prostitution is caused, not by female depravity and male licentiousness, but simply by underpaying, undervaluing and overworking women so shamefully that the poorest of them are forced to resort to prostitution to keep body and soul together.'[4]

In 1928, the year all women twenty-one and over got the vote in the UK, Shaw published a book called *The Intelligent Woman's Guide to Socialism and Capitalism*. Yes, that might sound like *Mansplaining Politics for Little Ladies* to us, but it demonstrates he really did want to engage women in the fight. Elsewhere, he wrote, 'The word "prostitute" should either not be used at all, or applied impartially to all persons who do things for money that they would not do if they had assured means of livelihood.' This white man, born and raised in Victorian times, sounds positively Gen Z: *Respect the rights of the sex worker and understand that if it's consensual, it's work.*

He wrote big meaty parts for women and was far more likely than most contemporary male playwrights to give a woman the titular role and the winning argument. *Major Barbara*, *Candida*, *Saint Joan* and *Fanny's First Play* are the tip of the iceberg. He frequently depicted both university-educated women (a new phenomenon at the time) and clever, disenfranchised working-class women who demand and deserve more. He actively fought against the trope of the 'fallen woman' who sins by fornicating and dies in the gutter (a standard of the Victorian melodrama).

In 1881, when he was twenty-five, Shaw took a stand for animal rights and became a vegetarian.[5] He protested against vivisection, fox hunting and game hunting.[6] In 1889, seventy-eight years before homosexuality was legalised for men, he wrote a letter to the editor of a London newspaper, advocating for gay rights:

> I appeal now to the champions of individual rights to join me in a protest against a law by which two adult men can be sentenced to twenty years penal servitude for a private act, freely consented to & desired by both, which concerns themselves alone. There is absolutely no justification for the law, except the old theological one of making the secular arm the instrument of God's vengeance. It is a survival from that discarded system with its stonings and burnings; and it survives because it is so unpleasant that men are loath to meddle with it, even with the object of getting rid of it, lest they should be suspected of acting in their personal interest.

This was a very brave thing for a Victorian to publish.

Shaw advocated for interracial marriage and against war.[7] He made arguments for a fairer, better world in both non-fiction prose and scripted drama. It's probable that without Shaw and his socialist peers working for social justice and change, many or even most of the current intake of RADA students would never have been inside the building. Shaw was a big part of influencing society to widen our collective circle of empathy. So why were students fighting to take his name off the theatre?*

Because George Bernard Shaw's brand of socialism had a dark side. It rested on the sinister premise that equality thrives best in a genetically elite society. He advocated for a sort of superman race not all that different to one strived for by another self-dubbed 'socialist'. *Nazism* is an abbreviation of *Nationalsozialismus* – or in English, *National Socialism.* In Shaw's own words: 'The only fundamental and possible socialism is the socialisation of the selective breeding of man.' Let those five final words linger for a moment. Shaw is suggesting that the way to achieve real equality is to breed out 'flaws' and breed in 'strength'. So yes, Shaw advocated for women's rights, gay rights, animal rights, workers' rights – *and* eugenics, the scientifically erroneous and morally grotesque theory of 'racial improvement' and 'planned breeding'. Watch his circle of empathy shrink before your very eyes. It's hard for us to imagine now, but Shaw thought he was being empathetic to future generations by 'perfecting' them.

Eugenics, which is mostly now linked in people's minds to the horrors of the Holocaust, was then a very popular idea that was seen as a kind of 'town planning' for the human race. As a mental exercise, I want to try to imagine where these people were in history and, even without our hindsight, how they could possibly have thought this was an acceptable idea. I'll explore later why I think it's really important to do this. For now, let's try to employ our cognitive empathy and find a (much more innocent) parallel from our lives.

---

* It should be noted that to date, the students have not been successful. At the time of writing, it is still the George Bernard Shaw Theatre.

Remember when we thought Covid was mostly carried on the hands, and we all had to sing two verses of 'Happy Birthday' while we scrubbed away? Remember that scientists then discovered it was actually transmitted by airborne droplets and the advice became all about wearing masks? They never really loudly announced, 'Hey, the hand-washing thing wasn't quite right,' because it's good practice to wash your hands and it definitely stops the spread of other diseases. They just stopped going on about it and we figured out it wasn't the key thing any more.

Well, now imagine you're living in a time where scientists have recently found out about the exciting new science of genes and, furthermore, you've read that some conditions like asthma, for example, are hereditary. Remember there is no effective treatment for asthma yet (Ventolin wasn't launched till 1969), so people die of asthma all the time.* The scientists say, 'This new discovery about genes means we've got a cure! Not for those already stricken with the condition, but if we tell everyone with asthma not to have children, then the next generation won't suffer from it and no innocent child will die of it ever again. Fixed!'[8]

Now obviously the scientists are wrong about this. It's not going to work like that because genes are far more complicated than that, and environmental factors play a large part. But *historical you* doesn't know that any more than *actual you* didn't know that coming home and singing 'Happy Birthday' near your housemate was much more likely to spread Covid than failing to wash your hands laboriously. You're just going along with the science. In fact, all your friends, leaders and

* My great-grandparents were told to emigrate from London to Australia in the 1920s because one of their children had asthma and the recommended treatment was 'move to a hot country'. In fact, asthma can get worse in extreme heat.

media outlets are telling you that you're being unscientific and heartless if you know a way to eradicate suffering and you don't participate in it and encourage it.

Of course, you are living in a moral minefield, because the scientists are effectively telling asthmatics that they are not serving the human race if they have children. Asthmatics should let themselves die out. How do you feel as an asthmatic person who wants children? 'No more broken humans like you, please! Don't pass it on!' Not so much 'wear a mask' as 'wear a condom'. Also, while the scientific and political leaders are saying their intentions are to rid humanity of unnecessary suffering and 'defects', they are setting themselves up as moral arbiter, judging what is and isn't a 'defect'. Almost everyone agrees that human beings in a civilised society would be foolish not to use this cool new science to make life better, but people disagree about what should be 'bred out' and what shouldn't. It doesn't stop with medical conditions. What else will be considered an 'undesirable trait' by the powers that be? Exactly what kind of genetic town are they planning here? Will people like you be welcome in it? And crucially, what means are they prepared to use to get there?

There were those who advocated for 'positive eugenics' – encouraging, coercing or forcing people to have children through 'selective breeding' – and there were those who advocated for 'negative eugenics' – stopping people having children through coerced or enforced segregation, sterilisation, forced abortion, euthanasia (though of course, without informed consent, 'euthanasia' becomes execution) and even genocide.

In a film for Paramount British Pictures in March 1931, our socialist, empathy-building dramatist friend Shaw, with no apparent irony, openly says to camera, in something that looks remarkably like a pre-war TED Talk:

> I object to all punishment whatsoever. I don't want to punish anybody, but there are an extraordinary number of people who I want to kill. Not in any unkind or personal spirit. But it must be evident to all of you, you must all know half a dozen people at least, who are no use in this world; who are more trouble than they are worth. And I think it would be a good thing to make everybody come before a properly appointed board just as he might come before the income tax commissioners and say every five years or every seven years, just put them there, and say, 'Sir or madam, now will you be kind enough to justify your existence? If you can't justify your existence; if you're not pulling your weight in the social boat; if you are not producing as much as you consume or perhaps a little more, then clearly we cannot use the big organisation of our society for the purpose of keeping you alive, because your life does not benefit us, and it can't be of very much use to yourself.'[9]

That's right – Shaw argued against fox hunting, but dreamed up the original *Hunger Games* for humans.

Many people assume eugenics was a right-wing movement, but almost every high-profile left-wing thinker and activist was in favour. The *Guardian* backed it and so did the *New Statesman*. Astoundingly, even Helen Keller endorsed eugenics for a time, saying 'some "defective" children should not be saved from a premature death because of their propensity to criminality.'[10] She was seduced into this way of thought for a time by Alexander Graham Bell, a mentor who wanted to discourage deaf people from marrying each other (presumably, in part, because deaf people did nothing for the sale of the telephone). That is how pervasive an idea it was among people who were, in other ways, liberal intellectuals best known as advocates for human rights.

Marie Stopes, the original British family-planning matriarch, whose centres are now synonymous with reproductive rights, was an enthusiastic eugenicist and fervently against mixed-race marriage.[11] One of her objectives was 'to furnish security from conception to those who are racially diseased' or in other words, mixed race. Yes – that's who your pro-choice Marie Stopes local clinic is named after.* She wanted some people to have no choice at all. Her ideology is in a different (fascist) galaxy from ours, and yet without her we may not have had the 'our body/our choice' policy we do.

Virtually every left-wing person from the early twentieth century you've ever heard of had a hot take that will leave you gasping. Socialist philosopher Bertrand Russell suggested the government dispense colour-coded 'procreation tickets'. In his masterplan, if you bred outside your ticket colour (race, class, 'ability') – you'd be fined.[12] In fact, some 1930s Fabian Society members went further than that and came up with the idea of artificially inseminating working-class women with what they considered to be 'high IQ sperm'.[13] Heavy shades of Gilead.

Left-wing intellectuals thought they were giving Darwin a helping hand without considering the ethics of this – or even more unthinkably, *while* considering the ethics of this. The theory of evolution was sweeping through society as a demonstrable fact, but it was still very controversial with both religious and scientific objections regularly put forward. Prior to Darwin, the most pervasive theory for the diversity of life was that propounded by a French biologist called Jean-Baptiste Lamarck. He believed that parents could pass on characteristics that they have acquired through their life: for example, a rower who develops strong muscles will produce a child with strong muscles. This mostly discredited theory was now

---

* Or was, until they changed the name to MSI Reproductive Choices in 2020.

revisited as neo-Lamarckism,[14] and proponents believed that 'fallen women' would pass on their immorality and 'moral disease' to their children, so it was inadvisable to foster or adopt such genetically hampered offspring. Eugenicists also strongly advised against taking in children from poor families who couldn't afford to keep them, as they were likely to prove just as 'incapable' as their parents.

In 1934, psychologists Harold Skeels and Marie Skodak were working at the Iowa State Board of Control, helping to place orphaned children with adoptive families. Their work included administering IQ tests to toddlers, and in one case described two young girls as 'doomed from birth' on the basis of their low scores. Guess who invented IQ tests? Eugenicists.[15] It helped them rate us all – even toddlers. Influenced by eugenics, Skeels and Skodak believed that the children had inherited their parents' lack of intelligence and should not be candidates for adoption. Instead, they were sent to an institution for the 'feeble minded'[16] and were put into the care of women who they described as 'morons'.[17] All of these terms which are now slurs were then official medical diagnoses. Under the care of these women, the IQs of the children rose to a 'regular score'. It's almost as if these so-called unfit women were, in fact, cleverer than the eugenicists that diagnosed them and that children respond better to tests if they're being nurtured and not prejudged. The idea that the children deserved love and human rights regardless of their test scores or intellectual potential never occurred to them.

Sick, disabled or homeless white people undermine the narrative that white people are superior, so there was a real desire to eliminate evidence of perceived 'white imperfection' through any means necessary. You know how 'Maggie Thatcher Milk Snatcher' took free milk from schoolchildren and everyone was shocked at her cruelty? The twist: we only had free milk in schools in the first place because eugenicists were trying to improve the teeth and bones of the breeding British working classes who'd struggled so much in the Boer War against stronger African soldiers. Milk for the poppets at break time was not out of concern for marginalised individuals, but rather an attempt to build a master race fit for warfare who would breed ever-more strong-boned soldiers. I'm not suggesting attempts at better nutrition are eugenics per se, but this initiative was specifically driven by the desire for 'better breeding', not social care.

Beatrice Webb, a socialist and social worker who came up with the term 'collective bargaining'[18] (the foundation of unions negotiating with companies), presented a policy to the government to 'secure a national minimum of civilised life ... open to all alike, of both sexes and all classes, by which we mean sufficient nourishment and training when young, a living wage when able-bodied, treatment when sick, and modest but secure livelihood when disabled or aged.' A universal wage and a welfare state – how frightfully modern. She was also really keen on her own genetic material being preserved over others, assuring her peers she was 'the cleverest member of one of the cleverest families in the cleverest class of the cleverest nation of the world'.[19] She believed in making a world full of people as 'clever' as she was by being an elite member of a society who got a say in who got to breed, and inflicting sterilisation on those who were poor or in any way deemed deficient.

It wasn't just white people who advocated for eugenics. Professor Kelly Miller, Dean of Howard University, a historically Black American college, wrote an article in *The Scientific Monthly* in 1917 entitled 'Eugenics of the Negro Race'.[20] It opened: 'The problem of eugenics is receiving much attention from students of sociology at the present time. The future welfare of society depends very largely upon perpetuating and carrying forward the best characteristics derivable from physical heredity and social environment.' The article goes on to examine why Black academics and intellectuals were having fewer children than working-class Black people, and sometimes no children at all.

He noted that while the faculty members of Howard had come from families averaging 6.5 children, they themselves were only producing on average 0.7 children per head. His suggested reasons included academics not wanting to bring children into a world of white supremacy and the hardship of recovering from the trauma of family enslavement while making the exhausting effort of social advancement. Miller's own mother had been enslaved. He also cited the financial pressures of maintaining an upper-middle-class lifestyle and, more heartbreakingly, 'The educated negro, especially when submerged in a white environment, is under a sort of social captivity. The effect of this psycho-physical factor upon reproductivity awaits further and fuller study, both in its biological and psychological aspects.' Both tragic and sobering.

His article reads, in some ways, not unlike a contemporary think-piece about Black trauma in America, but its opening assumption about the welfare of society and genes was just received wisdom at the time; it wasn't even up for debate. The thrust of his argument was that academic Black Americans must have more children, because those children are likely to be cleverer than other Black children. He at least acknowledges that environment is a factor, which many eugenicists discounted. He lived his values and had five children of his own. Some Black progressives like civil rights activist W. E. B. Du Bois went further and took the stance that 'only fit blacks should procreate to eradicate the race's heritage of moral iniquity.'[21] Dr Thomas Wyatt Turner, a charter member of the NAACP, promoted 'Assimilationist Eugenics', which proposed that 'The Talented Tenth' of all races should mix so that the 'best' black and white genes could be combined to create 'the best babies'. In fact, the NAACP hosted 'Better Baby' competitions. Astoundingly, proceeds from these contests went to its anti-lynching campaign.[22]

A great many of the people in the late nineteenth and early twentieth centuries who fought for civil rights, the living wage, votes for women, rights for sex workers, the decriminalisation of homosexuality, children's rights and social services were so enthralled by Darwin and intellectualism that anything that was 'science' was, to them, morally sound by default, because it was 'objective' and 'neutral'.[23] The survival of the fittest can't be immoral! It's natural. It's biological. And you can't argue with biology. They really believed they could help evolution out through eugenics, by projecting fitness onto human beings and then helping the 'fit' ones survive and thrive. Their ideas of who was fittest reflected their white (or white-informed), university-educated agenda in a deeply racist, colonised world.

Where does this leave George Bernard Shaw, a eugenicist among eugenicists but an outlier in so many other positive ways? It was in this deeply racist, colonised world that Shaw advocated for Black people and wrote a novel with a Black female heroine.[24] He sometimes argued for the rights of Jewish people and referred to antisemitism as 'hatred of the lazy, ignorant, fat-headed Gentile for the pertinacious Jew'.[25]

Perhaps he was a bundle of violent contradictions. Perhaps he just didn't care. But there is one way in which his outlier tendencies may have surpassed all others. George Bernard Shaw advocated for Hitler. And not when he was some little-known political dissident. He advocated for Hitler *after the war*. He did it after the horrendous photographs from Auschwitz and other camps had been widely distributed. Shaw argued that Hitler's eugenicist aspirations should not be tarnished by the antisemitism they were attached to. Terrifying images from concentration camps, he said, reflected not bad ideas, but bad execution. He blamed incompetent guards and poor nutrition (presumably for those who were deemed candidates for life but not breeding). It would seem Shaw's desire to eradicate poverty by genetically 'improving' the human race was an end that justified any means, including, apparently, genocide and the insurmountable suffering of Jewish people and other vulnerable groups. Are you cringing at the name of the George Bernard Shaw Theatre yet?

Does history repeat itself, or is it just that historians repeat themselves?

How do we reconcile any of this?

Well, we need to ask lots of questions and develop the muscles that will allow us to sit with uncomfortable, complicated answers. We need to understand that all human beings, including you and me, are complex, flawed and heavily influenced by our peers and the received wisdom of their time. We also need to acknowledge that sometimes the progress people fight for will develop beyond their intention so greatly, it will end up revealing them to be monstrous.

So, questions: some drama students want the George Bernard Shaw Theatre to be renamed – and we can understand why they're making that argument, having analysed his most appalling views. But say they achieve that. It's not a simple fix. Do those same actors upon graduating also refuse to audition for *Pygmalion*? I ask this not to catch them out. I understand their anger, but I want to think this action through to its logical next steps. What if the artistic director of the National Theatre calls up and asks them to play the lead role in *Major Barbara*? Do they turn it down, even though it is a big opportunity for them, and the play makes an interesting argument against capitalism and for compassion?

If RADA is to take Shaw's name off the theatre, should they also have refused his royalties (which coincidentally came to an end that year)?[26] What if that had meant there were less funding for academic or pastoral care of students, including members of under-represented groups? Where should those royalties have gone instead? Do those same students imagine that Shakespeare, who died more than three hundred years before Shaw, shared their value set more than he did? Will they only appear in plays by living writers who they know for certain have contemporary, progressive views? If so, their career as an actor is going to be limited to the freshest possible scripts (and even then – no guarantees!) as what we know as 'the canon' is written entirely by highly complex figures with some horrendous views. Will other actors and artists, who care less about progressive change and more about fast fame, take a more central place in their industry? And, if so, is that a positive step forward for the art our society consumes? While the powers that be continue to produce those shows, and bums rush to those seats, being a jobbing actor (for most) means taking the limited number of jobs offered.

So perhaps responsibility should lie less with the jobbing actor and more with the salaried producer. But the questions they face are no clearer cut. Do they start culling George Bernard Shaw from their programmes? Or is there a value in these plays which still have a feminist, class-challenging message and are written by an extraordinary talent? Do we need to separate the art from the worst flaws of the artist? If the work fits with our values, but the artist's views outside the work don't, how do we square this? Is it better or worse if the art seems to showcase the 'right' values, and the artist expressed the 'wrong' values elsewhere? The progress we have today was fought for exclusively by people we'd argue fiercely with now, so does their art have to be reconciled with our contemporary values to be performed, or can we find interesting and challenging ways to stage and explore old, complex texts?

I will make some moves towards resolving some of these questions, but answers are not my endgame. Far more important than the conclusion is the conversation. A conversation that is nuanced, empathetic and, most of all, self-aware. A conversation that is ongoing and ever-changing with each year, decade and generation.

This is not the same as advocating for all talk and no action. We do not simply have to sit with history, we also get to make it, and sometimes that means ceremonially dethroning historical figures who were wrongly put on plinths. Statues of men who enslaved human beings for profit are coming down and it's thrilling. When the Colston statue was pulled down at the Black Lives Matter march in Bristol on 7 June 2020, even the police officers who were present said that it wasn't the time to intervene. Bristolians had been petitioning to take it down for years. They'd filled out all the right paperwork and spoken at all the right town halls and been denied. Critics of the 'illegal destruction of public property' should realise that Colston's Wikipedia entry (at the time of writing) reads, 'During Colston's involvement with the Royal African Company from 1680 to 1692, it is estimated that the company transported over 84,000 African men, women and children to the Caribbean and the rest of the Americas, of whom as many as 19,000 may have died on the journey.' 'Transported.' 'May have died.' Not 'kidnapped and trafficked'. Not 'were killed under Colston's command'. All of Colston's crimes are presented under a section labelled 'Career'.

Imagine a man who kidnapped and enslaved thousands of white men and women, white little boys and girls with blonde ringlets. Imagine if he killed about a quarter of them in an unspeakably cruel way. Where would his statue be? Can we seriously suggest we think the account of him doing those monstrous things would be listed under 'Career' on his Wikipedia page? Or would it be under 'Captivity' like Fritzl's entry, or 'Deaths, Survivors and Eyewitnesses' like Jonestown? Or would it be under 'Atrocities' or 'Homicide'? The Chinese have an idiom: 'The beginning of wisdom is calling something by its proper name.' We can never begin to dismantle the poisonous views and impact of structural racism while statues of men whose sole 'career' achievement is barbaric cruelty.

The four protesters who brought Colston's statue down were found not guilty of causing criminal damage in 2022. A report by Professor Steven Cammiss and other academics who sat through the entire trial stated:

> It was Edward Colston and Bristol City Council that appeared to be on trial. The defendants and multiple witnesses argued that Colston's crimes were so horrific that the continued presence of his statue was offensive, abusive and distressing. The local council's failure to remove it, despite 30 years of petitions and demands from Bristol's African Caribbean community, in particular, also led to the defence claiming that the council's inaction amounted to misconduct in public office.[27]

Cammiss suggests that if the statue had been given context in the form of a plaque planned for 2019 that never materialised (because the wording was in dispute), the statue may never have come down in that way. 'Contextualising could have made a difference,' he said in an interview; 'with that lack of activity, I think [not guilty] was a justifiable verdict. What really came through in the evidence was the extent to which the community's disquiet with the Colston statue, in essence, just hit a wall.'

The We Are Bristol History Commission published its recommendations about the future of the statue, in the light of a survey of public opinion.[28] It suggested the statue is kept in Bristol Museum, lying down and 'in its current state', that is to say still covered in the protesters' graffiti, and 'that attention is paid to presenting the history in a nuanced, contextualised and engaging way, including information on the broader history of the enslavement of people of African descent.'[29] The M Shed museum, where the statue is currently lying, is now offering a walking tour of Bristol's thousand-year fight for abolition, telling this story from the point of view of those who do not have historical monuments in their name. The tour ends at the plinth where Colston's statue once stood.[30]

Why was there more public support for taking down Colston's statue than taking Shaw's name off the theatre? You might say having homicidal views isn't the same as violently enslaving and killing people. But you might also say having your name taken off a building isn't the same as having your statue thrown into a river. And they weren't just ideas. George Bernard Shaw was highly influential and very vocal about eugenics from as early as 1903. We cannot discount his influence on developments in the social landscape which lead to the eugenically motivated 'Feeble Minded Bill' of 1913[31] that created a dangerous and hostile environment for people with intellectual disabilities and (perceived) mental health issues in the UK.* Laws were passed that allowed the state to incarcerate people considered 'unfit' indefinitely, so that they could have neither a sex life nor children. Shaw was part of a culture which

* Winston Churchill was Home Secretary at this time and drafted this bill himself. He wanted to go further and sterilise people considered unfit.

endorsed and promoted a policy of cruelty in Britain and, by extension, worse horrors around the world.

I think the reason Shaw's name remains and Colston's likeness has been removed from Bristol's plinth is twofold. Firstly, story is everything. Shaw was a great teller of stories and the framing of him as an important Irish dramatist working in British theatre is deeply ingrained in our historical narrative. We edit out inconvenient truths if they get in the way of a long-held story that is serving us. It's hard to let go of the story of a hero, especially one who has shaped our cultural or personal identity. If our Obi-Wan Kenobi was working for the dark side all along, what does that mean for our journey as Luke Skywalker? (We've all got main-character energy. It's our life after all.) We want to look away from or justify anything that doesn't fit our story.

If you do not believe story can be as important as all that, think of this: the International Fund for Animal Welfare reports that every year, humans kill around a hundred million sharks.[32] Last year nine people were killed by sharks, but only five of those were unprovoked. Why do we have the *Jaws* narrative of the monstrous killer shark, hungry for human, so clearly locked in our psyche, when we are clearly the predatory, genocidal species? Because sharks have no Spielberg. Everything is story.

Secondly, context has a role to play. The RADA theatre was not named after George Bernard Shaw because of his views on eugenics. He is commemorated for being a skilled dramatist and for writing characters who shattered elitist stereotypes and shaped a kinder society. His name is on the door of a theatre, not a genetics lab. In 2020, University College London, located in the same neighbourhood as RADA, retitled two lecture halls and a building previously named after scientists and statisticians Francis Galton and Karl Pearson.[33] This move was not without controversy, as both men are widely seen to have been brilliant in many ways. However, Galton is known as 'the father of eugenics' (coining the term itself) and Pearson's ideas were exported to the US and used to justify (among other brutal policies) mass sterilisations of marginalised people. Given this, frankly, their excellent work in weather maps and stats pales. Eugenics is their largest legacy, and it overrides all else. It wasn't something they just advocated for but something they co-created and exported.

Had Shaw's name been on a science lab as a high-profile supporter of eugenics, I imagine it would have been removed at the same time. This is not to say that there is no further conversation to be had about the commemoration of historical figures and the reshaping of their narratives as generations reframe their actions. Each generation gains new perspectives on the past and that is how we learn from history – if and when we do. When we have the movie the sharks deserve, the narrative will start to shift, and different decisions will be made as a consequence.

Colston's statue came down because he is commemorated for the blood-soaked profit he spent as patron supporter of his own philanthropic ego. Colston's primary contribution to the world was glorified violence. His supposed philanthropy was nothing more than the gifting of stolen money taken from enforced labour of human beings to churches he agreed with and schools who put his name on them. Buying houses of education and worship with blood money needs must affect the lessons, values and historical accounts learned within those buildings. In other words, when you buy schools and churches, you buy the story that is told inside them. No matter how substantial his philanthropy, I don't believe it's relevant. If someone stole your child, sold them, and built a really lovely community library with the proceeds, how would you feel? Colston did nothing to widen society's circle of empathy, only to squeeze it to the point of gasping – which is not true of Shaw. When we take down statues of those who are exclusively celebrated for ill-gotten gains and enslavement and how they showed-off their profits, we are not destroying history. We are living it.

Why does no one get angry at Attila the Hun?

The further back in history we go, the less we expect to relate to the characters in it. No one wants to take down the Colosseum because enslaved people were made to battle to the death there. No one is trying to remove Tutankhamun's name from buildings because he used slave labour and had people sent to their deaths.[34] We know that the ancient world was cruel and harsh and while we have no desire to be friends with Genghis Khan or Henry VIII, we don't take their cruelties personally the way we do with historical figures from the twentieth, nineteenth and even the eighteenth centuries. Why? Caligula is as dead as George Washington and his crimes were worse, so why do they seem more abstract?

I think it is because we are closer to George Washington, so we expect more of him in the same way we judge our parents' failings more than our great-grandparents'. The further back in time someone lived, the less we imagine we should understand them. We are horrified by George Bernard Shaw's worst excesses precisely because he is not long out of living memory and his most modern views meant he was capable of writing *Pygmalion*! After watching his most compassionate, contemporary-seeming plays, we hear about his enthusiasm for eugenics, and we are angry with him.

Secondly, it is because we are still living with the legacy of transatlantic slavery, the Holocaust, colonisation and the class system. Some people in our society have inherited both trauma and a socio-economic position caused by individuals who are still venerated. Enslavement in the ancient world does not seem to have a direct impact on us in the same way.

One reason to engage with Shaw's work and legacy is that it forces us to ask, 'How could someone who got so much so right have been so unspeakably wrong about something like eugenics?' This is why I wanted to employ cognitive empathy earlier to figure out how he and his contemporaries could have got there. Because our next question is this one:

What will history judge us for?

If you are a progressive, left-wing, well-educated person now, it is highly likely that you would have argued for eugenics had you been around in the early twentieth century. What you might have disagreed upon were which groups made good candidates for breeding or whether positive or negative eugenics was the way forward. If you'd been against it, you'd have been fighting against your stamm all the way and might have been something of a social outcast. Even the scientists who argued with it did so on the grounds that they thought it wouldn't work, not that it was morally reprehensible.

There were some high-profile, outspoken opponents of eugenics though – mostly right-wing Catholics like Hilaire Belloc and G. K. Chesterton who found it to be antithetical to their doctrine.[35] Both of them were also outspoken antisemites. So let's examine where we might be coming unstuck now and not be so arrogant as to think future generations will only look back at us with admiration.

In a hundred years' time, people will likely be ripping our names off theatres for 'being an inter-species captor and murderer who cooked the flesh of our victims'. Or for being 'so-called vegans, who blithely aligned ourselves with others who ate the corpses of our prey'. Greta Thunberg might be lauded by some for her work in saving the planet (should that mission be accomplished!) but it's entirely possible that she will be judged harshly by others because she associated with flesh predators and there are pictures of her where meat was present on the table. In the film *#ForNature*, she says:

> The way we make food: raising animals to eat, clearing land to grow food to feed those animals. If we continue, we will run out of land and food. It just doesn't make sense.

How will her statement read to future humans who view us as the generation that failed to protect the rights of species who couldn't talk, because we were barbarians who kept captive and ate the muscle and young of our non-verbal friends?

Thunberg's words will probably hit future generations the way a statement about the abolition of slavery from the point of view of finance and agriculture practices would land with us today. 'If we continue' not 'we will be barbarians' but 'we will run out of land and food'. Thunberg does care about animal rights and teamed up with animal welfare charity Mercy for Animals to make a film.[36] In her quote above she was specifically appealing to leaders about sustainability for human beings and using the argument she thought would best persuade them. However, this statement implies that her reasoning for not keeping animals captive, ruthlessly killing and cooking them, and wearing their skins, is nothing to do with their welfare and everything to do with ours. Future generations may not be interested in the context, because their societal circle of empathy may be so much wider than ours. It may mean that their affective empathy for animals will be so great, people will have no ability to find cognitive empathy for us.

Thunberg, who is vegan, may well have had to sit with world

leaders while they devoured a rare steak on the grounds that they have agreed to discuss climate change with her. Will the animal-enslavement abolitionists of a century hence look back kindly on her, or will they judge her the way we might judge someone who didn't enslave anyone but worked or socialised with those who did? Will they acknowledge she was one of the forces who saved them from extinction, or will they take her name off lecture halls and demand to take down the plaques honouring her name? If you could advocate for her to future generations, would you? And would you ask them to take into account the context of the times she had no choice but to be born into? If so, should we not discuss historical figures within their context? Can we even compare Greta Thunberg's comments about animal farming to enslaving people, which we would never do?

On 10 May 2021, it was reported by human rights outlets that there was evidence suggesting that seven Apple suppliers in China were forcing members of the Uyghur population into slave labour through 'poverty alleviation programmes'. The enslaved workers are effectively working and living in prison camps overseen by guards in watchtowers.[37]

Laura Murphy, Professor of Human Rights and Contemporary Slavery at Sheffield Hallam University, commented: 'All state-sponsored labour recruitment programs in Xinjiang must be understood as compulsory labour because no minority citizen in the region has the ability to refuse to participate in the programs.' Reports say that those who refuse to 'participate' are sent to jail.[38] Apple claims it 'looks for evidence' of forced labour when inspecting suppliers but has not, to date, found any. Human rights groups counter that Apple relies on interviews with workers who risk their lives if they speak the truth.

In June 2020, Apple published an open letter from its CEO,

Tim Cook, on its website, which claimed to support Black Lives Matter and committed the company to 'pushing progress forward on inclusion and diversity' and vowing the company would donate to groups like the Equal Justice Initiative, 'which challenge racial injustice and mass incarceration'.[39] But in May 2021, the *Washington Times* described the company as 'continuing to use slave labor' and said that Mr Cook 'continually pushed back against Congress, lobbying to weaken a bill it was crafting preventing U.S. companies from using slave labor in China'. The article went on to say that a few months earlier, 'the Tech Transparency Project found one of Apple's most well-known iPhone suppliers was using forced Uyghur labor in its factories.'[40]

If you think you're exempt because your phone is a Samsung Galaxy, think again. The ASPI Report* (endorsed by Amnesty International and Human Rights Watch) based on analysis of government documents and local media reports, says, 'Under conditions that strongly suggest forced labour, Uyghurs are working in factories that are in the supply chains of at least 83 well-known global brands in the technology, clothing and automotive sectors, including Apple, BMW, Gap, Huawei, Nike, Samsung, Sony and Volkswagen.'

If you have a phone, laptop or car, or if you shop for clothes on the high street, it's most likely you rely on slave labour. But what are you supposed to do? This is just how our society works. We are locked into a system that forces our hand for economic and pragmatic reasons. We want to end it, but how do we sign a petition, raise awareness, donate to activist organisations and write to our political representatives without buying devices very probably made by enslaved people? If you're reading this on a device, do you know where it's come

* Australian Strategic Policy Institute, which is an independent think tank.

from? Do you want to know? If you're thinking there's nothing you can do, I get it – I've also got a number of electronic goods of unknown origins and two Apple devices and that's how life works right now – but it's disingenuous not to admit that this was very much the stance of some of America's Founding Fathers who we (correctly) judge so harshly.[41]

In 1775, Samuel Johnson asked in *Taxation No Tyranny*, 'How is it that we hear the loudest yelps for liberty among the drivers of [slaves]?' Are we just abolitionists compromised by association like Alexander Hamilton? Of course, we feel it is different. The conditions for those enslaved are different, we hope. The level of dehumanisation and torture is different, we hope. And crucially, in the case of Americans at least, the enslaved workers who make the things we want or feel we need are further away, despite the fact that we could jump on a plane and be there faster than many New Yorkers could've travelled to the South. It seems it is as easy for us to disassociate from the origin of our goods and the human beings who make them as it was for those in 1776. Are we better than Hamilton or just deeper in denial? Are you still sure we'd never enslave people?

If you're still feeling sick about how your own progressive movement backed eugenics and are grateful that your stamm would have nothing to do with that today, I have news for you. The workforce enslaved to make our devices in China is subjected to enforced sterilisation, forced abortion and compulsory contraception.[42] Between 2015 and 2018, the birth rate in most areas of China fell by about 9 per cent, but the birth rate in the mainly Uyghur regions of Hotan and Kashgar fell by more than 60 per cent. This is the Chinese government practising eugenics on people who work for us. Right now.

The Victorians used child labour, which we would never do, because we are enlightened and believe in the rights of the child. In fact, The International Labour Organization tells us that 160 million children are in 'child labour'[43] which the UN defines as 'work for which the child is either too young or work which, because of the detrimental nature or conditions, is altogether considered unacceptable for children and is prohibited.'[44] They are not up your chimney, but far away they are sewing sequins on an outfit for a child you protect, and mining minerals for the devices you use.

These are just some of my predictions about what we'll be judged for by future generations, before we even get to climate change which is causing humanitarian disasters and emergencies all over the world. These are just the things we are aware we are culpable for now.

Generational trauma or generational anger?

The truth is, no matter how young and plugged in you are now, your grandchildren or future relatives (should the human race be lucky enough to survive) will most certainly judge you for the way you talk, act and think now. Views we currently congratulate ourselves for will not be considered radical in the future. We don't even know what progressives of the future will despise us for yet, but it will certainly happen. When you're elderly, you may well argue with young people about the good you did and the changes you made that they don't appreciate. Don't believe me? Speak to some second-wave feminists. They had to stamm all the way up to figure out so much of the shit we take for granted. They're now being looked at with suspicion across the board. We'll look at some examples shortly.

Young feminists rejecting the previous generation is no new phenomenon. In the last conversation we discussed Emmeline Pankhurst breaking away from the suffragists to start the suffragettes due to political differences. Her own daughter,

Stella, fell out with Emmeline in turn over her classism, elitism and racism (that's right, we have another eugenicist on our hands). Pankhurst Jr rejected the activism of the woman most responsible for getting women the vote. Rich, married women over thirty first. Yes, of course that precluded many Black and Brown women, but it is our prejudice to think that no women of colour had property in the UK in 1918. And this was the only possible first step. The government wouldn't give all women twenty-one and over the vote after the First World War because so many men had died in battle, it would have meant there were more female voters than male – and they couldn't have that. What would women do if they were a majority? So they gave all men aged twenty-one and over the vote where previously only men who had property or significant wealth had that right. They also gave the vote to women over thirty with property and addressed the frightening gender imbalance threat.* A mere ten years later and bang! It was on for young and old, owners and renters, male and female.

Generations usually have a clearer insight into what their parents got wrong, but often it is because the generation before them had already expanded the circle of empathy. Emmeline Pankhurst asked the men to empathise with and therefore legislate for women like her – well-educated, upper-middle-class women. Imagine trying to get working-class women the vote when working-class men didn't have it. It wasn't just a practicality, however – it was a genuine feeling of superiority she'd been trained to have. Emmeline Pankhurst felt that middle-class women, once allowed into the political system, would fight for the rights of women of all classes. Her daughter

* There were some exceptions to these rules. Men who'd turned nineteen while in combat could vote. Women married to men who owned property or were university graduates themselves (no mean feat then!) could vote too.

demanded they make the empathy circle wider again and allow working-class people to advocate for themselves.

Generational anger is important – the fiery and motivating energy of youth is usually at the forefront of a social movement – but it often ignores the boring reality that progress is a process. Just as the contours of our coastlines have been shaped by wave after wave, so the contours of our feminism have been shaped by that steady, ceaseless beating on the sands of time. Let us not forget the work of the wave in whose wake we break. Let us ask ourselves first, why did they think the way they thought? We have to remember the context in which they were raised.

Some young people attempted to cancel Margaret Atwood for her comments in an article in Canadian newspaper *The Globe and Mail*:

> The #MeToo moment is a symptom of a broken legal system. All too frequently, women and other sexual-abuse complainants couldn't get a fair hearing through institutions – including corporate structures – so they used a new tool: the internet. Stars fell from the skies. This has been very effective, and has been seen as a massive wake-up call. But what next? The legal system can be fixed, or our society could dispose of it . . .
>
> If the legal system is bypassed because it is seen as ineffectual, what will take its place? Who will be the new power brokers?

Atwood's article is an argument for due process to be upheld rather than discarded altogether precisely because it has not been upheld.

The push-back from the internet could be summed up with the blanket statement: 'Believe women'. Similarly, Gloria

Steinem said in an interview: 'We should believe women but also women have got to be believable.'[45]

These could come across as grating statements to a generation horribly aware that in the UK, for example, five out of six women who are raped don't ever report it because they do not believe justice will be done, and they cannot face any more trauma – and this belief is not unfounded. Only one in a hundred rape cases reported to the police in 2021 resulted in charges, and charges don't by any means lead to convictions.[46] Far more guaranteed is re-traumatisation, stigmatisation and ultimate validation of the accused. Given that the Crown Prosecution Service's own calculations[47] say only 0.62 per cent of all rape cases are 'false allegations' (a figure that is probably overblown in failing to account for the likelihood of coerced retraction by the five out of six women who are raped by someone they know) just how much more 'believable' must women be? So why would these pillars of feminism say this?

Atwood was sixteen years old, and Steinem was twenty-one, when Emmett Till, a fourteen-year-old Black boy, was accused of sexually harassing a white woman in a grocery store and was consequently abducted from his bed by two white men, beaten beyond recognition, shot in the head and thrown in a river. The white men who murdered him, Roy Bryant and J. W. Milam, walked away with a not-guilty verdict from an all-white jury. They later confessed (but perniciously couldn't be tried twice for the same crime). Carolyn Bryant, Till's accuser, testified in 1955 that he had grabbed her hand, put his arm around her waist and propositioned her, saying he had been with 'white women before'. In 2008 she gave an interview to Professor Timothy Tyson for his book *The Blood of Emmett Till*, and he says she admitted to him: 'That part's not true,' referring to Till grabbing her around the waist and whispering obscenities to her (as if it would have justified his murder if it were!). In

August 2022, a grand jury in Mississippi declined to indict the eighty-eight-year-old Carolyn Bryant, despite the existence of a decades-old warrant for her arrest for the kidnapping of Till – issued but never served – which had turned up during a search for evidence in the basement of a Mississippi courthouse.

On 25 May 2020, a white woman called Amy Cooper got into an altercation with a Black man called Christian Cooper in Central Park, New York. Christian was a birdwatcher and Amy's dog was not on a leash. He politely requested she fix that, and she became irate and phoned the police, claiming she felt unsafe in his presence. He filmed it and it went viral. It was clear she was weaponising the story of her white womanhood and therefore her presumed vulnerability and innocence. She was also using his Blackness and maleness as markers for danger and potential violence for her own ends. She didn't want to be told what to do. She wanted to win the status battle. She knew that this was a power she had, and she disregarded the frankly lethal possibility of calling the police on a Black man in America and telling them she felt unsafe.[48] Unarmed Black people in the US are three times more likely to be killed by the police than unarmed white people.[49]

This happened on the same day that George Floyd was arrested and murdered by police. Christian's safety was truly at risk. These two strangers shared a surname. It is chilling to realise the reason Amy felt so empowered to phone the police in such a cavalier and unnecessary way that day, has the same root cause as them sharing a name ... Enslavement. At one point, a family like hers had 'owned' a family like his. 'Believe women' ... It's too short a catchphrase to embody the complexity of humanity.

Atwood and Steinem's comments point out the problems of youthful absolutes like this. Men do not have a monopoly on the abuse of power. They've just traditionally had more of it. Women are just as capable of lying and abusing power. Anyone who says otherwise is dehumanising us, because all varieties of human beings are flawed and can be corrupt, venal and dishonest. 'Believe women' is a hashtag attempting to right an avalanche of historical wrongs. But two words cannot take into account any exceptions to this disturbing pattern. When Margaret Atwood says, 'Don't forget due process', or Gloria Steinem says, 'But women have to be believable', they are speaking from the position of having lived long lives. They have spent time in the past. They remember how things were before most of us were born. They speak as women who've seen many changes in the feminist movement, and they are perhaps saying, 'Beware . . . we've been here before.'

When bell hooks criticised Beyoncé on a panel in 2014, saying 'I see a part of Beyoncé that is in fact anti-feminist – that is a terrorist, especially in terms of the impact on young girls,' not only was she speaking off the cuff, she was doing so in a multi-layered academic way because she was, in fact, an academic and a public intellectual. Her role is not to give unabated praise to a pop star. This was reduced online to 'bell hooks called Beyoncé a terrorist' and there was an enormous fury directed at hooks. However, if you watch the whole panel in context, hooks was really saying that few high-profile men in public life will rant against feminism now the way they did when she was a younger feminist. However, men who, for example, run the music industry, control the imagery that commodifies and reduces women to their sexuality and Beyoncé's aesthetic is a part of that stealth anti-feminist messaging – which she coded as 'terrorism' against the progress her generation made.

I understand what she's saying while not wholly agreeing with it, but hooks would not have anticipated unanimous agreement from her audience. She also praised Beyoncé in other ways and at other times. What is important here is that she was essentially saying: 'I'm from the past, where men were overt in their efforts to bring feminism down. Now the messaging is less likely to be, "a woman's place is in the kitchen and the bedroom", be alert for those ideas being brought to you in a Trojan horse – especially one that looks to be feminist.' That is an extremely valid point that we should take on board, especially if we are not old enough to remember more overtly sexist rhetoric from large media outlets. Expert capitalists often live by the mantra, 'If you can't beat it, sell it.' The entire counterculture of the 1960s that sought to eschew capitalism has been packaged and marketed back to us as expensive yoga studios, silent retreats, therapy and leisure wear. So hooks is correct to tell artists to be on the lookout for those who would use them as pawns, and for consumers and fans to be aware of what they're buying into, as well as what they're buying.

I have seen bell hooks written off as old fashioned and out of touch – and therefore seemingly disposable for any number of minor transgressions by young feminists whose whole worldview has been shaped by the intersectional way of reimagining feminism that hooks was responsible for. She wrote more than thirty books and endless papers and articles over her lifetime. It is unreasonable to expect that even she would agree with everything she said when she wrote so much over such a long period. Contemporary feminism owes her a great deal.

An older feminist might use words you don't like, but what is the thought behind the thought? What can she see that we can't because she's got a bigger piece of the picture, or even just a different piece? And what might you know when you're older that you may express in a way that is seen as clumsy and outrageous by younger people than you?

I'm not saying 'respect your elders and shut up'. Revolutions are usually hosted by the young. Wise older people know better than to think what they found radical was logical but what young people find radical is just ridiculous. I will unpack how people in different generations can better speak to each other and communicate about important things and teach each other in our final conversation. There are ways in which I think some second-wave feminists cannot see that they set a movement in motion and now wish it to stop where they think is best. Difficult conversations require participation from both sides, and you don't own what you shaped. It will be reshaped by every generation. Cognitive empathy must be employed, even if affective empathy seems out of reach. No one is beyond radicalisation and rabbit holes. Sitting with the present can be even more difficult than accepting the past.

In order to move on, we need to examine history's harmful and empowering truths. They invariably sit side by side in the mixed, chaotic bag that is the best and worst of humanity. George Bernard Shaw was wonderful and terrible precisely because he was human. We need to humanise him much as he humanised Eliza Doolittle and her marginalised ilk and learn from the terrifying way he dehumanised others through eugenics. We cancel the past at the risk of losing great wisdom. If we scratch out the George Bernard Shaws of our difficult past, we risk forgetting why they thought the way they thought and fought the way they fought; understanding these figures and their contexts will help us consider our own actions. To this end, I would like to suggest that instead of taking Shaw's name off RADA's theatre, in the interests of embracing uncomfortable uncertainty and critical thinking, we advocate that the venue should host the annual UnShaw Event, a debate or lecture that interrogates what we ourselves are unsure about and invites us to engage with our own thoughts and actions.

Perhaps this could be a cross-generational event. If we cannot appreciate what second-wave feminists accomplished (for example) that we take for granted, the younger generation will lose valuable allies with a wealth of experience who might have been open to conversations about current progress.

One of the conversations that is sometimes highly flammable between members of different generations today is about gender nonconformity or what the media often refer to as 'the trans debate'. If we are to speak about it so that genuine progress can be made, then we need to let go of the idea that history has some kind of simplistic 'right side' and see that it is a chequered and complex climb to the next peak with a clearer view. Usually that next view allows us to significantly widen our circle of empathy. What will that look like when it comes to gender? That is a question for our next conversation.

Conversation Three

The Conversation about Gender Nonconformity

What is the prediction machine between our ears?

When a stranger enters my flat, my cats are curious and a little suspicious until they determine whether this human behaves like the other keen-to-please humans they already know. My cats never attack or run because their experience of humans, so far, has been a positive one. When observation confirms that this one seems like the others, they relax. If they see a dog, no matter how sweet or nervous it is, they hiss or run. This is because of a combination of their encounters with scarier dogs and their innate fear of anything that might be a predator.* In other words, my cats are sweet, fluffy little bigots. They make assumptions about individuals based on other encounters with the same species.

Brains are prediction machines that are always active, working like the autocomplete function on your phone to guess

* Uniquely, cats can be said to have domesticated humans by moving in and hunting rodents in exchange for shelter. We didn't catch and attempt to train them. Perhaps that's why their assumption is that humans are cool unless they prove otherwise.

what comes next. Cats are less intelligent than humans, so they rely on their amygdala for predictions more than we rely on ours.* The amygdala is a very old part of the brain which deals with some of its most basic functions – predicting, identifying and responding to danger. Consequently, the amygdala is especially important in how we experience fear, disgust and aggression.

Most vertebrates have an amygdala. It's good for fighting, fleeing, feeding, fear, freezing up and fornicating. It's not really accurate to think of the human brain as carved up into neat little sections like this, each acting independently, but it can be a useful structure to have in mind as a layperson trying to get to grips with what drives us and how we make choices. You may have heard the amygdala described as the lizard brain, but it isn't the case that we have a lizard amygdala with a rodent cortex grafted on top, and a human neocortex grafted on top of that. Our amygdala has evolved in concert with the evolution of the neocortex, and in most cases, when something happens, lots of different areas of the brain get involved.

But my human brain does have structures that my cats' brains don't, and that difference means that I have the option to make predictions and decisions by consciously combining my values, experience and instinct – as well as my ability to learn from and react to the social and cultural conditions of the current historical moment – in order to choose a course of action. A cat can only make predictions and decisions by relying on an instinctive response, because her brain doesn't contain a thoughtful, pondering prefrontal cortex which allows her to consider the implications of her actions.† To get more

* Cats have instincts we don't, of course, but they can't work the remote control.

† To be clear, cats do have a neocortex – just not enough of one to be thoughtful and pondering.

detailed, the amygdala decides which predictions are most urgent, based on its assessment of what it suspects could be dangerous. Of course, human beings do also make decisions relying mainly on our amygdala. Sometimes it's useful, because it helps us get out of a burning building as quickly as possible or pull a child out of the way of a speeding car.[1]

We move through the world trying to predict what will happen next. We are always looking for signs that things are going to happen as we expect them to and it's why we are easily stopped in our tracks by innocuous things. If our bus driver is dressed like a clown, we double take. What's going on here? What might she do next? You might have just done a double take right now, because you'd predicted it would be a *male* bus driver dressed like a clown. Why? Most of the bus drivers (and most of the clowns) you've seen in real life and on screen have been men. When things are as expected, we pay less attention. Why? Because it takes immense cognitive resources to keep noticing and checking things, so when everything is familiar, we mentally 'switch off' and save some power for later, or for subconscious background functions. That's fine in theory, as an engineering shortcut, but in our socially complex world, it leads to problems such as confirmation bias and prejudice, and we need to be aware of when these instinctive problem-solving techniques are leading us astray.

We can and must do better when it comes to judging individual human beings if we take the time to employ executive function – via our prefrontal cortex, other parts of the frontal cortex, and parts of the basal forebrain. This is the most recently evolved part of our brain and, along with parts of the neocortex, it's responsible for language, conceptualising and reasoning. But these things require mental bandwidth, primarily in the form of readily available attention and the capacity to hold back the instinctive response. This can be difficult to do.

So a broad range of representation of any marginalised group is critical for society as a whole. If 10 per cent of bus drivers dressed like clowns for a year, you'd stop noticing. The more individuals from a particular group we are introduced to, the less individuals are likely to generalise about members of this group and the more they will make informed decisions, case by case. Representation retrains our brain's prediction machines – all these individual changes eventually amounting to a shift in the collective unconscious – and doesn't alarm the amygdala into an inappropriate fight-or-flight response. (Of course, even if the amygdala is activated, that doesn't mean that the neocortex shuts down – we don't use one part of the brain and not another. But when you feel something very strongly which is at odds with your values, you have to rely on the rational, reasoning part of your mind to 'talk you off the ledge'. And that's not easy.)

We'll get to gender nonconformity. First I want to analyse, in a detailed way, two other historical examples that we can learn a lot from. The first one we are more familiar with – gay rights. In a 2012 interview with NBC's *Meet the Press*, (then Vice President) Joe Biden said in his first open support of equal marriage, 'I think *Will & Grace* did more to educate the American public [about gay people], more than almost anything anybody has done so far. People fear that which is different. Now they're beginning to understand.'[2] This statement directly influenced then-President Barack Obama to support equal marriage as well.[3] That began a domino effect of other high-profile politicians joining them, and paved the way for the Supreme Court ruling making same-sex marriage legal across the US in 2015.

Will & Grace (as you probably know) was a sitcom about the relationship between Grace, a straight interior designer, and her best friend Will, a gay Manhattan lawyer. As well as the fairly 'straight-passing' Will (played, it should be noted, by a straight actor, Eric McCormack), the show featured ostentatious Jack, and a variety of other gay characters, all of whom middle America got to know and hold affection for. It was originally broadcast from 1998 to 2006, and while some criticised it for portraying camp stereotypes, or not doing enough to show sexual affection between gay men, its presence on network television, its depiction of lots of different kinds of gay men, and the way it allowed those men to be the leads of the show, contributed to wearing down what I like to think of as 'society's amygdala' – the alarm system which develops when the dominant group keeps reinforcing a negative consensus and raises their children to be fearful of and/or disgusted by a minority group.[4] (It is important to note that children not raised in this environment show no such fear or disgust! This isn't somehow 'natural', biologically driven or unavoidable.)

The original *Queer Eye for the Straight Guy* (2003–2007) featured straight male guests who habitually made fearful predictions about the gay male stars (or in other words were homophobic). The gay presenters then gave the straight men's wardrobes, kitchens and dating-lives friendly, much-needed makeovers. By the end of each episode, the formerly homophobic man associated the Fab Five with new haircuts and deep kindness. He'd greet them with open arms rather than flinching at the prospect of having to defend himself from unwanted advances or somehow 'catching queerness'.

While the show was criticised for flamboyant behaviours that played into gay stereotypes, the evidence that it contributed to eroding homophobia lies in the new *Queer Eye*, the 2018 series reboot on Netflix, which now includes a much wider variety of people for the team to support with soft furnishings and makeovers of the heart – none of whom exhibit any kind of gay panic.* The new show can't operate on the same frequency as the old show because too much of the world has changed. Startled homophobes in Texas, Toledo or Tokyo would now just look bigoted on our screens, because too many people have learned not to make negative predictions about gay men based solely on their sexuality.

This is not to minimise the very real homophobia and often physical danger gay people live with all around the world.† But I am noting a profound societal mental shift that has, in large part, occurred due to a drip feed of positive or non-negative representation – there is much academic research that supports this.[5] The other knock-on effect of this is that more people have felt safe to live their truth out loud because of mainstream models. The percentage of adults in the US who identify as LGBTQ+ (or at least who are willing to say so in a survey) more than doubled between 2012 to 2022, from 3.5 per cent to 7.1 per cent.[6] This almost certainly means that more people know (and love) out gay individuals in person. Consequently, our brains are more likely to recognise gay people as local, friendly and individual, rather than 'other' or even dangerous.

Modern Family was another American sitcom featuring gay characters, specifically two gay men raising an adopted child. It ran from 2009 to 2020, and quickly became an important part of the social landscape because it helped mainstream America to understand that, for instance, gay men in the gym will most likely do exactly what straight men will do – chat about their

---

* While one could still argue that the new show perpetuates stereotypes about gay men being emotionally literate and good at aesthetics, it continues the old show's work of broadening understanding of gay men as human beings, as opposed to merely the 'other'.

† It's important to say that homophobic hate crimes are on the rise again due to factors I explore elsewhere in the book but it's unarguable that overall attitudes have got better since the mid-twentieth century.

family, try to lift slightly more than they should, and worry about their receding hairline. Some members of the LGBTQ+ community feel the show is reductive, narrow in the scope of its representation, and that it creates heteronormative goals (aspirations of marriage, kids, monogamy, the nuclear family) but perhaps that's one reason it has contributed to calming the gay panic to which many Americans were prone and which were used for relatable laughs in shows of the 1990s and early 2000s like *Friends* (as discussed in our last conversation) and *Seinfeld*. You will no doubt remember tropes of male characters who exhibited neuroses about their friendships having homo-romantic qualities (pulling back quickly from a sincere hug and covering with macho behaviours) and expressed manic anxieties about being mistaken for a gay couple by strangers. ('Not that there's anything wrong with that!', as Jerry and George were fond of archly qualifying in *Seinfeld*.)

Between 2001 and 2009, Gallup polls reported annually that only 40 per cent of Americans were in favour of same-sex marriage.[7] That number did not move during that time. In 2011, after *Modern Family* had been on the air for two years, this number had shot up to 53 per cent. By 2021, a year after the show came off the air, a Gallup poll reported that an all-time high of 70 per cent of Americans were in favour of same-sex marriage.[8] While there were obviously many contributing factors that led to both the legalisation and widespread acceptance of equal marriage – largely the hard-working activism and legal fights of some members of the gay community and their allies[9] – the impact of 60 per cent to 70 per cent of Americans watching at least some episodes of *Modern Family*, and its Emmy-winning, mainstream cultural acceptance on network TV, is an example of these campaigns, cultural shifts and representations working in parallel to make real-world change.[10]

What could be more normal or natural?

Let's go back a little further in time, but still in very recent memory, to explore the sinister origins of this gay panic and resistance to equal rights. I described in our previous conversation that one of the defining ideas of the early twentieth century was eugenics. To recap, this is now understood to be a vile attack on autonomy and individuality, but then was widely seen as a powerful force for societal good. By identifying a template for 'perfect humans' and then making it a goal for genetics to move further and further towards that prototype, it was thought that a perfectly harmonious world could be created. How did this attempt to make 'perfect humans' treat queer people? The Eugenics Archive of Canada explains:

> One of the consistent facets of eugenics over time and place has been an interest in regulating sexual behavior, sexual orientation, and gender expression. Indeed, this is one area in which the insidious quest of normalization associated with the eugenics movement is very evident.
>
> A quick review of the earliest cases of institutional sterilization in Indiana, which passed the world's first sterilization law in 1907, confirms this. Sodomy, which most likely encompassed a wide variety of male same-sex interactions, was the infraction listed for approximately one third of male inmates identified by Dr Harry Sharp at the Jeffersonville Reformatory for vasectomy in the early 1900s.[11]

In the US, partly as a legacy of the eugenics movement (which was practised through widespread enforced sterilisation up to and throughout the 1970s[12]) homosexuality was officially declared a mental illness between 1952 and 1973 and, for men, homosexual practices were not decriminalised even in the relatively liberal state of New York until 1980. (These laws had been in place since America was colonised.) In fourteen states, it wasn't decriminalised until 2003, and then only because state legislatures were overruled at a federal level by the Supreme Court. The rhetoric around the sexuality of gay men and lesbians was that of 'sexual perversion' and the public was encouraged to be disgusted by the thought of same-sex people in bed. This societally trained disgust encouraged widespread shame and fear among gay and bisexual people.*

If you are too young to remember the 1980s and 1990s, many people genuinely feared that gay men and women would ogle or attack them and consequently many wanted them banned from single-sex spaces like fitting rooms or changing rooms. Many straight men in the 1980s, who didn't have relationships with any out gay men, only knew what was shown in television, movies, print, religious and political communications, and family lore – and those depictions tended to be effete and/or predatory. Their prediction machines only had that information to go on, and so it was common for them to conclude that any man sharing their locker room who exhibited 'signs of effeminacy' might be about to make an unwanted pass at them or even physically attack them.

Out gay people in society were new in the 1980s, because decriminalisation was new, and so the press was also happy to vilify them. During this time, a journalist called Terry Sanderson highlighted homophobic rhetoric in his Media Watch column in the *Gay Times*. This was in the UK, where the media landscape was similar to the US at the time, and

* This was complicated by the AIDS crisis and the ignorance and bigotry around it, exacerbated by cowardly leaders and resistance to even acknowledgement, let alone education.

serves as an excellent record. These are genuine headlines and quotes from his Media Watch archive:

> 'Is it wise to share a lavatory with a homosexual?' *The Times*, 1985

> 'Given an inch, the homosexuals demand all. Granted legality, they have advanced boldly, noisily, immodestly, without shame, flaunting and organising themselves, proselytising vigorously, demanding ever-fresh "rights", privileges, handouts, immunities, special representation.' *Spectator*, 1985

> 'Why was the Reverend Gregory Richards, a homosexual, employed as a chaplain in the prison service? God knows how many people he has infected with the disease [he was HIV positive]. Equal rights for homosexuals cannot operate in sensitive appointments when such risks as AIDS exist.' *Express*, 1985

> 'Martina Turns Girls Into Gays: A huge scandal exploded over women's tennis last night when senior players were accused by a former Wimbledon champion of seducing young players on the circuit. Margaret Court said the example set was so bad that young girl players were scared to go into tournament changing rooms . . . [Court said]: "It's very sad for children to be exposed to homosexuality . . . There's no doubt there's a lot more of it than when I finished playing. There are players now who won't even go to the tournament changing rooms."' *Sun*, 1990

We needed fresh stories to alter these bigoted predictions. The stories we consume inform the laws we make, and then the laws we make inform the stories we can tell. Over time, the majority of a population responds to both representation and legislation by recalibrating their assumptions.

One of the key shifts in the Western understanding of homosexuality in the last five decades is that it is now widely recognised as something that is 'natural' and not 'unnatural'. The definition of 'unnatural' is usually something along the lines of not being in accord with nature or consistent with a normal course of events. Progress is slow and human beings are fearful of it. If you're reading this book and you identify as gay, lesbian, bisexual or queer, I am sure you already know that others have revealed (or concealed) a level of discomfort with who you're attracted to and your imagined sex life – or possibly even how you dress or behave socially. I am equally certain you have felt the hurtful ramifications of that.

All of this seems bizarre, especially when you first learn that homosexuality is everywhere in nature among non-human animals. Fifty per cent of the sexual intercourse male bison have is with each other. Monogamous female pairings are common among macaques and even the norm in some populations. They sometimes mate with males but they're homoromantic, coupling with other females. About 30 per cent of Laysan albatrosses in Hawaii are females in same-sex relationships. They find male birds who are already in committed relationships to father their chicks, but they raise them as same-sex female couples. Male swan couples adopt abandoned eggs. We should note that academics – such as anthropologist Eimear McLoughlin – have cautioned against anthropomorphising animal 'sexualities', and of reducing the complexities of human sexuality to biological essentialism.[13] It's not the whole picture but it's a piece of the puzzle. Same-sex 'romance', monogamy and promiscuity is abundant in the natural world.[14]

Communities that vilify homosexuality have artificially

trained their societal amygdala for fear, shame and disgust. There are still sixty-five countries that criminalise homosexuality – twelve of those countries punishing it with the death penalty.[15] Many of them formerly had or included societies that embraced homosexuality, until Western colonisers introduced a rigid form of Christianity which demonised it.[16] In countries where gay people finally have the right to marry, there are still bakers who refuse to make their cake. American anthropologist Ruth Benedict wrote: 'We make a profound mistake when we equate our local normalities with the inevitable necessities of existence'.[17]

Shame and disgust are understood to be evolved and interconnected solutions to differing adaptive challenges. Sexual shaming is probably a combination of other people's bodily functions being suspect,* the need for sex to be a private act hidden from children and imposed (arbitrary) moral codes in which human beings demand conformity within their stamm. Almost all children have a disgusted response when they first learn about sex of any kind. 'You put what where? Gross!'[18] Curiosity abounds but their responses range from giggling, to rejecting the idea out of hand, to making vomiting noises. This response makes sense before adolescence, when sexual urges kick in. If you don't have a biological driver to exchange bodily fluids with someone else, you can see why it might come under a 'possible contamination' disgust response.[19] The idea of kissing someone you don't want to kiss can be repulsive, but with someone you fancy it can arouse you.

If we do not wish to live in a society with the sophistication of a seven-year-old hearing about sex for the first time, then we need to normalise sexual acts between adults who want

* And our own, too – Mary Douglas's *Purity and Danger* and Julia Kristeva's *Powers of Horror* are both classic texts dealing with the theory of abjection.

and enjoy them. Arbitrary disgust that normalises shame for healthy libidos, aroused by a variety of harmless stimuli, has no place in an evolved society. There is a great deal of evidence that a healthy sex life improves our quality of life, self-esteem and reduces stress and depression. Given that a sex act between consenting adults usually doesn't affect anyone else negatively, communities that show opprobrium for those who do not conform to the dominant group's idea of what is arousing are creating a *learned disgust response* in their population.[20]

Learned disgust can even be a response to changing fashion in gender expression, which scrambles that stamm's understanding of what men and women look and behave like (or in other words 'the gender binary'). This is completely arbitrary. We know this because when women in the West boldly pioneered wearing trousers in the first half of the twentieth century, Western society's amygdala expressed its full-throated repugnance, even though (unnoticed by them) women had worn trousers in Asia and the Ottoman Empire for hundreds of years.

In 1933, Marlene Dietrich, the bisexual film star famous for wearing a scandalous tuxedo on screen, was both refused service in a Hollywood bar[21] and threatened with arrest in Paris for wearing trousers.[22] As late as the 1960s, star Mary Tyler Moore had to fight her TV network to be allowed to wear trousers in the popular television sitcom *The Dick Van Dyke Show*,[23] and a woman in New York was thrown out of traffic court because the judge complained she wasn't dressed properly.[24] It's hard for us to imagine now, but it seemed genuinely repulsive to some people and alienating to others when women started to co-opt what was regionally traditionally men's fashion.

Similarly, when men started to grow their hair long in the 1960s, it read as gay or feminine to many and some men were violently attacked. But long hair on men was common before the First World War. Do a Google image search for 'long hair Victorian man'. Pages of images will come up and none of them will seem unfamiliar. Short hair on men became the norm in the First World War to curb lice in the trenches. Michael Antony in *The Masculine Century* writes that 'Men for the next half century had to measure themselves against the war veterans, to try to give themselves and others the impression that they too could have endured the trenches.'[25] Again, it's hard for us to imagine anyone cared so deeply but in 1964, a seventeen-year-old David Bowie (then Jones) founded The Society for Prevention of Cruelty to Men with Long Hair and appeared on the television programme *BBC Tonight* complaining that they'd often be taunted on the street with gender-based heckles such as 'Darling' and 'Can I carry your handbag?' The presenter introduced the teen Bowie and his friends as a group protesting because 'they're tired of persecution, losing their jobs, being sent home from school and college and even being refused the dole'.[26] The young men who appeared on the show mostly had hair that didn't even hit their shoulders, and a couple of them had short hair with floppy fringes, but it genuinely gave the people in charge of their opportunities a gender-scrambled 'ick' response and so cost those young people some of their human rights.

Binary signifiers can become the sticky norm, when in reality they are no more than fashion. And, though fashion is laden with ideological assumptions and semiotics around societal gender roles and class signifiers, it can change fairly swiftly. A man with long hair or a woman in trousers no longer scrambles the binary for most twenty-first-century brains. It is so common now, we've collectively recalibrated. In turn, people aren't burdened with shame for these arbitrary choices any more.

Who will buy these unwanted children?

Thinking about how society's amygdala has evolved in regard to sexual orientation and gender expression reminds me of another way in which society has changed, connected to my own life: how we think about adoption. This is the second historical model I want to look at before we get to today's landscape of gender nonconformity. When I was a child, people often commented that I looked exactly like my mother. That was evidence to me that people see what they want to see, because I was adopted at ten days old and had never even seen a picture of anyone biologically related to me. My older sister and younger brother are both the products of my parents' combined DNA and yet my mother has often commented that I am more like her than either of her biological children, in our tastes and talents.

Have you ever seen that viral picture of a tiger suckling piglets who've been dressed in stripy jackets in an attempt to fool her into thinking they're her own?* It's possible I'm such a piglet and the ways I'm like my mother are my attempt at a stripy jacket. It doesn't feel that way, but human beings are intricate and complicated, and we rarely understand ourselves completely. All I can say is, I am very much my mother's daughter. Mind you, that wouldn't help her if she needed a kidney, because biologically I'm not hers.

When I met my birth mother a decade ago, I discovered that I look exactly like her. Her cosmetic genes are strong in me. But in almost every other way, I am more like my mum than my biological mother. Sometimes people refer to my birth mother as my 'real mum' and I always assume they are

---

* This viral picture may not indicate that the tiger was fooled but she was suckling them and you get the point.

talking about my mother who raised me. Personally, I have never met an adopted person who says 'real' when they mean 'biological'.* To our people (in the main) real and biological are very different things.

Historically, many societies around the world have recognised birth parentage as 'natural' and superior, and adoptive parentage as 'unnatural' and inferior. The most famous and OG ancient adoptee is Moses. The Egyptian Pharaoh's wife or daughter (depending on the text you consult) secretly adopts him when the Pharaoh orders all the male newborn children of the minority enslaved Jewish population to be killed. Moses, who is treated as a biological son in the royal Egyptian household, eventually reveals himself to be a cuckoo in the nest and rises up against the Pharoah, killing his adopted father or grandfather in the process. One moral of this story is, beware when taking a foundling into your home: he'll put his 'natural' kin first and end up killing you.

The main purpose of adoption in virtually all known ancient societies was to provide an apprentice and/or heir if one was lacking, which was entirely intended to serve the needs of the adult. For example, in the Byzantine Empire, which existed from 395 to 1453 CE, there was an annual market festival in mid-September which boasted, along with agricultural produce, livestock, jewellery and clothing, 'a brisk trade in children whose impoverished parents sold them into slavery'.[27]

Later the 'abandoned child' moved from being a fiscal opportunity and became society's scapegoat – an individual without a past, family connections or status. Such children garnered disgust and distrust and were reviled as 'criminally prone' people. This was exacerbated (again!) by eugenics.

---

* Some adopted people feel differently and have a strong presence online – this is my personal experience. Everyone's relationship with adoption is different!

Colonisation, also under the influence of eugenics, split up many Indigenous families. Indigenous children were taken from their homes and put into boarding schools to be assimilated, often violently. They were stripped of their familiar clothing, punished for speaking their own language and suffered appalling abuse and neglect. Many of them never returned to their homes.

Previously, there was no concept of 'an orphan' in Native American societies, because kinship extended far beyond the model of the nuclear family. In the Cheyenne tradition, for example, paternal uncles and maternal aunties are responsible for their nephews and nieces in the same way that parents are for their children. In fact, the words *náhko'éehe* (my mother) and *náhko'e* (mother) are used when addressing 'my maternal aunt' and 'aunt' respectively, and the words for paternal uncle and father have a similar relationship.[28] The same kinship and linguistic tradition exists in Australian Aboriginal cultures,[29] the oldest uninterrupted Indigenous societies in the world, so we know that it is fundamentally and deeply human.

The Mosuo people of China are matrilineal and as such maternal uncles are more important and present than fathers. Because of this, children form different attachments, and it is unlikely a child will ever be an orphan because even if both their parents died or left, their attachments to close caregivers would continue. We are sometimes so sure our familial models are 'natural', when really they're just what is familiar.

In Victorian Britain, children were sometimes adopted by a family of a higher social class, but not in the way that we'd recognise adoption. They were often neglected, treated unkindly, put to work and forbidden to play with or often even talk to the 'natural' biological children in the house (in case they infected them with criminality, or a perceived moral or mental weakness). Other orphans were sent to so-called schools provided by 'philanthropists', but the conditions were so unsanitary and the punishments so harsh, many ran away to a life of crime on the streets. Around 60 per cent of the Victorian British criminal population were orphans. Orphans were also massively overrepresented in sex work.

Charles Dickens spent three years of his childhood forced into labour in a factory, when his parents went to debtors' prison. Inspired by this hardship, he began to change the public perception of parentless children through his fiction. In one of his most famous books (first published in 1837–9), young Oliver Twist's mother dies after childbirth and we are encouraged to look through his hungry, abandoned eyes as he's sold into indentured servitude and pressed into a life of crime.

Charlotte Brontë's *Jane Eyre* (1847) invites us into the relatively more fortunate life of a Victorian adoptee. Jane's adopted brother (who is the biological child of Jane's guardian, Mrs Reed) catches her reading one of the family's books. He chides her for it: 'You are a dependent, mama says; you have no money; your father left you none; you ought to beg, and not to live here with gentlemen's children like us, and eat the same meals we do, and wear clothes at our mama's expense.' She is told by the maid: 'You are less than a servant, for you do nothing for your keep', and when she is sent away to a terrible school for parentless children, a teacher publicly humiliates her and tells everyone:

> This I learned from her benefactress; from the pious and charitable lady who adopted her in her orphan state, reared her as her own daughter, and whose kindness, whose generosity the unhappy girl repaid by an ingratitude so bad, so dreadful, that at last her excellent patroness was obliged to separate her from her own young ones, fearful lest her vicious example should contaminate their purity . . .

These novels were big hits in both the UK and America, asking the literate public to rethink the demoralising effect of prejudice on the psyche of orphans and the social impact of the mistreatment suffered by children in orphanages. Not many years later, there was a movement to recognise the importance of child welfare, especially those vulnerable and parentless. In that way, *Jane Eyre* was the Victorian *Modern Family* for orphan representation. In fact, it could be argued that Jane helped light the touchpaper that changed our minds about adoption and, without her, there's no way Cam and Mitch could have accepted their adopted child Lily as entirely their own.

Partly because of the power of stories like these, and partly because our circle of empathy is expanding, modern society finds the idea of adoption as a financial transaction repugnant and the idea that orphaned children should be grateful to their adopted caregivers archaic. The agreed upon purpose of adoption is now, almost always, to serve the child and put their welfare first.*

In 1851, America became the first country in the world to recognise and codify the legal practice of adoption, although it was much more *Jane Eyre* in spirit, in as much as the children were still referred to as wards and the parents were referred to as guardians. The UK followed suit in the 1920s. During this time children were slowly but increasingly seen as deserving of rights and protections, because philosophers and thinkers take a long time to convince legislators and society at large. In the twentieth century, adoptions went from 'open' to 'closed', which was seen as progressive because it was a move to give the child equal rights and equal dignity with children cared for

---

* The reality of adoption is not always in the best interest of the child, but society agrees that it should be.

by their biological parents. It was believed that keeping birth records sealed was beneficial, and it became standard practice for children to not even know they were adopted.

Over time, this was recognised to be damaging for adopted children, who deserve transparency along with acceptance and empathy but, with all its failings (and sometimes disastrous consequences), in some key ways moving from 'This is my illegitimate ward' to 'This is my daughter' marked a huge moral step forward. The term 'birth mother' (to replace the terms 'natural mother' and 'real mother') became commonplace in the 1950s and '60s. Some people don't like that term now, but at the time it was seen as a move away from: 'I'm not your real mother, Cinderella!' In 1979, pioneering social worker Marietta Spencer wrote 'The Terminology of Adoption', which solidified language designed to make children feel part of their new family.

A hundred years ago, it would have been completely acceptable to consider me and refer to me as an illegitimate, unnatural – and therefore inferior – child. If my parents had told people they were my mum and dad and people had found out 'the truth', it would have seemed as if they were fantasists or liars. I have never encountered this view in my lifetime. In my family, it was 100 per cent fact that my parents and siblings were mine. In the wider world, I am legally my parents' child and if people discover I'm adopted, while they may misunderstand who my 'real mum' or 'real dad' is, they don't seek to undermine my relationship or argue I deserve a downgrade from mother/daughter to guardian/ward. They do not suspect that I'm morally inferior or that I'm gaslighting society with my lies. They don't assume I'm a cuckoo in the nest or that children like me are dangerous and grow up into untrustworthy adults.

And yet all of those things would've been said and believed

of me some decades ago. If you think I'm exaggerating and that these views about innocent children could not have been commonplace, consider this. In 1936 (a peak time for eugenics), Eleanor Garrigue Gallagher, the head of an adoption agency, insisted, 'It is a fallacy that a girl who has had extra-marital relations is mentally subnormal, or has low morals or ungovernable passions, or a low degree of education . . . ' She was fighting the good fight against this fallacy, which was received wisdom (while obviously using ableist language and assumptions).

Despite some social progress, the shaming of 'fallen women' was widely extended to their offspring who were seen to be predisposed to that 'immorality'. Adoptive parents were still not expected to treat orphans the same as their biological or 'natural' children. Activist Vera Connolly responded to Eleanor Garrigue Gallagher with the most horrendously racist, ableist statement imaginable: 'Parents who adopted an unknown infant have found themselves saddled with a child who is diseased, partly Negro, or perhaps an idiot.'[30] At that time, people in America usually did not adopt outside their racial group. You surprise us, Land of the Free! Society's amygdala was burning up with fear of adopted infants and racist and ableist as hell, just to rub a horrible amount of salt into the wound.

I have to wonder, had I come into the world at this time, how would that assumption of otherness and moral degeneracy and criminality have affected my self-esteem? My opportunities? Would I have believed those things myself? Would they, to an extent, have become true because they were agreed upon and because the power structures would have reinforced them? Would I have even lived long enough to find out if the things assumed about me were true, or would I have been so under-resourced and neglected I'd have died? (The death rate was high for children in general in Victorian times but higher for orphans.[31]) If I'd somehow survived and got ahead despite my circumstances, would I have spent my life in exhausting activism to improve conditions for other adopted, illegitimate children, trying to prove that I shouldn't be 'society's scapegoat', and neither should those from my stamm?

I can guess at some of these answers simply because some of my contemporaries weren't as lucky as I was. When I found my birth mother, I discovered that some babies of my generation went to orphanages, and I phoned the Australian adoption helpline to talk it over. I was devastated by the emergence of this sliding door I could have so easily been pushed through. The overly frank advisor told me, 'You wouldn't have wanted to go to an orphanage, they were terrible places.' She explained that all of her clients raised in orphanages struggled in adulthood. I asked her what my chances were, and she said, 'It was a matter of supply and demand. Depends on the year you were born.'

As she put me on hold to look up the stats, my blood ran cold. What if she came back and said it was a close call? That would mean I'd effectively taken someone else's spot in a loving family. I got the winning lottery ticket while they'd gone to a cold dorm with no secure attachments. When I heard her say, 'You're all right – the year you were born no babies went to orphanages in your state,' I burst into tears and cried for about forty-eight hours because it was the first time in my life I'd recognised myself as an 'orphan'. Many people assume that orphans are children with no living parents, but that is only one definition. The word has a history of being used to describe those whose parents and wider families cannot or do not wish to look after them. Over 90 per cent of children living in orphanages worldwide today have at least one living parent.[32] Oliver Twist, probably the most famous fictional orphan, is the illegitimate son of a 'fallen woman' who dies in childbirth – but his father is a rich man (married to someone else) who is alive at the time of his birth.

I feel extremely lucky to have been adopted by a family, and so fortunate to be born in a time after orphans and adoptees were categorically demoralised, criminalised and marginalised. It is important to highlight here that the NSPCC report that children in the care system (which means foster care rather than permanent adoption) still experience being singled out and stigmatised at their schools and in their communities. They caution that the language we use for care-experienced children really matters.[33] Care-experienced people are also massively over-represented in the juvenile judiciary system and far more likely to be incarcerated as children and later as adults. The Victorian legacy for children without active parents has by no means disappeared, even though the rights of the child are recognised, but it is much diminished for children who are legally adopted, especially at birth, because they are no longer perceived as orphans or somehow 'other'.[34] Personally, I feel I have not been treated any differently in society as an adopted child ever and a few generations ago that would not have been possible for any orphan.

There, but for the seemingly arbitrary grace of God, go I. While no one bothered to record comprehensive statistics on Victorian orphans, we know from what records we have that many children who came before me had shorter lives, more mental health problems and no proximity to influence.[35] Although adopted children do have unique issues, and often have severe attachment anxieties, society's collective agreement that we get to be unilaterally accepted as full children, call our caregivers Mum, Dad, Granny and Grandpa – and believe it – gives us rights, recognitions, dignity and entitlements that embolden us and allow us to live at full mast.

No adoption is perfect. Not every adoption works. (Not

every biological family works either, but in different ways.) Some adoptees find their biological families and withdraw from their adopted ones, feeling more at home with their genetic kin. None of these things are reason enough to deny that I'm my mother's daughter. I am grateful every day that society agreed that biology, in this case, wasn't a priority or even relevant. In my case, we argued with biology and won.

Are you who you say you are?

If someone challenged me and said I was a fraud, that I was lying when I said I was my parents' real child, and that I was eroding the rights of biological sons and daughters, I hope you'd be my ally. I hope you'd tell them that in all ways that are meaningful, I am my parents' daughter; that biology wasn't key here. I hope you'd point out that it is 'natural' because animals adopt orphaned young – sometimes even between species. Sometimes whales adopt a dolphin, or a dog adopts a duckling. Sometimes piglets wear stripy jackets and get tiger mums. We know these chosen kinships can even mimic biological relations, for example, where incestuous taboos exist among animals – mother and son bonobos, for example – adoptees obey those same rules.

I hope you'd tell them that while adopted children have some different needs, it doesn't make us less than or other. We're still entitled to the protections of the law and the use of inclusive language. When an adoption is high profile, sometimes the press focuses on this each time they mention the child, as if it's somehow gossip-worthy, reflecting the attitudes of a bygone era. Whenever I see a newspaper printing something like: 'Famous film stars arrived at the premiere with their son and adopted daughter,' I shrink. This language seems structurally violent, or at least horribly abrasive, to me. Why do you need to say they're adopted? I'm not ashamed of being adopted – it is an important part of my identity and my story. But when you repeat it in irrelevant contexts, it sounds like somehow we're not 'real children' – we're hangers on, or even imposters. This goes against the trend for full inclusion. It's an example of how language can grate, hurt or exclude and it stands out precisely because it's no longer the norm.

In every generation it seems there are new marginalised groups whose members are gaining traction and visibility and are unnecessarily treated with suspicion, fear and even hostility. When I was growing up, it was gay people with emerging rights and representation. Luckily for me, before my birth, it was adoptees and orphans who were gaining ground and receiving push-back from those who feared the intrusion of the new. Society's amygdala was activated against both of those groups among others. This is far from inevitable but there is a parallel with the way both adoptees and gay people have been treated and distrusted to the way gender-nonconforming people's identities are being called into question today. There is a new visibility of trans, non-binary and gender-nonconforming people – and not just as punchlines on sitcoms, perceived as outliers who can be othered precisely because they don't conform to gender norms.

The increased visibility of trans people in our society is scrambling the gender binary, and as it has in the past, seems to be disrupting society's amygdala, and this needs to be addressed. To be clear, I'm not suggesting trans people wish to be 'normed' but rather that they deserve the same dignity and acceptance that they see other people getting as a right.

Despite this new attention, gender-nonconforming people make up a very small minority of our society. And in order to see if there are meaningful lessons to be learned about the social progress of adoptees and gay people when it comes to this conversation, we need to ask, are gender-nonconforming people really a cohort who have always been with us and are currently marginalised? It is hard to know exactly how many people are trans or gender nonconforming as sometimes there are arguments about how the surveys are framed and many may not be willing to say, but the last census in England and Wales said 0.5 per cent of the population aged sixteen years and over reported that their gender identity was different from their sex registered at birth.[36] Scotland's best estimate is the same and the figures in Northern Ireland are unknown. Most countries with reasonable rights and protections for LGBTQ+ people currently report that between 0.1 per cent of their population and 1 per cent of their population are gender-nonconforming.[37] So even if we assume that as trans people get more rights and representation that number could double or even triple, gender-nonconforming people are a tiny minority.

There have always been people who exist outside of the Western gender binary. You may have heard that many Indigenous societies have people who identify as a 'third gender'. However, many scholars who belong to Indigenous cultures argue that the idea of a 'third' gender implies a Western binary that does not exist in Indigenous cultures in the first place. For there to be a third, we must begin with the concept of two, which isn't the assumption of most, if any, Indigenous societies. Native Americans have 'Two Spirit' people. That term was coined in 1990 by queer Native Americans at a conference, attempting to replace the slur word 'berdache', imposed upon them by people who colonised their land.[38] They were trying to explain something to people who could only understand gender through a Western lens, and to recognise a long, illustrious, queer culture of their own.

There are many models for thinking about gender. Contemporary non-binary British artist and thinker Travis

Alabanza says, 'I'm trans because language is limited. In another time, would there be the need to say it?' and I think it helps to think of it this way – we might describe someone as 'old' or 'young', but we understand those are relative terms. As comedian Sara Barron says, 'I'm forty-two now, which might sound old but it's all relative. It isn't old for a tree or a mountain or . . . a man.' We get that while some people are very young (literally born yesterday), and some people are very old (102) most of us are on a spectrum. Most of us are old to someone and young to someone else, and how old or young we feel or are perceived as depends on our state of mind, the activity we are doing and the company we're in. Being twelve years old might be seen as very grown up in a primary school and being seventy might be seen as a veritable spring chicken in a retirement home.

We have lots of concepts like this. Colours are dark or light on sliding scales. Is the music high or low? Loud or soft? Some people are more 'masculine' and some people are more 'feminine', and some are a (sometimes changing) blend, and that doesn't necessarily correlate with body parts. Australian Aboriginals have the concept of brotherboys and sistergirls.[39] A brotherboy is a gender-diverse First Nations person with a masculine spirit. It is someone who in Western contemporary discourse would be said to have been 'assigned female at birth', but according to Aboriginal tradition also has a 'boy spirit'. They may have a masculine gender identity or gender expression. In Western terms, one brotherboy might be a lesbian and another might be non-binary and another might be a trans man. How do you know what kind of brotherboy you're talking to? You don't. They may or may not reveal those things to you as you get to know them, but you don't really need to know.

Amao Leota Lu is a Samoan *fa'afafine* (gender-diverse person who lives 'in the manner of women') performance artist and activist who also identifies as a trans woman in a Western framework. In an interview in the *Guardian*, she says, 'It can be problematic going into Western settings because there's the expectation that we are one or two genders rather than three, four or five, or anything in between. In the West I seem to be stuck in a world that seems to challenge my own indigenous identity.'[40] Amao told me *fa'afafine* are not seen as sacred or special in Samoan culture. She said, 'We just are. It's no big deal.'

Much like the concept of being an orphan doesn't really exist in Indigenous societies that don't use the model of the nuclear family, our way of looking at gender is just what is familiar to us. It isn't 'the truth', there is no one objective valid expression of kinship or gender. However, we live when and where we live, and many of our ideas and laws construct our reality. So, what is it like to be gender nonconforming today? Let's activate our cognitive empathy and explore the landscape.

What's it like to be trans today?

In 2018, UK employers were surveyed and one in three admitted they were 'less likely' to hire a transgender person than a non-transgender person.[41] Almost half (43 per cent) said they were unsure if they would recruit a transgender employee. The survey found the retail sector had the highest number (47 per cent) of businesses unlikely to employ a transgender person. Information Technology was just behind and then hospitality and manufacturing. So, you're probably going to struggle to get a job in a shop, coding in a cubicle, waiting tables or on a factory line if you don't identify with the gender you were assigned at birth.

Other industries weren't much better. The same report showed that only 3 per cent of the 1,000 employers polled from a cross section of industries had an equal opportunities policy that clearly welcomes transgender people to apply for jobs. Only 8 per cent of the employers who would actually consider hiring a transgender person think they should have the same rights to be hired for a job as everyone else. Why trans people are not perceived as having the basic human right of being considered for a job is not clear. I imagine it's the same reason people didn't used to want to hire gay people or orphans. Misinformation. Fear. Decisions made with society's amygdala, incorrectly trained to guess at trouble.

In the same survey, few employers consider their workplaces liberal enough to tolerate transgender workers, with only 4 per cent declaring their workplace culture diverse enough for transgender people to 'fit in'. If you are hopeful things might have improved since then, according to a 2021 report by UK recruitment firm TotalJobs along with YouGov, almost two-thirds of trans people believe it is necessary to keep their identity secret from colleagues to feel safe and secure in their jobs, whereas five years earlier, just over half of trans people felt this way.[42] We will examine why things have become worse soon.

Anecdotally, an acquaintance of mine, who I understood to be a progressive person, told me a trans woman had applied for a job in his company driving a delivery van, but he felt it might put his clients off because they wouldn't know how to deal with 'the situation'. He said they might be confused by her, so he'd given the job to someone else who, he reassured himself, was more qualified anyway. Obviously, he had not told her what his biggest reservation was, but my guess is she at least suspected. A 2021 survey said that 56 per cent of trans people had found getting work challenging, difficult or impossible.[43] In this context, employ your affective empathy and imagine being a transgender person trying to get a job. Imagine being a Black transgender woman, for example, and going for interviews.

Not for your dream job. Just a minimum-wage job. Do you feel hopeful? Another 2021 poll conducted by advocacy group TransActual found that 72 per cent of trans people surveyed reported experiencing transphobia when trying to access goods or services, and 99 per cent of trans people surveyed had experienced transphobia on social media.[44]

According to a study by the Williams Institute at UCLA School of Law published in 2021,[45] trans people are four times more likely to be the victim of a violent crime in the US. There are 86.2 attacks per 1,000 people compared to 21.7 per 1,000 people for cisgender people (we'll unpack this word, and my initial resistance to using it, later, but for now for those unfamiliar with it, 'cisgender', sometimes shortened to 'cis', is the current term for someone who is gender conforming).* The study also reveals that transgender households have higher rates of property victimisation (214.1 per 1,000 households) than cisgender households (108 per 1,000 households). It's almost twice as likely that someone will come and damage your home or steal your things if you're trans. The study author, Ilan H. Meyer, Distinguished Senior Scholar of Public Policy at the Williams Institute, said: 'Research has shown that experiences of victimisation are related to low wellbeing, including suicide thoughts and attempts ... The results underscore the urgent need for effective policies and interventions that consider high rates of victimization experienced by transgender people.'

Rates of suicidal ideation are much higher in the trans community than with other cohorts – in 2020, the US National Library of Medicine reported that 82 per cent of transgender individuals have considered taking their own life, and 40 per cent have attempted suicide.[46] This compares to 0.7 per cent

---

* Gender conforming simply means you identify with the gender the doctor declared you at birth.

of the general public who have attempted suicide.[47] While all evidence available indicates the transgender community is the most targeted group in the LGBTQ+ community,[48] the UK has not yet found a way to reliably record and publish stats on violence against trans people because we have a smaller population, and the Office for National Statistics says, 'Releasing this information could be equivalent to releasing individual personal details which we are legally obliged not to do.'[49] The percentage of the UK population that is trans is so small, releasing data could reveal details about individuals! You'd never guess there were so few trans people, given how many column inches are devoted to stories – generally negative – about how gender-nonconforming people are changing our society. Trans people are clearly a marginalised minority, and the cultural conversation surrounding trans rights is growing more toxic. Why?

What's the origin story?

A November 2020 study by the Independent Press Standards Organisation (IPSO) in the UK showed a 400 per cent increase in reporting on trans issues in the mainstream press from 2009 to 2019.[50] While the study showed some trends towards respecting pronouns and more sensitive, inclusive language, it also showed an increase in negative or 'concerned' (asking questions that imply negative answers) reporting. That trend appears very much to continue from 2020 till now with no sign of abating. According to Ell Folan at Novara Media, in the month of January 2013 there were six articles in the *Daily Mail* about transgender people and none of them were negative. In January 2023 there were 115 articles about trans people and 87 per cent of them could reasonably be categorised as negative.[51] That's 115 articles in one publication in one month. Remembering that the trans population in the UK is between

0.5 per cent to 1 per cent, the estimated 13,500 articles in the mainstream media written about trans people in the last seven years seems like an extraordinary focus.

We need to examine some specifics about attitudes and reporting. In 2015 the first transgender actor appeared on *EastEnders* and the IPSO report found almost 70 per cent positive reporting and just over 30 per cent neutral reporting, with absolutely no negative or 'questioning' reporting.[52] Before that, in 2004, Nadia Almada appeared on reality show *Big Brother* and won, in a cultural milestone that was reported with near-unanimous positivity.[53] Let's compare that with recent reporting of the first transgender actor to play a transgender character in *Doctor Who* in December 2023. Even articles that reported this mostly neutrally or even somewhat positively often also included comments such as 'the Family Education Trust [is] saying that it promoted a "cult of gender ideology" for young people watching the TV show'.[54] Some headlines were not about the character herself, but specifically about complaints from viewers about a trans character appearing on their screens at all.[55] The *Telegraph* devoted around 760 words to a claim that the BBC had 'hidden tweets from gender critical viewers' and painstakingly quoted those tweets: 'Why is this show anti-woman? Humans cannot change sex' and 'My partner, a biologist, says sex is immutable and binary . . . Stop gaslighting us'.[56]

It is remarkable that there seems to be no such recorded outrage or even questions being asked in 2013 when Sophia Burset, played by Laverne Cox, came onto our screens as a trans prisoner, sharing facilities with non-trans female prisoners, in the global hit *Orange is the New Black*. I was an avid fan of the show at the time and don't remember thinking it would cause concern that a trans woman would be housed in a female prison, nor that she should work one on one with cisgender female prisoners in her own beauty salon. I can't remember one conversation about this character in relation to women's safety either in person, on socials, or in the press, which seems unthinkable in today's landscape with a heavy focus on how trans prisoners are housed (a topic we will come to later). Furthermore, I have searched X/Twitter's back catalogue and can find only positive tweets about the character of Sophia and the issues her character highlights for trans women both in prison and society. I'm not saying there was no negative reporting or social media action, but if there was it was not significant and it is very difficult to find.

Even more remarkable, in retrospect, are the positive articles from the *Daily Mail*. One piece from June 2015 about Laverne Cox and her co-stars doing a glamour shoot has ten comments from readers, all resoundingly positive, including: 'These women are awesome' and 'all the women on [the show] are beautiful'.[57] Another article was published in 2015 with the headline: 'The heartwarming moment the actress Laverne Cox gives advice to another transgender girl – who is aged just seven.' The public comments on this are mostly positive, with no comments that read as alarmed or angry.[58] This is an unimaginable response in today's landscape.

There are also many articles and interviews in the *Telegraph* around this time celebrating Laverne Cox and what she is doing for trans rights. The articles even highlight Cox's recommendations that trans teens have access to gender-affirming care, including the use of puberty blockers. She describes her own painful puberty and says medical care can be life-saving.

Consider an article in the *Telegraph* from November 2015 that opens this way: 'TV bosses should offer leading roles to transgender actors, [Conservative Party] culture minister Ed Vaizey has suggested. The minister said the success of transgender star Laverne Cox in Netflix series *Orange Is The New Black* and the Amazon Prime show *Transparent* showed broadcasters "the sky is not going to fall on your head" if they pursue a diversity agenda.'[59] The article reports that Vaizey is also concerned about online trolling against trans people, arguing more must be done to stop this, including representation of trans people on TV who happen to be trans rather than making their gender identity the most important part of their story: 'Not seeing this as somehow exotic but completely mainstream is really important,' he said.

Vaizey was not a Tory outlier in this. Prime Minister Theresa May (who had historically not been a friend to LGBTQ+ rights!) gave a speech at the Pink News Awards in 2017 in which she said:

> We are determined to eradicate homophobic and transphobic bullying. We have laid out plans to reform the Gender Recognition Act, streamlining and demedicalising the process for changing gender because being trans is not an illness and it should not be treated as such . . . I am committed to seeing that work through.

Jeremy Corbyn, the leader of the opposition at the time, went further and said that Theresa May was not promising enough, and that she would have his support if the requirement for trans people to undergo medical tests was scrapped.[60]

In her book *The Transgender Issue*, Shon Faye identifies the 2010s as a time in which many campaigners and activists in the trans community hoped that a new understanding would come out of 'visibility politics'. She hoped for better representation after many generations of trans people being at best the butt of the joke, and at worst violently dehumanised. This time of new hope was most alive when Laverne Cox was on the cover of *Time* magazine in 2014 alongside the caption 'The transgender tipping point. America's next civil rights frontier.' This was a significant, iconic moment, especially as the US is such a cultural thermometer for the rest of the world.

The accompanying article in *Time* about Cox by Katy Steinmetz reads:

> Almost one year after the Supreme Court ruled that Americans were free to marry the person they loved, no matter their sex, another civil rights movement is poised to challenge long-held cultural norms and beliefs. Transgender people – those who identify with a gender other than the sex they were 'assigned at birth,' to use the preferred phrase among trans activists – are emerging from the margins to fight for an equal place in society. This new transparency is improving the lives of a long-misunderstood minority and beginning to yield new policies, as trans activists and their supporters push for changes in schools, hospitals, workplaces, prisons and the military. 'We are in a place now,' Cox tells *TIME*, 'where more and more trans people want to come forward and say, "This is who I am." And more trans people are willing to tell their stories. More of us are living visibly and pursuing our dreams visibly, so people can say, "Oh yeah, I know someone who is trans." When people have points of reference that are humanizing, that demystifies difference.'[61]

Steinmetz seems to be saying that trans people had taken a number and waited for gay people to have all the rights afforded straight people, and while that hadn't eradicated homophobia and wasn't likely to usher in the first gay president, things were much better – and so it was time for trans people to step forward and ask for more. Cox's answer was, in short, that people's affective empathy needed to be activated through story and humanisation.

Much has changed since then, as we have already seen from the seeming 180-degree turn from the mainstream press. The Conservative Party has also made a complete reversal on trans rights, including May's promised reforms to the Gender Recognition Act. In 2023, Conservative Prime Minister Rishi Sunak actually invoked unprecedented powers to block Scotland's Gender Recognition Act Reform bill, which had passed in Scotland by a large majority. Keir Starmer, as leader of the opposition, also rolled back Labour's support for trans people.

What are the consequences of this? Well, inevitably, society's collective amygdala has been activated. The story has changed, so the fear response has changed. In 2023 the Home Office reported an increase in hate crimes against trans people by 11 per cent in a year, and by 186 per cent in the last five years.[62] The Home Office briefing admitted, 'Transgender issues have been heavily discussed by politicians, the media and on social media over the last year, which may have led to an increase in these offences, or more awareness in the police in the identification and recording of these crimes.'[63]

The same report stated that while in 2019 some 53 per cent of people agreed that a trans person should be permitted to change the sex on their birth certificate, in 2023 that figure had dropped to 30 per cent. In 2019, 82 per cent of people described themselves as 'not at all prejudiced' against trans people. In 2023 only 64 per cent of people could say that. In other words, as a nation, we are becoming more prejudiced to trans people. What's happened? Why was this promising new frontier at a time of greater visibility and cognitive and affective empathy for trans people seemingly so quickly stopped in its tracks?

Was a backlash inevitable all along?

In part, it is a phenomenon that occurs with many movements which are gaining rights that I think of as 'The Empire Strikes Back'. In January 2017, in response to Trump coming to power in the US, after he'd been caught on tape talking about sexually assaulting women, women marched in protest in countries around the world. The #MeToo movement followed, which resulted in Harvey Weinstein being sentenced to twenty-three years in prison, and other men being publicly called to account for predatory and sexually criminal behaviour. The Time's Up legal defence fund raised about $20 million for lower-income women seeking support for sexual harassment or assault.[64]

The cultural conversation, in turn, has changed remarkably, as I'm sure you've experienced. Is the consequence more rights for women and more male allies for feminism in a straightforward trajectory? On the contrary, as discussed in our first conversation, in June 2022, the American Supreme Court overturned the Roe v. Wade ruling which guaranteed the right to an abortion resulting in (at the time of writing) a total abortion ban in fourteen states, a partial ban in two states, and other states 'in flux' with outcomes to be determined. Campaigners warn birth control is also under threat. As we also explored, young men are falling down online 'rabbit holes' and being radicalised by commentators in the 'manosphere' resulting in targeted violence against women. In other backlash news, UN Women warns that gender disparities are worsening around the world with many countries clamping down on feminist movements. This makes life harder for women, meaning at this rate it has been estimated by UN Women that it could take '286 years to close the global gender gaps in legal protections for women and girls'.[65]

To be clear, I am definitely *not* blaming the women's

movement. We are right to make visible protests and clear demands and celebrate wins, and must push on in defiance of and opposition to these threats to our rights. As Susan Faludi says in her excellent book *Backlash: The Undeclared War Against Women*, 'A backlash against women's rights is nothing new . . . It returns every time women begin to make some headway towards equality, a seemingly inevitable early frost to the brief flowerings of feminism.' She unpacks how for every period of progress, there's a spate of political push-backs and TV shows that tell women the freedoms they've gained have left them alone and exhausted and they were better off in the kitchen, leaving it to Beaver. She likens women's progress to a corkscrew rather than a ladder, with even some powerful second-wave feminists recanting or backtracking from their radical '70s rhetoric in the 1980s – perhaps feeling exhausted, defeated or naive. In fact, 'the manosphere' has its roots in the '70s and '80s in opposition to feminism.

Let us consider the Empire Striking Back for gay rights in the UK. After decriminalisation in 1967,* there was of course an expanding visible population of gay people. Once you're no longer legally obliged to stay in the closet, you can protest for more rights. This led to a fear of social contagion, especially for children and teens who were seen to be vulnerable to the 'gay agenda' of recruitment.† This seems ludicrous to us now. It's obvious to most of us that children seeing role models on

* Or rather, partial decriminalisation – the age of consent was placed at twenty-one for gay people, and 'street offences' were met with far heavier penalties. It was also illegal for gay men to have sex in a hotel room.

† And, as activist Peter Tatchell recalls, there was a significant uptick in arrests for gross indecency directly after decriminalisation: 'In 1966, the year before partial decriminalisation, 420 men were convicted of gross indecency. To my shock, I found that the number of convictions soared by over 400 per cent to 1,711 in 1974. The authorities were determined to ensure that the limited liberalisation of 1967 did not give a green light to

television and in their own communities helps them understand their own feelings, or the feelings of others, and potentially think, 'People can date guys and/or girls!? That's a thing! Cool!' At the time, however, the media and influential people and politicians created a landscape where people were very frightened of gay contagion, no doubt conflated with the AIDS crisis.

Three years later, in this media landscape which both raised society's amygdala against gay people and lowered empathy for them, Margaret Thatcher's government introduced Section 28. This legislation ruled that a local authority 'shall not intentionally promote homosexuality or publish material with the intention of promoting homosexuality' or 'promote the teaching in any maintained school of the acceptability of homosexuality as a pretended family relationship'. After some legal wins and positive cultural shifts, Section 28 ushered in fifteen years of an even more hostile environment, and pushed some gay people back into the closet. *Blue Jean*, a 2023 feature film inspired by a true story, follows Jean, a lesbian working as a PE teacher and netball coach in a secondary school during Section 28. She has to hide her personal life, diminishing herself in the process, sneaking into gay bars and sometimes bumping into lonely, confused queer or questioning older teenage students without being able to help or mentor them or stop them from being bullied. She is always in fear of her job. I recommend watching it as a way of enhancing your affective empathy for those who suffered through Section 28, which was introduced in the name of 'protecting children'.

Trans people were affected by Section 28 too. Trans people marched and protested and were arrested along with gay men,

---

what they still regarded as a vice.' https://www.petertatchellfoundation.org/1967-the-myth-of-gay-decriminalisation/

lesbians and bisexuals. Imagine being a trans teacher in the UK in 1988! That is rarely considered as that movement is usually considered to be a struggle for gay rights, liberation and visibility, in truth because that was the focus. It is easy see the parallels between the struggle for gay rights then to the fight for trans rights now. New visibility. Some ground gained. More people coming out as trans. Children and teens having a language to say how they're feeling and role models to engage with. In turn, those children and teens get more visibility and people panic that children are being converted and need to be protected. Rights are taken away. We've talked about today's media landscape for trans people broadly. Let's compare it directly to the British media we've already looked at leading up to and during Section 28.

These are exactly the same publications:

> 'Is it wise to share a lavatory with a homosexual?' *The Times*, 1985

> 'Unisex loos make me wish for the bad old days.' *The Times*, 2019

> 'Given an inch, the homosexuals demand all. Granted legality, they have advanced boldly, noisily, immodestly, without shame, flaunting and organising themselves, proselytising vigorously, demanding ever-fresh "rights", privileges, handouts, immunities, special representation.' *Spectator*, 1985

> '"Pride" is no longer a movement that is simply fighting for the rights and liberties of people who have faced prejudice and discrimination because they don't happen to be straight. It has morphed into something altogether more controversial and political – it is promoting the trans

agenda that undermines longstanding concepts of sex and gender . . . Am I the only BBC journalist who still believes in two genders? . . . the only one who thinks there are far more urgent problems . . . than the supposedly terrible plight of a vanishingly small number of people who aren't happy with their sex, gender or identity generally?' *Spectator*, 2022

(The audacity of the *Spectator* not to own that they actively fought gay pride for as long as possible, as they now clutch their pearls and use gay rights as a weapon against those seeking trans rights.)

'Why was the Reverend Gregory Richards, a homosexual, employed as a chaplain in the prison service? God knows how many people he has infected with the disease. Equal rights for homosexuals cannot operate in sensitive appointments when such risks as AIDS exist.' *Express*, 1985

Compare the perceived risks in law and order then and now:

'Female police officers could have to strip search trans women . . . It opens the door for drunk males under arrest to demand a strip search from a female officer by claiming to identify as a woman.' *Express*, 2022

'Martina Turns Girls Into Gays: A huge scandal exploded over women's tennis last night when senior players were accused by a former Wimbledon champion of seducing young players on the circuit. Margaret Court said the example set was so bad that young girl players were scared to go into tournament changing rooms . . . [Court said] "It's very sad for children to be exposed to homosexuality . . . There's no

> doubt there's a lot more of it than when I finished playing. There are players now who won't even go to the tournament changing rooms."' *Sun*, 1990

Compare fears of contagion and danger in changing rooms with these headlines:

> 'Is changing gender the new anorexia? ... According to Dr Littman, rapid onset gender dysphoria may be driven via social contagion – the spread of behaviours and attitudes within a group through imitation and conformity.' *Sun*, 2018

(This theory has since been thoroughly discredited[66] but not retracted by the *Sun*.)

> 'Gender-neutral changing rooms aren't safe – they just appease the trans lobby who won't accept you if you don't conform to their views.' *Sun*, 2017

Something that makes this backlash different from Section 28 is that it has occurred during the age of social media. In our first conversation, we examined some of the cult-like tactics that are used on the internet to force fast conformity in your stamm, and to insist you have more empathy for fewer people. You must affectively empathise with your stamm but you must not even cognitively empathise with your counter-stamm. This has happened dramatically on this issue.

Some (often young) people have demanded others (often members of an older generation) start using new language and take on new ideas wholesale. Others, angered by calls for exclusion, or even sometimes questions, suggestions or debate that they feel fan the flames of exclusion, at times use threats of harassment or sometimes even threats of violence. At the same time some people who see trans rights as an encroachment on other people's rights speak very violently too.

A cursory scroll through social media searching for hot-button topics will certainly provide any number of examples, calling for a 'final solution' to the 'trans problem', public castrations and executions, and *in utero* testing for transness in order to ensure a trans-free population. All eugenics tactics, often delivered with extra slurs and graphic language.

It's key to note that this 'debate' is by no means taking place on a level playing field – on one side there is a marginalised and oppressed group, seeking to be treated with dignity and respect, while on the other side there is an empowered establishment demanding the right to continue not treating them with respect. But the upshot is that the most angry and radical members of both stamms seem incapable of creating a dialogue or attempting to find cognitive empathy for those in the other stamm. The most vocal and definitive members of both groups do not represent every member of the wider stamm by any means, but the way stamms work, there is now a deadlock. How is this different from the way Section 28 was fought?

The people who were being demonised by a constant press campaign representing them as predators and deviants despised the journalists writing such things and the MPs legislating against them. Their response was neither quiet nor polite. The reporters and politicians saw that fury as more evidence that they were grotesque and had a clear agenda of corrupting young people into deviance: 'We're not saying you can't choose your deviant lifestyle – just leave the children alone!'

What's different now is that while Section 28 protesters were furious and intense, the nature of the time meant there appeared to be some leadership with the messaging. The internet allows us to see every single thing being said by every single person and for individuals to message public figures directly and publicly. I am sure that journalists and politicians received a lot of hate mail throughout the Section 28 era that was read by assistants and/or binned, but it wasn't out on a wall for everyone to see. Also, you couldn't fire off a quick insult or threat in a rage. You had to get a pen and paper, and if you'd gone to all that trouble you probably at least tried to articulate your thoughts. (There were no doubt many inarticulate messages too!) The nature of rapid-fire communication now, coupled with the fact that sending messages is both free and frictionless, means there is much violent talk online in every direction on many issues.[67]

I once saw a comment under a Billy Joel video from a poster who said they were thrilled to have discovered Joel's music through the popular high school television comedy drama *Glee*. The response underneath was shockingly abusive and graphic and threw slurs at the person who originally posted, claiming they didn't deserve to know Joel's music if their reference point was *Glee* and that, in fact, they should consider ending their life. The original poster countered: 'I'm only nine.'

That abusive comment to a child excited to have found the original 'Uptown Girl' was every bit as abusive, horrendous and dehumanising as I've seen from gender critical people (or sock puppets and bots) towards trans people and their supporters. And as abusive or horrendous as threats I've seen from trans activists and people supporting trans activists (or sock puppets and bots) towards gender critical posters. But instances of online abuse by trans activists are then bundled up and used as proof that trans people (women especially) are violent predators crashing into women's spaces at every opportunity to take over and inflict terror, which then becomes the presiding narrative. Given that only approximately 18 per cent of the UK population is on X/Twitter, and abusive tweets represent a vanishingly small fraction of that discourse, using slights on X/Twitter as a metric for how trans people feel in the real world is unfair and misleading – especially given that, since owner Elon Musk's deregulation of the platform in pursuit of his libertarian take on 'free speech', it is increasingly difficult to tell if those posting are bored teenagers, sock puppet accounts acting in bad faith, or bots. As a result, many trans people have left the service – further warping and skewing its relevance.[68]

We have to imagine that the same thing would have happened in 1988 if LGBTQ+ people had had access to the internet as well as the stationery shop and the post office. I do not excuse this behaviour. Even if it is done in arch irony or righteous indignation, it's nasty and works directly against any point anyone is hoping to make. But it is not evidence that trans people are dangerous and must be stopped, unless we are also going to mount a big campaign about the dangers of Billy Joel fans and any number of other people or groups on the internet.

If you doubt some seriously salty tweets would have been dashed off in 1988, please remember that when the House of Lords passed Section 28, a group of lesbian protesters abseiled from the viewing gallery down onto the floor, which must have been quite scary for the people underneath. The protesters were arrested, as were their colleagues who'd stayed above. Another group of lesbian activists broke into the BBC News studio as the news readers were live on air. Some were wrestled to the ground. One handcuffed herself to the camera. The press responded predictably that these are the people who are threatening our children and wanting to recruit them. We also have to acknowledge that there were a series of videos and articles celebrating these brave activists as heroes in 2018, on the thirtieth anniversary of these startling physical protests, from the very publications that were vilifying trans people in the same week.

How would the press represent trans women if they broke into public spaces in a threatening way when they were legislated against? What would the narrative be?

Gender critical people would argue that lesbians, being women, do not have the same upper-body strength or potentially high testosterone levels as trans women who've been through a male puberty.* They argue that trans women are more of a physical threat and specifically to cis women. But people did say in 1988 that lesbians were stronger and more manly and were a predatory, physical danger to women and that gay men were a physical threat to men. I remember it well. It was said to me personally. People wanted gay people out of single-sex spaces because they were frightened that they were physically dangerous predators.

A note on this – I was raised in Queensland in Australia, a state in which male homosexuality wasn't decriminalised till 1991, the age of consent wasn't equalised till 2016 and equal marriage wasn't passed till late 2017. While my religion didn't focus on homosexuality much, when it was mentioned, it was always in the context of a sin with the possibility of a redemption arc. For some reason, despite that, I never felt homophobic.†

---

* It's important to acknowledge that many trans women would identify as lesbians, but for the purposes of this passage I want to focus on the framing that a gender critical person would use.

† This doesn't necessarily mean I wasn't homophobic at the time; internalised queerphobia being something it's extremely difficult to notice or examine. I was always drawn to queer people and spaces. When I moved to Sydney in the 1990s, home of the Mardi Gras, two out of three living in the cool Eastern Suburbs at that time were said to be gay (safety in numbers!). I was still a Jehovah's Witness but strangely in my element. I once confessed on the quiet to an elder who seemed more sophisticated than the others that I wasn't

It was in this climate that I was told to be physically scared of lesbians. They were depicted as larger and stronger than other women and highly predatory. I remember Jehovah's Witness men posturing fear around gay men. In fact, lesbians and gay men were much more likely to be the victims of violence then, as they are now. Trans people are too. Many trans people feel extremely physically vulnerable, and we've seen the hate crime stats already.

The other difference today compared to 1988 is that the internet has created the kind of surround-sound power that we discussed in our first conversation (and that we will unpack more in our fifth conversation around cancel culture). Where cancel culture is accountability, and where it amounts to harassment and coercion, is a big and complicated topic, but it is foolish to think that gay men, lesbians, bisexuals and trans people fighting Section 28 wouldn't have pressured the newspapers to stop printing the work of journalists in favour of the bill if they could have. Would people have been fired or moved on to other jobs in increasingly right-wing publications if queer people had had that power? Of course. It was affecting the lives of the LGBTQ+ community heavily. They were fighting for it to stop and using all they had.

Is this the right no-platform?

The practice of no-platforming speakers in universities is also seen by the establishment commentariat as evidence that millennial and Gen Z trans activists are censoring and silencing those who are just asking questions or wanting a debate. Young people counter that there is so much misinformation now

homophobic and he smiled and said, 'Neither am I' which certainly wasn't something we could ever say into the broom-handle mic!

entering their campuses via screens that inviting individuals in person whose ideas may exacerbate structural and physical violence is not acceptable and they have a right to push back. Whatever you think of no-platforming, young people didn't invent it. Baby Boomers did and Gen Xers used it too. The National Union of Students introduced the 'no platform' policy in 1974 to stop racists and fascists speaking on campuses, mostly members of the National Front, and it has also been used to stop homophobic speakers.[69]

In 1987, a year before Section 28 was brought in, a Conservative councillor called Richard Lewis who had spoken out against gay rights was asked to come and speak at the Conservative Association at Swansea University. Student Magazine *Bad Press* reported:

> Jon Lloyd-Owen, the Union Treasurer, informed Mr Lewis that he was not welcome in the building . . . the entourage eventually moved out of the building and across to a lecture theatre, followed by some 60 protestors . . . [Mr Lewis's] speech was drowned by cries of 'OUT OUT' from angry students.

Lewis 'condemned the behaviour of the Student Union members saying that it was an infringement of his freedom of speech'. Lloyd-Owen countered that Lewis was 'a dangerous homophobic bigot, whose antics pose a threat to all students and in particular those already oppressed by racism and anti-gay hysteria'. The student union president told the student press that Lewis was 'reactionary, opportunistic and misinformed' and that his 'ignorant views' were 'a danger to us all and generations to come'. The student union then disaffiliated the Conservative Association, causing a great debate about freedom of speech. Evan Smith recounts in his recent book *No*

Platform: A History of Anti-Fascism, Universities and the Limits of Free Speech:

> After over 30 academics from across the university signed a letter defending the protest against Lewis, [the university principal Brian] Clarkson stated that freedom of speech was 'the foundation of a University society and is not one which can be qualified in any way'. But Colwyn Williamson, a philosophy lecturer at the university, asked 'is there anyone who honestly believes in an unqualified right of free speech?' As the letter by the numerous academics pointed out, 'freedom of speech is not an absolute right in our society' and one that is legally curtailed on several levels.[70]

There's nothing new here. Just a different generation with a different human rights demand.

What do you do with witches?

What about lesbians' place within feminism? Does trans people's struggle to be included find any parallels there? American writer and activist Betty Friedan has often been called 'The Mother of Second-Wave Feminism' and her book *The Feminine Mystique* was groundbreaking in its examination of women's lack of rights and representation. In 1966, Friedan, Pauli Murray and Aileen Hernandez co-founded the National Organization for Women (NOW). NOW's mission statement was 'to bring women into full participation in the mainstream of American society now, exercising all the privileges and responsibilities thereof in truly equal partnership with men.' NOW's objectives, as outlined in the *New Yorker*, included 'securing the enforcement of anti-discrimination law; gaining subsidized childcare, abortion rights, and public-accommodations protections; and passing the Equal Rights Amendment. NOW was able to bring about changes large and small—to hiring policies, to credit-granting rules, to laws—that improved the lives of American women.'[71]

Who was included in 'American women'? Generally speaking, white middle-class women – largely not working-class, Black and brown, Indigenous, immigrant, unhoused, chronically ill or disabled women – and not lesbians, whom Friedan referred to as 'the lavender menace' in an interview with *New York Times Magazine*. In fact, she orchestrated a 'purge of lesbians' from NOW. The *Advocate* writes on this:

> Lesbians were perceived as 'man hating' and mainstream feminism was intent on presenting the movement as pro-woman, not anti-male. Lesbians were still viewed as perverts and even as mentally ill. It would be several more years before the psychiatric community's DSM would change its view that homosexuality was a mental disease. As Hannah Quayle wrote in a blog post about the purge, 'Lesbians were placed within an unnatural category of the 'third sex.' This 'third sex' was associated as a gross abnormality which violated female anatomy, heterosexual desire and gender behaviour by associating masculine features upon the female body. In this sense, lesbians were not considered 'real women,' and stood outside the category of 'woman' in a physical, sexual, personal and political sense.'
>
> Quayle asserted that within the mainstream feminist movement and NOW, 'Lesbians had to find an effective way to address the accusation that their masculinity was somehow complicit with men and the patriarchy, and that lesbian influence would not in fact dismantle strict heterosexual categories as it was widely believed. Heterosexual feminists excluded lesbians from the feminist movement

> in the 1960s based on this discomfort towards their sexuality.'[72]

This was all despite the fact that lesbians had helped found NOW and had always been central to feminism.

In response to the 'purge', at the 1970 Congress to Unite Women, lesbian feminists protested, crashing the congress and rushing to the front of the room wearing 'Lavender Menace' T-shirts. The parallels between lesbians then and trans people now are clear.

I recently listened to a high-profile podcast series called *The Witch Trials of J.K. Rowling*[73] in which Megan Phelps-Roper examines the current debate around trans rights, spending hours talking to Rowling, who is arguably the most high-profile advocate for the gender critical movement. On the face of it, you'd think I'd like this show. Phelps-Roper left a far more radical and bigoted cult than mine – the notorious Westboro Baptist Church, famous for picketing funerals and shouting homophobic slurs on the street. She says that compassionate people online took the time to talk to her about her beliefs and credits that with her deradicalisation. So far, so good. However, her conversations with Rowling are an extraordinary example of a performance of civility and politeness while shaping a narrative to tell a story. It's brilliantly done, and it is the equivalent of wiping away soot from a tiny spot on a window and claiming what you can see through it is the entire view.

I am not imputing motive. Perhaps getting Rowling was such a coup for Phelps-Roper that she did not want to offend her. Perhaps she agrees with her. What is clear is that the trans rights protesters are represented throughout as a baying mob. Audio file of activists shouting insults and threats punctuate the show. On the other hand, Rowling and the gender critical movement are presented as a collection of reasonable women who are 'just asking valid questions'.

Natalie Wynn, a public intellectual and YouTuber known as ContraPoints, contributes (later she said that she wishes she hadn't because she now feels used in what is anti-trans propaganda) as well as a young man called Noah, who seemed cherry-picked by the producers to appear naive and manipulated by an ideology. They were the only trans voices on the six-hour show. For this reason, I highly recommend if you've listened to the podcast that you also watch ContraPoints' YouTube video essay in rebuttal[74] and video essayist Shaun's YouTube riposte, 'JK Rowling's New Friends'.[75]

I have already outlined how much structural violence trans people live with and how small they are in number, but that is not mentioned in Phelps-Roper's podcast. *The Witch Trials* makes a case for civility above all – as if trans activists are the first to get angry or show up in numbers at protests when every human rights movement that has created social change has done the same, and many before them have been militant. Again, I'm not endorsing threats of violence. In fact, my view is that threats of violence, insults, death threats and acts of violence are wrong and extremely counterproductive. They also take up space and misdirect from the issues. As Amnesty International says, one infringement of human rights doesn't legitimise another.

Personally I do not use the word 'terf', which stand for Trans Exclusionary Radical Feminist and which some people use to describe gender critical feminists (although I do find it slightly ironic that they get irate at not being called the thing they have asked to be called!). However neutral its origins, it contains the plosives and fricatives of a curse word, and now functions for many as an insult. Language labels people, rather than asks them why they're thinking in a certain way. Because of the nature of the internet, it's now thrown at people who may be exploring this issue or following someone with gender critical views. It boxes people and sends them towards a stamm who are telling them, 'Those people don't like you – they'll label you'. It's not designed to get anyone to ask questions or elevate the discussion above the statements the tabloids are shouting. We need people to think critically about this. The word 'terf', like anything that functions as an insult, will activate the brain in an unhelpful way. No one changes their amygdala. They change their mind.

Just as I am appalled when I see people wishing violence on trans people, watching trans activists at protests with signs that read 'punch terfs', for example, chills me. It's grotesque and speaks to the kind of rabbit-hole-style radicalisation we explored in our first conversation.

To explore this further I talked to Dr Gina Gwenffrewi, a lecturer in transgender studies and English literature at the University of Edinburgh who co-wrote an impressive paper on trans feminist perspectives titled 'Beyond cisnormative understandings of the digital public sphere'.

When we spoke, Dr Gwenffrewi told me that these kinds of signs at protests are brought by very rare outliers, which are then photographed and memed endlessly to smear the wider group of peaceful protesters. She pointed out that a sign which read 'Behead terfs' was carried by one very troubled outlier but it's been photographed and shared so much some people are under the impression that it's the norm.[76]

Dr Gwenffrewi said:

> It's very frustrating for the vast majority of trans activists who go to protests that these signs become the predominant narrative. Nirmal Puwar, a senior lecturer at the department of Sociology at Goldsmiths University, writes about this in

her work *Space Invaders* (2004). She talks about the burden of representation for minoritised groups and how one example will be used to associate with the entire demographic.

A useful example of what Dr Gwenffrewi is referencing here might be this – in 2018 a video went viral of a cisgender man at a reproductive rights rally, taunting and then roundly kicking an anti-abortion protester who was filming him. Shortly after striking the anti-abortion protester, the man can be heard saying, 'I meant to kick your phone'. Regardless of what he meant to kick, it was a clear case of violent assault. But, while the man in question was castigated for his actions both online and in the real world (he lost his job as a result), he has been rightly treated as an unrepresentative outlier.[77] Most of us do not reference this incident as proof that all reproductive-justice advocates protesting for their rights are violent, or that men in general shouldn't be at these rallies. Nor should we draw these conclusions about trans people when outliers say violent things – to my knowledge, nobody has kicked anybody in the face, and I feel quite strongly that I would have heard about it any number of times had it happened.

Dr Gwenffrewi went on to say:

> It's very frustrating because all it takes is one person with a placard. I was at Pride in Edinburgh and I saw someone with a placard that said something like 'punch terfs' and I rolled my eyes. It was like two young transmasculine people. Looking back, I think, 'Should I have intervened?' Why didn't I intervene? Because I thought, 'This is going to come back at trans women. It won't be transmasculine people. I know that they have their own negative stereotypes to deal with, but not generally in relation to violence. It's trans women who always get stigmatised as violent.'

I agree that it plays into the very stereotype we are fighting against, that trans people are somehow dangerous. There are definitely signs we could tell people that they couldn't carry if they wanted to be at our protest. We would tell someone they couldn't carry a racist sign, so I'm not sure why we are allowing threats of violence.

Dr Gwenffrewi said, 'I think it should be explicit in the literature when you're advertising the protest: "We're here to protest peacefully and firmly. We don't want to feed into that narrative that trans women are violent so expressions of violence aren't welcome here."'

Cisgendered people holding signs threatening violence are helping shape that story for the press. More amygdalas are activated when those images appear in the papers. With all this said, it is disingenuous to suggest that trans activists are the first group demanding human rights to do any of these things. There will be more on how we might proceed in our final conversations. For now, let's look at some of the issues concerning people who have good-faith questions.

What do you mean I'm 'hetero'?

I admit when I first heard that I was a 'cisgender' woman – a word coined to describe someone who isn't transgender or non-binary* – I had an emotional reaction to it. I'll be honest and say it felt so fully imposed by some people on social media, it reminded me of the 'New Light' from the Watchtower Society, delivered without any permission to ask questions or time to consider this new language and what it might mean. As I've explained, I am very sensitive to any expectations for intellectual

* The prefix cis is Latin and means 'on this side of'. Trans is Latin for 'across, beyond, on the far side'.

sharp turns that must be taken on wholesale, because of my life experience.

I'll talk you through how it landed for me and where I arrived, because it might help others who are thinking through this or other ideas or language. If you're irritated that I didn't immediately accept it without any emotion or thought – stop and consider why, and whether you're looking for obedient stamm members or contemporaries with understanding and intellectual rigour.

At first, it felt like being asked to use the prefix 'cis' was a request to qualify my womanhood for someone else. I needed to sit with it for a while and talk about it with other people who offered a safe haven for discussion. I looked at the contexts people were using it in and realised no one was asking me to identify as a cis woman per se, but rather to use the word in situations where I needed to distinguish myself from trans women, precisely because we had different needs and circumstances.

Then I had the idea to look up the origins of 'heterosexual'. It was coined in 1869 by thinker, writer and human rights activist Karl Maria Kertbeny, to define someone with a 'morbid' or excessive sexual desire for those of 'the opposite sex'.[78] This was at a time when the most common categorising of sex was 'procreative', which equalled good and proper, and 'non-procreative', which was deemed as deviant. This is an unfamiliar framework to us, but was completely standard and the only way most Victorians knew how to look at it.

At the same time, he coined 'homosexual' for those attracted to people of the same sex. Previously, Westerners hadn't seen sexual orientation as a part of their identities. 'Buggery' or 'sodomy' was an act – and a crime at that. The idea that your libido made you a certain sort of person was entirely new. Kertbeny also came up with 'monosexual' for those who masturbated, although interestingly no one is asked to define themselves as either monosexual or not monosexual today. That's a category we've abandoned, perhaps because we feel it's unnecessary because it's assumed that almost everyone does it.

By the 1930s, 'heterosexual' had evolved to mean someone attracted to the opposite sex. Some people pushed back against that too when it was popularised – because, they insisted, they were 'normal' and didn't need a new identity. People in my community when I was growing up balked at the idea of being 'straight' or 'hetero' rather than 'just a normal non-deviant person'.

I'm sure, given the resistance to orphans and adoption, the same was true when the term 'biological children' was introduced into society. Although it's hard to find documented evidence for this, surely at least some parents would have said things like, 'My child is my child! I don't need to qualify that by saying they're *biologically* my child!' Naturally, they were not being asked to do that unless it was to distinguish between biological and adopted sons and daughters, but in their minds sons and daughters were exclusively biological and all others were waifs, strays, orphans and bastards, so I can see why some people might have felt a bit offended at hearing that turn of phrase and having to apply it to their offspring in any context at all.

All this helped me think through the idea of using the word cis to describe myself. I realised I didn't need to say that I was cis any more frequently than I said I was straight (this was before I was sure I was bisexual). I realised I was comfortable with 'straight' or 'hetero' because I'd heard these terms since I was a teenager, and they didn't seem threatening to me. I only needed them in specific contexts. These words didn't change my life. They only made room for other people. I am bisexual.

I am an adopted daughter. For that language to make sense, other people have to be cool with being straight, and being biological children. The only logical conclusion here is that I need to own being a cisgender woman.

At the end of these thought processes, I revisited my original emotional resistance to the prefix 'cis' and analysed where it had come from. I think it was fear that I was losing something and that something had control over the way I defined myself. But after I'd thought it through, I didn't feel that way. No one was taking control from me. Instead, I had extended my model for thinking about how the world worked. In fact, this was something I needed to think about, because I hadn't always done that in the past.

Before the movement for transgender rights and identity had become so visible and mainstream (and a few years before I started *The Guilty Feminist* or had engaged with activism much), my stand-up comedy tour manager was a transgender woman called Charly. I never questioned her womanhood. When we were on the road, people were occasionally snide or prurient behind her back. I always felt defensive of her. I resisted those remarks and made it clear that Charly was both a woman and my friend. I never let anyone misgender her. I don't remember anyone in academic or journalistic public discourse saying 'trans women are women' or arguing that they weren't, at this time. In 2009 and 2010, I just felt intuitively that Charly was who she said she was.

At the same time, I don't remember being horrified that one of my favourite sitcoms, *Friends* (again!), portrayed Chandler's trans parent in a risible way. The characters misgendered her and the gag was that it was emasculating and humiliating for Chandler. Embarrassingly and shockingly, I myself used the word 'tranny' to describe a hypothetical character in a comedy improvisation scene in a book I co-wrote in 2008. Years later, some college students in the US, who otherwise loved the book, had their professor write to me to ask why I had used this word. I was mortified. I had no idea I'd thrown out a slur like that in the 2000s. In the second edition, I removed this word and replaced it with an example of an improvised scenario that included the name of their college as a thank you to them for reaching out. A trans friend (*very* kindly trying to make me feel better!) pointed out that it was a constant part of the landscape at the time, with gay-friendly show *Ugly Betty*, for example, throwing the term around. Gay character Marc, played by Michael Urie, famously referenced manipulating trans character Alexis by remarking it's 'like taking candy from a tranny'. This is a salient reminder of the landscape that trans people were obliged to live in, that I participated in, and perhaps you did too.

It's for this reason we need to really consider the language we use and how it might land with everyone, not just us. I have a friend who was raising money for period poverty on social media, and she referenced 'people who menstruate' in a short post and the abuse she was flooded with from gender critical people was so extreme that she closed down her account. I understand people feeling that the word 'woman' is being erased, and that that is dangerous given the history of the world and current state of play for women everywhere. But I don't think it is. This is why.

When I was a kid watching after-school TV, and there was a phone-in competition, the presenter would say, 'Don't forget to ask your mum and dad before you use the phone!' When I was working as a nanny in the 1990s, I noticed this had changed to 'Ask the bill payer!' Notes home from the school were no longer addressed to 'mums and dads' – instead they went to the 'parent or caregiver' and more recently I've seen 'your grown-up'. When I was a kid, the doctor or government services referred and/or wrote to the child's 'mother or parent' whereas now in shorthand, it's sometimes 'primary carer or caregiver'. I can understand why some mothers who'd conceived a child, carried it in their womb for nine months, and then given birth to that human being – with both the toll it takes on the body and also the bonding all that implies – might have felt really annoyed to be called a 'bill payer' or a 'primary carer'! Honestly, in retrospect, that could feel a little like it was in danger of erasing mothers and fathers.

Why did it happen? Well, it was two things. The Gay Agenda™ and Big Orphan. When I was a kid, it wasn't legal or socially acceptable for same-sex couples to be out, or adopt a child, or have a surrogate* – so there was no reason to say 'parents' instead of 'mums and dads'. Single parents just weren't really thought about, because they were less common and not centred in our society. 'Parents' instead of 'mothers and fathers' is used to include children who don't have both a mum and a dad, because their family doesn't look heteronormative. Foster children, or children who live with a grandparent or other extended family, need to understand that they should ask someone in charge if they can use the phone or go on a school trip. It saves confusion and makes children who are already different feel more like their life is one people understand and acknowledge.

We haven't lost the word 'mother'. We haven't stopped loving our mums and calling them 'Mum'. No child says, 'Primary Caregiver! Can I have a biscuit?' 'Bill Payer! Can I call *Blue Peter*?' We still have WhatsApp groups called 'School Mums' which include the odd dad, granny or caregiver (although some kind people might change the name of the group chat to 'School Legends' or 'School Mums and Derek' to make

* There are still some parts of Australia where it is illegal for same-sex couples to use a surrogate. Only heterosexual couples and single women may apply!

everyone feel loved). We haven't lost anything, but some people have gained loads.

If you've given birth to and raised a child, that's amazing and it doesn't take anything from you that that wasn't the way my childhood worked and that I called someone who didn't give birth to me 'Mummy' when I was a little girl. There are more than 100,000 children in the UK who really appreciate terms like 'caregiver' or 'your grown-up' and not having to wince when they keep being reminded that they're not cared for by their mum or dad.[79] It doesn't make my mother any less of a mother or any more of a primary caregiver or bill payer.

A 2023 study published in the *British Medical Journal* based on analysis of thirty-four studies from countries where same-sex relationships are legal, compared the development of children raised by heterosexual parents with those brought up by lesbian and gay parents – and some studies also included the families of bisexual, queer or transgender parents. It found that, 'Contrary to many concerns . . . most family outcomes were similar between these two family types, and sexual minority families have even better outcomes in some domains, such as child psychological adjustment and child-parent relationships.'[80] I'm certain this would not be possible if we kept reminding these families that they were odd or abnormal with our language.

In truth, we are called all sorts of things all the time. If you're on a train, you're addressed as a 'passenger'. If you're in a doctors' surgery, you're a 'patient'. That doesn't undermine your womanhood. It's just the most relevant thing about you in that instance. I understand that the deep connection many women feel with their period and reproductive organs might make this issue more emotional, so I say 'women and other people who menstruate' which is a bit of a mouthful. I understand many women don't menstruate, including women who've had hysterectomies, and women who've been through the menopause, or perhaps are living with eating disorders, or having cancer treatment, or are elite athletes, but I say it because the vast majority of people who do menstruate are women and because of another aspect of inclusion. Some women, especially those whose first language isn't English, will not necessarily understand what 'people who menstruate' or 'people with uteruses' mean. We need to include immigrants, especially displaced people who are still learning the first language of the country they are in.

It's important that we find some form of language that includes everyone, because I have friends who menstruate and have uteruses, and womanhood is not a part of their identity. They feel painfully excluded in a society that already doesn't see who they are. I'm not going to make a point of making them feel worse, so I will continue to say 'and other people who . . . ' because that is as valid as me wanting to be referred to as 'my mother's child'. You can absolutely argue with biology and win. I'm living proof.

Much like no one is addressed as 'Bill Payer!' by a loved one, no one says, 'The people who menstruate and I are going for drinks tonight'. Womanhood isn't going anywhere. We are just finding a way to include people who've never been included in these conversations before.

Each issue has to be thought through critically. Pink 'pussy hats' which women knitted and wore on women's marches were criticised for being transphobic because they imply your genitalia 'makes you a woman' and racist because they represent the vaginas of white women.* Krista Suh, the co-founder of the Pussyhat Project, told NBC Out in 2017:

---

* To be clear – this is again a minority of voices, but it did become a sticky 'telling off' point.

> I never thought that by calling it the 'pussyhat' that it was saying that women's issues are predicated on the possession of the pussy . . . I think 'pussy' refers to the female anatomical part, but it's also a word that's used to shame people who are feminine . . . whether they are men, women [or] genderqueer. And I think what it comes down to is that femininity is really disrespected in our society.

She added that it was a direct response to Donald Trump talking about 'grabbing women by the pussy'.[81]

Krista Suh, who is not herself white, said, 'My belief is that pink is considered a little bit frivolous, girly, weak, soft, effeminate, and honestly, I don't think it's the color, I think it's a code for women . . . if it's a color associated with women, it will be mocked.' Perhaps the iconography didn't land as well as it might have, but most of the women who marched have a vulva and if they wish to express their feelings about how that might play into their experience of womanhood through headgear, as long as they're not coercing other people to wear it, it feels to me like projecting a dogma to tell them not to. There's nothing wrong with pointing out what else might be coded by women wearing them en masse (despite the founders' intentions) either, but this feels like a subject we could talk through and find some plurality on.

What about puberty blockers?

In 2021, 0.058 per cent of young people went to discuss gender-affirming care with doctors in the US. Most just had conversations about how they felt about it and perhaps switched to preferred pronouns or names. Only just over 0.001 per cent of the total population went on puberty blockers. To give you the numbers, there are 72 million children in America, 42,167 came in to talk about care and only 1,390 went on puberty blockers – that is, hormonal medications which essentially act to pause puberty by suppressing its effects while taking the medication. Why is the number of children on puberty blockers relatively small? Because only children who are so distressed by the idea of puberty that their lives are seen to be at risk are put on them.[82] This study is based on insurance, so there may be more who paid out of pocket, but that number is unlikely to be significant.

In 2022, in response to many US state bills banning gender-affirming care for young people, *Scientific American* reported:

> The truth is that data from more than a dozen studies of more than 30,000 transgender and gender-diverse young people consistently show that access to gender-affirming care is associated with better mental health outcomes—and that lack of access to such care is associated with higher rates of suicidality, depression and self-harming behavior.

Michelle Forcier, professor of paediatrics at Brown University was quoted as saying, 'Those laws are absolutely incorrect' and that '[inaccurate information] is there to create drama. It's there to make people pick a side.[83]

The article goes on to say that parent connectedness is associated with greater resilience among teens and young adults who are trans or gender diverse. Doctors cited make it clear their role is not to encourage a path to hormones and surgery. Joshua Safer, executive director of the Mount Sinai Center for Transgender Medicine and Surgery in New York City, says:

> It is talking and watching and being conservative. Only once children are older, and if the incongruence between the sex assigned to them at birth and their experienced gender

has persisted, does discussion of medical transition occur. First a gender therapist has to diagnose the young person with gender dysphoria.

Only after a diagnosis of gender dysphoria would hormones become a possibility – with any puberty-suppressing medication not intended to be used indefinitely.

> The Endocrine Society guidelines recommend a maximum of two years on GnRHa therapy to allow more time for children to form their gender identity before undergoing puberty for their sex assigned at birth, the effects of which are irreversible.

The evidence is there that safe, careful, family-connected care to socially transition and in a minority of cases to delay puberty and/or medically transition is the best route for trans, non-binary and gender-nonconforming children and teens. It is true that more young people are coming forward and that is what we'd expect to see as more gender-nonconforming role models come forward.

That is the evidence. Like any healthcare, it is best left between doctors and their patients. If doctors are coercing or rushing teens into puberty blockers (and on the contrary, waiting lists are astronomical, with waiting times of five years or more for a first appointment[84]) that is malpractice and should be stopped, just as it should if teens were coerced or rushed into abortions or any other kind of medical procedure. The medical profession must always be on guard for malpractice, but we can't legislate for no abortions in case people are rushed into it or regret it.

In July 2022 the BBC reported that the NHS was to 'close the UK's only dedicated gender identity clinic for children and young people', at The Tavistock Centre in London. The report said 'There were rising referrals and a long waiting list but at the same time some former staff were raising concerns about the way it operated.'

The findings included:

- the service was struggling to deal with spiralling waiting lists
- it was not keeping 'routine and consistent' data on its patients
- health staff felt under pressure to adopt an 'unquestioning affirmative approach'
- once patients are identified as having gender-related distress, other healthcare issues they had, such as being neurodivergent, 'can sometimes be overlooked'.

Wherever important checks and balances are not in place or active malpractice is occurring, that requires immediate attention. We are all aware the NHS is understaffed and under resourced and the healthcare professionals within it are operating under great pressure as seems to have been the case at Tavistock.

However, that doesn't mean we rush to end all care for trans youth as is now being suggested by many, in the same way that we wouldn't close wings of hospitals if we found malpractice in one. We would fix it. We would add resources.

The Cass Report was commissioned by NHS England to make recommendations on healthcare, clinical approach and interventions for young people who are questioning their gender identity or experiencing gender dysphoria. You have probably heard about it and you may have read extracts of it yourself as it was widely reported on in the media and there has been much discussion and analysis of it in the United Kingdom. It identifies that more than anything young trans and questioning youth need consistency of care and many clinicians need better training and more clarity in clinical guidelines which, of course, is welcome. However, some of its other recommendations have raised concerns.

It is too long and involved a report to cover in a detailed way here (a deep analysis would require its own chapter or perhaps book) but one of its key and most controversial recommendations is about moving away from the 'affirmative' pathway of puberty blockers and hormones to a service based on psycho-social support until more research can be done. At the same time it recommends great caution when children wish to socially transition.[85]

I spoke to Dr Reubs Walsh, Neuropsychologist and Postdoctoral Research Fellow at the Einstein Lab of Cognitive Neuroscience, Gender and Health, University of Toronto, who is herself trans, and she said:

> Fundamentally, the 'risks' to which the review refers when making its (predominantly) harmful recommendations, is essentially 'if we affirm trans kids they will grow up into trans adults', while refusing to recognise that if we don't, it's not that they'll grow up into happy healthy cis people. It's that they'll be in a closet of one sort or another, and maybe they survive like that, maybe they eventually come out, but maybe they're not okay ... different people will be different, but Cass' recommendations, whatever her intentions, especially as both the current and shadow health secretaries would implement them, will cost lives, and inflict untold suffering.*

The idea that because the research is insufficient you

* At the time of the interview, the health secretary was Conservative minister, Victoria Atkins and a Labour successor was anticipated.

> should stop treatment, or coerce research participation by conditioning treatment on it, is transparently absurd. By this rationale, trans people can't be given any medicine that behaves differently in the presence of different sex-related biological variables, full stop. Cis women would be ruled out of a huge amount of medical care if this same standard were applied.

She added, 'There are already confirmed reports that families are being brought in and threatened with a safeguarding referral if they don't immediately stop using puberty blockers and socially detransition.'

People often point to regret over transitioning or cases of detransition as evidence that young people should never transition. A 2019 survey in the UK of 3,398 attendees of a gender identity clinic found that just sixteen – about 0.47 per cent – experienced transition-related regret. Of these, even fewer went on to actually detransition and become detransitioners.[86] There is evidence that most who express regret say that their feelings stem from a lack of societal or family support: it's harder to get a job, it's easier to be ridiculed. Other countries report similar stats. By comparison, the best stats we have say about 5 per cent of women and other people who get abortions express regret, possibly many for reasons of societal shame. An abortion is irreversible in a way that transitioning, while difficult to reverse, is not. There are also studies that look at regret after gender-affirming surgeries alongside different, unrelated surgeries. The *Journal of the American Medical Association* places trans regret at less than 1 per cent, while general surgery regret is around 14.4 per cent.[87]

Most of us don't for one minute suggest we should deny people surgeries, or women and other pregnant people abortions. We would especially not deny teenagers abortions. This is not a direct correlation with transitioning but there are significant parallels. I have friends who've told me that every year they imagine how old their child would be and what they'd be like. Even though they think they did the right thing for their younger selves, they have an emotional response they can't shake. I also have friends who say it was the best decision they've made, and they never think about it. There are certainly other people who regret it altogether. That doesn't come into play when we fight for legislation for women having the right to choose, and nor should it.[88]

What about prisons?

Tabloids seem to particularly salivate over stories of men 'gaming the system' in prison to be housed in 'cushy' women's facilities so they can rape and assault them.[89] If you listen to the media, this problem is widespread and growing. Images are drawn of an army of criminals lining up to incarcerate themselves with women so they can prey on them in prisons. If you have a moment, see if you can estimate how many trans women there are, according to the most current data, housed in female prisons in England and Wales.

I'll tell you. There were 'five or fewer' trans women in prisons for women in 2020–21.[90] There were six trans women in female establishments in 2021–2.[91] In 2022–3 there were five (plus two who self-identified as non-binary or other).[92] The data is clear: this situation is neither widespread, nor growing.

In an interview in *Pink News* in 2023 Andrea Coomber, chief executive of the Howard League for Penal Reform, was baffled: 'I have yet to go to a prison where anybody has raised the experience of cis women in the estate dealing with trans women, as an issue. I don't think the public understand just how few trans women are actually kept in the women's estate – I mean, it is a handful of women.' Instead, she suggests considering the real issues: vulnerable women who have been abused or are suffering from addiction, subject to dehumanising conditions; often far from family, including their own children; often suffering from extremely poor mental health, frequently self-harming and even sometimes tragically taking their own lives. In our sixth conversation we will pull back and examine the wider impact of incarcerating women in more detail and question our assumptions about prisons in general and how we might reframe any campaign which seeks to protect the women who are in them. If we are truly concerned about women in prison – and we should be – it will not be a single-issue rethink and it will not start with half a dozen trans women.

For now, let us remember that there are about 75,000 male prisoners and 3,200 female prisoners in England and Wales in total. It seems like with those numbers the transgender inmates could be afforded their own cells. There is already a policy in place to determine whether any individual prisoner is a suitable candidate to share a cell because they are deemed dangerous or, in fact, vulnerable. There is also the important argument that trans people are victimised, assaulted and killed in prison,[93] a fact we rarely hear about in the press. To be totally, incontrovertibly clear: everyone deserves to be safe.

In the US, trans women are similarly often incarcerated with male prisoners. A 2007 study from the University of California found that transgender people in prison were thirteen times more likely to be sexually assaulted than a random sample of incarcerated men: 59 per cent of transgender prisoners reported having been sexually assaulted within a California correctional facility compared to just 4.4 per cent of the incarcerated population as a whole.[94]

Clearly any rape is horrific and, of course, prisoners everywhere – whether cis, trans, male, female or non-binary – must be protected from rape. Safeguarding is crucial. However, the constant gender critical lobby against trans women being housed in women's prisons to protect women comes under scrutiny when you find this out: Askham Grange Prison in Britain has ten female and ten male officers. Downview Prison has fifty female and forty male officers. Drake Hall has forty female and twenty male officers. Eastwood Park has seventy female and sixty male officers ... and the list goes on. Only one prison in Britain has exclusively female officers, and it's a very small open prison for women and young offenders. Most American prisons are the same.

If people are genuinely concerned about women being locked up with trans women or men somehow pretending to be trans women, why are we not campaigning to get rid of male prison officers who have the keys to the cells? A female prisoner may not even feel it's safe to report a male officer who has assaulted her. She may not be believed or heard, and she may well feel vulnerable to continued attacks or worse if she speaks up. How can we truly say we are worried about women imprisoned with people who've been through a male puberty, when women are guarded and told what to do by men every single day?

In September 2021, it was reported that a male prison officer had been jailed for six years and nine months for 'engaging in sex acts with' prisoners at a women's jail. Teesside Crown Court heard that while employed at HMP Low Newton between 2011 and 2016, David Whitfield behaved 'inappropriately' with twelve residents, using his position of power to 'extract or encourage' them to commit sex acts. The judge said Whitfield 'methodically, routinely and cynically took advantage'. He was cleared of sexual assault on one woman. I do not know the details of the court case but if it was his word against hers, it is not an unreasonable assumption that her testimony was not imagined to have the same credibility as his.

Criminal records are not a definitive bar to becoming a prison officer, and decisions on suitability are made on a case-by-case basis. Mark Fairhurst, the national chairman of the Prison Officers' Association said, 'It's very rare. Less than 1 per cent of our staff are corrupt, but it does happen.' The *Daily Mail* reported on this case, but I cannot find any evidence of the broadsheets doing so. I feel strongly that if a trans woman had done what David Whitfield did, this case would have been endlessly discussed.[95]

Reports indicate that violent acts inflicted on female prisoners by male wardens in the US are frequent, sustained, mercenary and brutal and I won't distress you by describing them here, but a cursory Google will make you feel physically sick and no American campaigner claiming to care about women's safety in prisons should be focusing on the limited number of trans women in prisons when there is such widespread and well-documented abuse from male officers.

Likewise, in the UK, there has been a huge campaign to not allow trans women into female hospital wards. At the same time the *Observer* reported at the end of 2023:

> data from NHS England shows thousands of breaches of [single-sex spaces] for patients every month, mixing cis men and women, with patient dignity and safety put at risk. Between July 2017 and July 2023, 126,404 mixed-sex accommodation breaches were reported. The monthly figure for July 2017 was 899, and 3,211 in July this year.[96]

The Met police recorded 1,753 sexual offences in NHS hospitals between January 2019 and September 2022, 511 of these rapes.[97] This is due to overcrowding and underfunding. The issue of keeping an extremely small number of trans women out of single-sex NHS spaces is clearly not about safeguarding women. The column inches devoted to this issue would make the average reader believe that single-sex spaces in hospitals are extremely safe except for the tiny percentage of trans women who are admitted, which consistently creates the narrative that trans women are predators. No one ever thinks that perhaps trans women, trans men and non-binary people, especially those who are pre- or mid-medical transition, would like privacy and prefer a space of their own.

The same can be said for refuges. In talking to trans friends, academics and activists, I find that the most common view is that it would be ideal if refuges were plentiful, well-funded and welcoming for all with some areas where trans women can have privacy, some areas where cis women can have privacy and some communal shared spaces. Women are turned away from refuges all the time due to excess demand and underfunding. In fact, in 2023, Woman's Aid wrote a report demonstrating 10,000 women had been turned away in England alone in the previous year.[98] Many have no choice but to sleep rough or go back to their abuser. Studies show that trans women are at an increased risk of intimate partner violence and also need somewhere to turn.[99] The greatest danger to all women seeking refuge is clearly underfunding.

Where it comes to public loos, I will just say this – in 2010 *The Times* ran an opinion piece complaining about the increase in gender-neutral loos on the basis that they smelled and were dirtier than women's loos.[100] There was no mention of the danger of male violence and none of the high-profile commentators who are angry about gender-neutral toilets now, and were working then, seem to have joined into that conversation or raised the issue of safety. At that time trans women had used women's loos for generations without comment and were obviously keeping them as clean as any other women were or weren't. In 2019, the Old Vic Theatre in London put in gender-neutral loos. I visited and found I didn't have to queue at all, the way I used to at that theatre. They were extremely clean with doors from floor to ceiling that made it feel very safe, and the block on the left, sans urinals, seemed to be where the women went and the other block seemed to be where men went by default.

Personally I have popped into men's loos over the years, in a pinch, when the women's were full and I've been desperate, so I quite like the idea that I have the option. I commented about the Old Vic's great new loos on Twitter and various commentators replied that they would be boycotting the theatre because it wasn't safe. I don't really think anyone is truly worried about being attacked in a crowded loo in the interval of *Waiting for Godot*. My strong preference is to pee without anyone watching me at all, so that's why I enjoy the 'locking-door feature', but I'll wash my hands next to anyone. I've honestly never noticed the trans women I've shared the loos with all my life.

The new alarm around trans women and possible men in women's loos has resulted in many butch lesbians and other women with masculine or androgynous gender expression 'being questioned', which they continue to report publicly. A close friend of mine with short hair, wearing jeans and a T-shirt, was questioned in a long queue for the women's loo that spilled out into the corridor at the Royal Albert Hall. It was embarrassing and it made her feel fearful and excluded. In his PhD, academic Rowan Douglas points out how scary using public bathrooms can be for both trans women and trans men, with transmasculine participants reporting extreme fear and anxiety in public loos, and some experiencing harassment and aggression. And as University of Washington professor Justin E. Lerner's research shows, many trans people simply 'hold it in' and avoid public bathrooms altogether.[101] The whole thing seems really unfair and unreasonable to me.

On the issue of sport, I wish we were in a climate where

we could have reasonable conversations about it. I agree with ContraPoints (the public intellectual and YouTube essayist I referenced earlier) who says it would seem sensible to take each sport on its merits and have conversations about some sports and not others: 'weight-lifting but not figure skating'. I would love sporting experts, including trans experts of course, to have meaningful conversations about how to resource all women in sport, including trans women who have long been left out of so much in society, while making sure there is a fair playing field.

Discussions are certainly beginning in rethinking the way we approach some sports as a two-category event. There are sports that are already mixed-sex – showjumping and marathons, for example. Some sports have handicaps and weight classes, like golf or boxing. Ten-pin bowling is traditionally split by gender, but Kelly Kulick was the first woman to ever win a Professional Bowlers Association (US) tournament – and on her first outing. There are two women on the list of top ten rock climbers, because flexibility and strength-to-weight ratio are more important than upper-body strength alone, however there are many sports where muscle mass and testosterone levels can give an athlete an advantage and it would be good to look to a future where trans women, and women with DSD (differences in sex development), could compete without being obliged to medicate and lower their testosterone. This will all require careful consideration and change in process, structure and strategy.

It is clear now that most trans women are currently extremely marginalised and often made to feel unwelcome in society in a way that would not resource them for the exhausting full-time demands of training, especially sports that demand relentless attention from a young age like tennis. Therefore we see very small numbers of trans women in sport, and when they do participate they usually do not win.* However, it would be good to look to a future where trans girls and women are happier and better understood and so more able to focus on other things and less on their gender identity and how it conflicts with the power structures of the world.

It would be a great thing for those with the expertise to explore changing models that would overturn our assumptions on how sport has to be done. This would require cooperative good-faith research and discussion. However, it feels impossible in a landscape that is so flammable and in which trans people are so often being depicted as the enemy and even as predators.

I think whatever we do going forward, we have to acknowledge that we do rethink our models when the world changes, all the time. We need to fit our models around the human beings who exist in our society, not exclude the humans we have as if the models are somehow rigid, because they are traditional. There was a time when women were excluded from rugby and football altogether, for example, and we had to create a new shape of things to accommodate women. Little League Baseball in the US only allowed a girl to join a boys' team because of a lawsuit.[102] There have been mixed netball teams at some levels of the game for years because there sometimes aren't enough men to form their own teams. This has never been commented on because it wasn't conflated with an argument about trans athletes.[103] There are also mixed doubles in tennis but that's been standard for so long no one notices. (I

---

* As Rowan Douglas points out, if around 1 per cent of the population are deemed to be trans, one might expect trans people to also make up around 1 per cent of athletes. Indeed, if the argument is that trans women are dominating women's sports, one might in fact expect trans women to make up significantly more than this. This would have resulted in around 100 trans athletes among the >10,000 competitors at the Tokyo 2020 Olympics – but in reality, four openly trans athletes were present, of whom only two were trans women.

feel if we tried to introduce those things now, there'd be headlines about it.) There are different issues at play in one woman playing someone who's been through a 'male puberty' at tennis, especially if they didn't medicate, but human beings are smart and I'm sure we could figure something out if everyone was willing and fair and kind. Ironically, we could reshape sport if no one was point-scoring off the field. We often reshape our world for a changing, more compassionate, fairer society. Why would we stop now?

On this matter more generally, I can understand why feminists who have worked hard to change society want conversation and analysis about how to change it again. I think it's hard for young people to imagine just how binary the world was in the 1960s, '70s and '80s. The gendered violence, expectations and restrictions were extreme. So much so, some women went into separatist communes. The women of Greenham Common who camped out protesting against nuclear weaponry had pig's blood thrown on them, and were called all sorts of gendered and homophobic slurs by some men who really hated them. Famously, women fought to be able to get a mortgage or even a credit card without a male relative co-signing it for them. Gender lines were so sharp you could cut yourself on them, and were always considered by the power structures to start and end with biology, so I can understand how some women are struggling with being told that those lines are blurred now without conversation or time and space to consider.

I admire second-wave feminists very much. And if you feel I'm teaching my grandmother to suck eggs here, I apologise. But you are the giants whose shoulders we're standing on. When you said 'We're not doing that, wearing this, working in that role or doing what you tell us,' you were the David who let go of a stone in a slingshot to take down that patriarchal

Goliath. Anyone who doesn't get what you went through needs to read more books from that time and seek out and listen to more women who lived through it.

The thing is, when the stone left your slingshot, it was only ever going to have one arc. You couldn't see it at the time. How could you have known? But young people today are telling you by living it: it was always going to sail right over biology. Many of you know this and are right on board. Others of you aren't.

Young people are often the most radical voices leading the way and some of them don't feel the word 'woman' or 'man' fits them exactly. They want a new framework to talk about themselves and currently have settled on non-binary and sometimes different or new pronouns and they are making it happen for themselves. There are visibly gender-nonconforming people in every generation. It's nothing new – but the embracing of it is. Some of the language is. The self-acceptance by a generation and their peers is. Without you letting go of that stone, they'd never have got there. Society would not have got here. You were a radical voice in your generation. What you thought and wanted broke moulds, and older people didn't understand it. They thought you were wrong and entitled and ruining the world.

It feels like every generation tells that same story, but yours doesn't have to. Of course, you may be delighted by the radical changes the young people are making, even though at times they're doing them with what feels like some draconian glee. In that case, please talk to other people in your generation. If you don't get it and think young people have lost the plot and are in the grip of social contagion, can you approach them with curiosity and ask them to explain and listen to the answers and then think on it?

There is an urgent reason for us to come together and be patient with each other and listen while engaging our empathy. Cis women's rights are not to be undermined in this struggle.

We are under attack on all fronts, all around the world. I have written a whole book about this. But the cis feminist and trans communities must align because our rights are inextricably linked and we are being manipulated by our common enemies. To analyse this further, we need to ask . . .

Where has our new hope gone?

Why *have* we stopped now when just ten years ago trans people were being resourced and accepted for seemingly the first time in Western society and the media and even governments were talking about 'a new frontier for civil rights?[104] Remember Neil Datta from the European Parliamentary Forum for Sexual and Reproductive Rights from our first conversation? He and his colleagues, along with academic and policy advisors all across the world who are researching the far-right religious anti-gender movement have the answer. (As a reminder, the 'anti-gender movement' is actively campaigning against abortion and gay rights including equal marriage, and is essentially against anything that might be sought after as a move towards equality in 'gender studies'.)

Neil explained to me in our interview in early 2024:

> There has been a scepticism about trans rights coming from within feminism for decades. It was a very marginal thing, but it was there. What is new is that the anti-gender actors have picked up on contesting trans rights. And this is a new phenomenon that we can date back to maybe six, eight years ago . . . They pick trans rights, specifically in context or countries which are too progressive to raise the issue of abortion or gay rights. They know that if they raise those issues in certain countries, they're not going to get anywhere, whereas an entry point can be trans rights.

> It's newer, it's less well protected because the demographic community is so small, and people tend to know much less about it, both in the general public and the political class, so it's easier to spread misinformation, whereas it's much harder to do with classic sexual minorities, LGB rights. It's harder to do with abortion rights or women's rights.

Neil told me that it's become very toxic in the UK, but we see similar developments also happening in Spain, which is very progressive on abortion rights and equal marriage and other gay rights. There is evidence the anti-gender movement are using trans rights as a culture war in Sweden, Norway, Belgium and in the Netherlands. What do these countries have in common? They are all very progressive, so it is very difficult to make headway on abortion rights or gay and bisexual rights, but they can try through beginning with trans rights.

He says it's clear from reading the anti-gender movement's correspondence that they have access to, that 'breaking up the feminists and the overall progressive communities and their sense of cohesion is their primary objective'. When anti-gender activists saw that trans issues got media attention, they decided to invest in it. He explains that the people in the anti-gender movement see no difference between gay and trans people: 'In their mindset, it's all equally against nature. It's simply opportunistic what they will target in a given time and place. If the situations were to change in the UK, they would switch to another target area.'

The Office of the United Nations High Commissioner for Human Rights report on the anti-gender movement agrees:

> Resistance to expanding notions of the term 'gender' to include transgender and gender-nonconforming people has been integral to pro-family efforts to defend the nuclear

> family formation and heteropatriarchal social arrangements. Replacing much of the explicitly intolerant and hateful anti-gay and anti-feminist rhetoric that has historically been associated with conservative sexual politics, the new family-centred vocabulary functions to create a guise of decency and respectability around anti-rights discourse and agenda … Pro-family actors have defined what they call the 'natural family' as 'the fundamental social unit, inscribed in human nature, and centred around the voluntary union of a man and a woman in a lifelong covenant of marriage'. Within their advocacy, the gender binary is cast as a fixed, biological 'truth' that is required for the social fabric and economy to remain intact because of its importance to the nuclear family model. The concept of the 'natural family' positions heteropatriarchal norms and social arrangements as universal, apolitical, and ahistorical – a matter of 'common sense'.[105]

In other words, the transgender issue is a wedge issue and is part of a much bigger plan.

If you're wondering why you've not heard of this (assuming you haven't), it is because the press are not focusing on it very much at all (at least at the time of writing), perhaps not grasping the scale of the operation.

Agenda Europa was created in January 2013 out of a meeting that took place in London involving approximately twenty North American and European anti-abortion leaders and strategic advisors who aimed to 'develop a Christian-inspired European think tank' and 'devise new strategies for European anti-abortion movements'. Why 2013? Because both the UK and France were in the process of legalising same-sex marriage and that was the breaking point. The anti-gender movement's decision to act was born out of fury, but their focus was achievable goals. They started to ask not 'what do we want?' but 'what can we have?' Again, they are using cognitive empathy to work out who they're dealing with and how they might manipulate us.

Once we allow the anti-gender lobby to shape our policy and become people of influence in our society, they will use that position to get the other things on their agenda. Documents have been uncovered that reveal a detailed, extremist strategy called 'Restoring the Natural Order: an Agenda for Europe', which seeks to overturn existing laws on basic human rights related to sexuality and reproduction, such as the right to divorce; for a woman to access contraception, assisted reproduction technologies or have an abortion; equality for lesbian, gay, bisexual, trans or intersex (LGBTI) persons; and the right to change one's gender or sex without fear of legal repercussions.[106]

Neil Datta and his team predict that the next issues they attack in the UK will be surrogacy and sex work because there is already some dissent in the feminist community on these things. Their arguments about the sacredness of women's bodies as far as surrogacy and sex work goes will lead neatly into abortion: 'While we're up in your uterus anyway, we've got some notes.'

This is real. This is happening. You have probably heard of Project 2025. The American Civil Liberties Union describes it as 'a federal policy agenda and blueprint for a radical restructuring of the executive branch authored and published by former Trump administration officials in partnership with The Heritage Foundation, a longstanding conservative think tank that opposes abortion and reproductive rights, LGBTQ rights, immigrants' rights, and racial equity.' And it goes on to say 'Project 2025's largest publication, *Mandate For Leadership*, is a 900-page manual for reorganizing the entire federal government agency by agency to serve a conservative agenda.' It is impossible to know how much of this agenda Trump will drive forward or be able to enshrine in law, but the values are largely in line with the anti-gender movement (and it is difficult to believe there is no crossover) as you will see if you look at The Heritage Foundation's website.[107] Some academics and policy-makers are trying hard to tackle it and currently engaging with the danger of the anti-gender movement in a number of ways. In 2021 there was a public hearing on 'Foreign interference on the financing of anti-choice organisations in the EU' which was hosted jointly by the Committee on Women's Rights and Gender Equality (FEMM) and the Special Committee on Foreign Interference in all Democratic Processes in the European Union, including Disinformation. Their focus was the anti-gender movement.[108] In 2023, UN Women, in partnership with the Generation Equality Action Coalitions on Feminist Movements and Leadership and Gender-Based Violence, met to discuss protecting our rights from the anti-gender movement.[109] LSE is currently funding a project called 'Transnational "Anti-Gender" Movements and Resistance: Narratives and Interventions', which is a research network that will come together for four transnational workshops, inviting theorists, activists and policymakers already working on 'gender ideology', with the explicit understanding that transgender issues are being used as a wedge issue to remove gay rights and reproductive rights.[110]

The Centre for Feminist Foreign Policy in Berlin, which is a human rights think tank, produced a rigorous report in 2020 called 'Power over Rights: Understanding and Countering the Transnational Anti-gender Movement'; this was funded by the German Federal Foreign Office and the Finnish Ministry for Foreign Affairs and their work in this area continues.[111] In 2023, the University of Bergen hosted a debate organised by the Centre for Women's and Gender Research (SKOK) at UiB, SAIH and Litteraturhuset i Bergen between senior academics about how the anti-gender movement is affecting research and activism in Norway.[112] Academic papers and symposiums on the anti-gender movement are happening all over the world discussing their agenda.

To be clear, I am not suggesting all women who identify as feminists and believe trans rights conflict with non-trans women's rights share other values with the anti-gender movement. Deep in the heart of the anti-gender movement there are drivers that would chill to the bone anyone who cares about the liberation of women. These include *Handmaid's Tale*-style ideas on sex being for reproduction not pleasure, women being exclusively in the home and even 'men's natural state is to be at war'. White supremacy and extreme homophobia is at the heart of this movement and this is openly acknowledged and discussed in all the academic and policy forums I've referenced and many others you can find for yourself. The anti-gender actors are using trans people as a pawn to divide the feminist community, but that is not their goal. It is a first move. Trump's 2024 campaign included a TV ad depicting Harris as pro-trans, ending with the tag line – 'Kamala is for they/them, President Trump is for you.' This aired over 30,000 times in every swing state, costing more than ads for the economy, immigration and housing combined. Why? Most people don't even know an out trans person. We are being manipulated to support their agenda.[113]

There are some people who have fallen so deeply down the rabbit hole that is set against trans people that they will not be able to accept this or act upon it. But I am hoping most feminists will be extremely keen to research this further, discuss it and mobilise. We cannot be infighting endlessly about how to move forward when those who would take all our hard-won rights are being pragmatic and making alliances wherever they can, keeping an eye on their end goals while making gains. We cannot allow them to scapegoat the rights of a tiny percentage of the population because it is deeply unfair to trans people, who are already extremely marginalised. In addition, we cannot allow those who would threaten all the rights that women and LGBTQ+ people have ever fought for, to throw us into chaos and distraction so they can further their attack.

One caveat: in an ever-changing world, we will always need to have conversations about logistics and practicalities. I believe trans people and non-trans people want to have practical conversations about a small number of issues that could be better for everyone as more trans people are able to be out living their best lives. It would be weird if no accommodations were going to be made for how spaces might look a bit different in the light of any social change. But right now any conversation about logistics and practicalities is being held under the glare of a far more sinister agenda and being used to fuel a fire that wasn't started by anyone in our camp, even if some have poured fuel upon it. The parameters of our conversation about trans rights must change as a matter of urgency and as a matter of fact. We need to lower our amygdalas to have these conversations. We must not leave this conversation for academics and policymakers alone, although I believe it should be led by those who know most about the anti-gender movement. We must take it into our communities and crucially into the media for immediate analysis and scrutiny. We need to understand the forces behind what happened in the 2024 American election and join the dots between the erosion of women's rights and LGBTQ+ rights and the intersections of the two. Crucially, we need to recognise that this is a global agenda. We need to bring to light who's been shaping our stories, because if it is our enemies, we cannot be repeating them over and over, until they become our reality. If we do, we are sharing 'New Light' for those who wish to plunge us into darkness.

In our next conversation we will explore freedom of speech, something that we must not lose if we are to take on this fight.

Conversation Four

The Conversation about Comedy and Freedom of Speech

Are you in on the joke?

One night, sleeping in my bed in London, I was woken by a phone call from my sister in Australia. She said that my father had had a stroke, and I should fly back home as soon as possible. She passed the phone to a nurse at the hospital, and he told me in an almost cheerful Australian lilt that I wouldn't make it: 'It'll take you twenty-four hours and he'll be dead by then.' My dad was relatively young and had always taken care of his health, so it was a great shock. There was no Wi-Fi or signal on the plane, so I just had to hope every second that he was waiting for me and that the nurse was wrong. I felt hysterical and arrived tear-stained and completely unkempt from the long-haul flight. When I walked into the hospital my mother looked at me and said, 'You've changed your hair.'

This is a line from *Out of Africa*, a film we'd watched together in which Meryl Streep takes a journey across a hazardous Kenyan desert during a war, fighting lions and sandstorms to get to her husband. It's the first thing he says to her, and it makes her laugh. When my mother said it to me, we fell into each other's arms laughing and crying. This is how I knew that the nurse was wrong. My father was still alive. I got to sit with him and was told he could hear me as I held his hand and told him what a wonderful dad he'd been. He died a few hours later.

That night, after my mother went to bed, my siblings and I sat on the kitchen floor and drank schnapps. And we did something else completely instinctive and primal as we sat as close to the earth as possible, weighed down by grief and gravity – we laughed. We laughed so much we cried, and we cried so much we laughed. We told funny stories about my father and shared memories and jokes from our childhood that only the three of us would understand. You'd be shocked by how much we laughed the night my father died, unless you've been through the same thing.

The next day, when the people from the funeral parlour came and gave us depressing brochures about cremation and burial, I made an aside to my sister that made her giggle. The funeral director laughed as well. He leaned in as he slid a blue urn across the table. 'Would your dad look good in navy blue?' Silence. 'Little funereal humour there.' We all stared. 'They give you a book of jokes when you train. For awkward moments.' We ended the meeting soon after. Who the fuck does this guy think he is, making light of our father's death?

Finding dark comedy in a desperate or hopeless situation, otherwise known as gallows humour, is an extremely relatable human experience. Laughing and crying are both reactions to heightened emotion. It's possible that crying when laughing or laughing when crying is the body's attempt to find equilibrium. More than that, if a condemned person is literally headed to the gallows, a moment of breaking the tension with wit gives them power – for a moment, they are in charge of the situation. Human beings can refuse to be completely consumed by our tragic lot, if we take mastery over it with a joke.

Now if the hangman makes a gag about the dead-man-walking, that's just cruel. He's a sadist who is reinforcing the homicidal violence of his all-powerful position and humiliating the victim at the end of their life. It's hard to think of anything worse. In other words, the same joke can be empowering or dehumanising. The ownership of a joke is key.

Nothing captures the paradoxical virtues and vices of freedom of speech better than comedy. Free speech is dear and indispensable in our democracy, but it can also be a driving force for hatred, fake news and polarisation. Comedy is the final frontier of freedom of speech because context, authority, irony and parody are all at play. But comedy can also be a Trojan horse for sticky and powerful ideas that can play a part in shaping our world-view. Comedy can make damaging ideas palatable and portable. Comedy can make those who are already disempowered seem risible to those in the dominant position. Comedy can also be an arena to release tension and say the unsayable, fearful things that lurk in the shadows. It can be a place to air and even mock damaging societal fears.

Screenwriter Nora Ephron used to say, 'Everything is copy.' She went on to explain that to mean that things that seem shocking, devastating or appalling when they are happening to you can be turned into a story you will later tell for the entertainment of others. If you fall over, you might be the butt of the joke at the time, but if you later tell the story of the fall, it's your laugh. Words that are malicious and hurtful in most contexts, when owned and reframed by a comedian, can be an ironic reversal of hate speech. So, let's talk about jokes.

Have you heard the one about . . . ?

There is currently an enormous debate among comedians and comedy audiences about whether the current push-back on jokes which seem to 'punch down' rather than 'punch up' is censorship from an overly sensitive, faux-offended minority with more clout than they deserve, or a sign of social progress in which comedians are held accountable for systemically violent statements like anyone else would be. Even comedians who in many ways seem progressive don't agree on free speech. Here's a sample of some recent remarks from the current crop of outspoken comedians, showing the range of viewpoints:

> 'Far-left political correctness is a cancer on progressivism.' – Bill Maher[1]

> 'If something as benign as political correctness can kill comedy, then comedy's already dead.' – Hannah Gadsby[2]

> 'Comedians have a responsibility to speak recklessly. Sometimes the funniest thing to say is mean. Remember, I'm not saying it to be mean. I'm saying it because it's funny.' – Dave Chapelle[3]

> 'I do think it's important, as a comedian, as a human, to change with the times. To change with new information . . . I think it's a sign of being old when you're put off by that.' – Sarah Silverman[4]

> 'I don't think the extreme left has done anything to inhibit the art of comedy. If you're Lindsey Vonn, if you're a champion skier, you can put the gates anywhere you want on the mountain – she's gonna make the gate. That's comedy.

Whatever the culture is, we make the gate. Does culture change? And are there things I used to say that I can't say? Yeah. But that's the biggest, easiest target. The accuracy of your observation has to be a hundred times finer than that to just be a comedian.' – Jerry Seinfeld.[5]

'I think that comedians deserve context in what they say. You shouldn't just "cancel" out of context, but I also think comedians have a responsibility to evolve and to try to push things forward. And pushing the envelope doesn't mean digging your feet in while the envelope moves forward – you should be ahead of that envelope, that's how you should be pushing it.' – Patton Oswalt[6]

I think, overall, this range of views is a good sign. Convergent thinking is undesirable. It stifles creativity, flattens innovation and homogenises diverse voices. It's also essentially impossible for comedians. One of the biggest roles of comedians in society is to think of something you haven't already thought of and surprise you with a new way of looking at the world. Even if a comedian is reinforcing the status quo, they have to have a twist on the everyday because a punchline is a surprise by definition. That requires leeway and bandwidth in a creative space, but that space, as is true of almost everything in life, is neither infinite nor fixed.

You and I may both have hard lines on jokes we consider unacceptable, but those lines might be different. So how do we decide which line is the right line? Do we even want some kind of groupthink on that? How do we (or should we) ask speakers to be responsible without returning to top-down censorship?

Part of the reason I want to analyse freedom of speech through the lens of comedy is that hate speech is often clear to see when it *isn't* intended to amuse, provoke or subvert. There are strong anti-hate-speech laws in many countries which will punish people for using slurs in public. But comedy seems to operate in a grey area, where things which are manifestly unacceptable somehow get a pass because the intention is to entertain and provoke laughter. Sometimes the comedian is using irony, so the literal meaning and the message of the joke might be at odds. For all these reasons, comedy is an excellent space to analyse the power, purpose and policing of free speech.

No one really knows why we laugh, but academic studies suggest that laughter plays an important role in social bonding. Academics Guillaume Dezecache and R. I. M. Dunbar suggest that human communities, being much larger than those of other primates, require more time for social maintenance – and that laughter is a means of providing additional bonding capacity by expanding the 'grooming group'. Their study demonstrates that laughter enables a threefold increase in the number of bonds that can be maintained simultaneously, which has the potential to significantly increase the size of bonded communities.[7]

Baboons pick lice off each other to bond and reinforce social structures. Humans, who are usually lice-free and running in larger packs, use jokes and laughter instead. It makes sense when 'making fun' is about raising and lowering each other's status in jest. Grooming among animals can be an act of affection or dominance, much like teasing someone you love. You know if someone is a friend because if they ask you to get them a cup of tea you can say, 'Yes, Your Majesty' (raise) or 'Are your legs painted on?' (lower). You wouldn't say that to your boss's boss or your new boyfriend's mother. This makes sense of why you endlessly rib your own mum but no one else is allowed to do it. It's why being given a (friendly) nickname in a new workplace or friendship group is a sign you're starting to belong. It's why your best buddies are generally the people you laugh with most often.

The more you're surrounded by like-minded people, the more this bonding effect will work. Bob Dylan will crash and burn at a heavy metal night and Iron Maiden will get booed off if people have come to see acoustic folk. Comedy operates in a similar way. Stamms count. Creating *The Guilty Feminist* as a live comedy show, not just a studio podcast, was a direct response to my experience in comedy clubs where I rarely felt 'in on the joke' and often felt like the butt of it. In the 1990s and 2000s in the UK it was very normal to go to a club and see a line-up of exclusively male comedians. It still happens, but usually people mock it now. Same with all-white bills. Comedian Lolly Adefope will often point this out by posting a picture of the exclusively white faces with a line like 'I'm thinking of painting my living room this colour.' I remember going to clubs in the 2000s which were predominantly run and populated by heterosexual men and hearing lots of jokes in which girlfriends were 'bitches', and women more 'other' than human.

When I started doing stand-up comedy around the same time, I once went on stage after a man had talked for fifteen minutes straight about women in a pejorative way. The routine ended with the twist that the girlfriend he'd been ranting about had actually been buried in his back garden for six weeks. This was a variation of an old-fashioned trope comedians refer to as a 'then I got off the bus' joke. The comedian tells a story in which they're naked, but fails to reveal they're in public until the punchline. He hadn't (I hope!) really hurt anyone. It was only words. But words that reflected a very real power imbalance in our society, and which felt really loaded in the room. I could see women shifting uncomfortably. Possibly they were themselves survivors of violence, consistently vigilant for danger.

I – a fortunately still living, breathing woman – had to follow him and go out in front of the same audience. It felt humiliating. And more than that, it felt like I was starting behind the eight ball with some of the audience, because I seemed to be in the category of 'victim'. No matter how good your sense of humour, no matter how willing you are to take good-natured teasing at your own expense, it's super-hard to be 'in on the joke' if the punchline is your own violent death.

Once in the 2000s at a comedy festival, I was invited by a famous comedian to see his show. It contained a great deal of rape material – including a number of jokes that seemed to excuse or endorse rape and one that implied the comedian would have raped a woman if he'd known he'd have got away with it. He laughed it off in the bar afterwards: 'Bit too rapey tonight, I thought.' It made me uneasy. At least one in four women in his audience will have been raped and they came out to be entertained.

That night his assistant texted me saying he wanted to see me in his hotel room. I declined and she said he was very insistent. I said no again but I always wondered what would have happened if he'd known my room number. He was famous and I had no profile at that time. The landscape was very different for women then. I doubt I'd have had the courage to shut the door in his face. I have no evidence at all he'd have hurt me or even touched me, but the show made me feel like I wasn't one of the community members he intended to bond with.

If I build it, will they come?

This was the environment that inspired me to leave and create a new space. Festivals and comedy clubs felt othering and sometimes threatening. Despite this, I was always told if I couldn't cut it with the male baboons by getting them to delouse me thoroughly, that was on me for not being talented and hard-working enough. This made me interested in the social 'architecture' of the space.

Through podcasting, we've built a community of female baboons and there's not a louse in sight. It's hard to do comedy well if you're not exhibiting enormous confidence,* and it's hard to project that if the environment is one where male baboons are picking lice off each other, but only engaging with female baboons by showing signs of dominance or sexual posturing. How does the female baboon hope to fit in? By pretending she's one of the boys and snacking on their fleas, even though they keep giving her the side-eye and pushing her off? Instead, we designed a space where women were celebrated and made to feel both safe and wanted: the environment men were conditioned to expect as standard in the clubs they played in.

Occasionally I've had men on the podcast, and usually the audience have been polite but not effusive. My stamm makes men earn their place and I have seen them get nervous when no one has come to see someone like them. The effect is immediately flipped, even though the man in question might have enormous experience and cachet in the wider comedy world.

Sometimes, in order to make our spaces feel safe, people suggest bans on certain topics for comedy – like, for example, male violence. I do not agree that whole topics or areas of conversation are 'off limits' for me or guests on my show. This is why ownership of the jokes is so important. We can make comedy out of terrible, shocking, hateful events or ideas, but we are operating in an environment where our value set seeps through into the punchlines.

In my recent solo show, I had a routine about getting men

* Even if you're playing with a nervous persona as a stand-up comic, as a performer you need to own the room.

to talk to each other about violence against women. Women, of course, know that it is *not all men*. One hundred per cent of the men I've been alone with have not killed me.* However, psychologists tell us that the men who do hurt women truly believe that all men either do it or want to but are not 'man enough'. When those violent men sit in a comedy club and the men around them laugh at jokes about men hurting or killing women, that endorses their view. They can't tell that most of the men (we assume) are laughing at how shocking and edgy the joke is, so it reinforces their violent views and potentially their actions.[8]

In the routine I suggest that straight cis men tell those guys, 'Hey, it's not all men, you know!' I want them to bring up male violence in social situations with their friends and have created 'conversation starter' cards that I ask an audience volunteer to practise with. We role-play being at the pub with a male friend and casually bringing out cards that read . . .

- 'Ninety-six per cent of homicides are committed by men. Why do you think that is?'
- 'Embezzlement is committed at a fifty-fifty split between men and women. So it's not that women are more moral than men, just overwhelmingly less violent. Why do you think that is?'
- 'Almost 100 per cent of mass shooters are white straight cis men. Do you think our people have an anger problem more generally?'
- 'If men stopped killing, killing would stop. Discuss.'

Although the facts are horrendous, the idea of schooling men to bring up these facts over beers using formal

* This doesn't mean they haven't hurt anyone, but the point still stands.

conversation-starter cards is funny, so the laugh comes from the role-play, not the violence. The fact I'm coaching them in public reverses the patriarchal gendered status gap that is the very tension in the material.

The question is not so much what are we laughing at but why are we laughing? These are valid questions, especially if comedians have hopes of reaching a wide audience. Banning jokes by subject matter means that some routines that can have a positive power and encourage an important conversation would not be possible. Censoring words or themes can be reductive and counterproductive if your mission is to help shape a more compassionate, less violent world.

How good were the good old days?

The earliest kind of solo comedians, akin to stand-up comics, were jesters, appearing on the scene in the 1300s.[9] Interestingly, jesters in the Middle Ages and Elizabethan times were always some kind of outsider, in a marginalised position, often dressed in risible clothing. Some were chosen because they were 'old and ugly' serfs – that is to say, people in forced servitude to rich landowners. Others were excommunicated monks – isolated and then shunned.

Ironically, it was probably easier to be a woman in comedy then than in recent times, presumably because she-fools or jestrixes seemed outsiders almost by definition. Mathurine de Vallois, a sixteenth-/seventeenth-century French jester, was famous for her crowd-work and biting wit, and there are legendary stories about her. A lady-in-waiting is said to have complained that she did not want a fool at her right-hand side. Mathurine immediately jumped onto the lady's left side and quipped, 'Well, I don't mind it at all.'[10]

While no one else dared offend the court or monarch

because the punishment could be capital, jesters were given something known as 'comic dispensation', a 'freedom from all constraint'. The jester could do a routine in rhyme about the monarch's disastrous foreign policy, which was a way of keeping their ego in check, and presumably releasing the tension about their warmongering or exploitation of their subjects. Many jesters were little people; it's easier to punch up if you're physically smaller than the aristocrats. You're not seen as a physical threat, so you're given more leeway to mock the mighty. Some jesters were neuroatypical people who were seen as truth-tellers because they didn't always censor the same way as neurotypical people.[11]

The most important point here is this – jesters were always at the mercy of the wealthy and powerful who they were employed to tease. One of the reasons only truly marginalised people could apply for the job of jester was that they were deemed so powerless, they were the only ones able to laugh at everyone with impartiality. That is not the same dynamic as the comedy landscape of today, led by extremely wealthy men in designer clothes, driving sports cars home to their mansions in Primrose Hill and Malibu, all paid for by Netflix stand-up comedy specials, in which they often mock groups of people who have little to no visibility.

This remains true even as comedy line-ups become gradually more diverse. The best-paid people in comedy are multimillionaires, regardless of their background or identity. There is no cap on what a comedian can earn, especially with global streaming services able to pay out sums the Elizabethan aristocracy couldn't imagine. Wealthy and powerful people want to be friends with comedians, so their proximity to influence can be astounding. President Obama guested on *Comedians in Cars Getting Coffee* with Jerry Seinfeld when he was in office. I have a comedian friend who was invited to go in a private jet to Jeff Bezos's island (also private), where he holds some kind of exclusive event with talks, lectures, networking and conversation for the most glamorous celebrities.

That's not to say a medieval or Elizabethan court jester's lot couldn't improve if they were good at their job. Hamlet's 'Alas, poor Yorick' speech is an homage to the royal family comedian fondly remembered and seemingly living a life of at least some intimacy with his regal employers. This doesn't imply he was paid well, but clearly he had social capital in the house and no doubt benefited from it. Court jesters weren't wealthy in the main, but they could have big paydays and be gifted real estate and horses. Some were so beloved they were buried in ostentatious monuments. In some ways, the million-dollar Netflix deal is nothing new. The difference is that the locus of power never shifted with the gifts handed from king to jester: any illusion of favour was fickle and could be taken away as quickly as it was given. There was no democracy. Literally no one but the king really had freedom of speech. And if the king turned against you, cancel culture could mean your whole head.

Some mentally or physically disabled people were 'kept as jesters' but treated like pets. They were referred to as 'innocent fools'. They were not paid and made to sleep on the floor till they no longer amused the family and then cast out and pensioned off with alms or forced to beg.[12] If you're horrified by this, then you're an Elizabethan progressive and Renaissance comedy lovers think you're a snowflake.

A large king on a golden throne mocking the serfs wasn't called comedy; it was just daily life. Entertainment came in the form of one outsider serf, given permission to mock the king. Just as with my dad's funeral, as with jokes about violence against women – who tells the joke can be as important as the joke itself.

Is it my right, nay my duty, to offend?

I've heard comedians talk about knowing that money and fandom has made them unrelatable. They used to do material about catching the bus. Now it's 'Isn't it awful when your limo's run out of champagne and your chauffeur won't stop talking?' In fact, Ellen DeGeneres's comeback stand-up special was called 'Relatable' for that reason. The same goes for mocking the powerful, which for many younger comedians means the previous generation. I remember Stephen Fry being asked in middle age if he and Hugh Laurie would ever 'get the band back together' and do sketch comedy again. He replied, 'Sketch is a young man's game. Once your friends are High Court judges, you can't be mocking the establishment any more. You *are* the establishment.' Hugh Laurie added in a different interview: 'I'm actually older than most of the Cabinet in Britain at the moment. I think their average age is about 45. So it starts to mean a different thing.'[13] Age isn't necessarily a barrier, but Hugh Laurie went to Eton and Cambridge, and so shares wealth and class privilege with many of those in leadership roles in this country; I think he's implying that many of them feel like 'younger boys' to him, which impacts how he feels about being qualified to mock the establishment.

Some comedians want to reserve the right to ridicule everything and everyone but not at the expense of cutting themselves off from an opulent lifestyle and proximity to power. They want their coke and they want to snort it too, ideally in the company of the great and the good. I'm not suggesting a comedian needs to deride the powerful, and I'm not saying you can't be friends with the Clintons if you also want to make people laugh. I'm saying if you're not making fun of the truly powerful, how can you justify mocking oppressed groups? We may no longer live in a world in which one man on a throne alone has free speech, but that doesn't mean freedom of speech is equally distributed. There remains a hierarchy of status and wealth, and with it, unequal access to opportunities to share and air one's views. If those at the top use their platform to ridicule people who cannot reply with equal volume, their freedom of speech encroaches on those other people's freedom to defend and speak for themselves.

Some argue that freedom of speech must include a right to offend. That there can be a thrill in comedy that plays with societal rules of propriety and punches down in jest. That 'shock comedy' is a legitimate version of the form. Human beings can really enjoy being shocked, the way we enjoy going on a roller coaster to be scared. It's a kick, and we get a free physiological buzz. What's the harm in a bit of shock or a bit of offence, if it makes us laugh?

I'd like to analyse two routines explicitly designed to shock and look at the impact of them. The first is in Jimmy Carr's 2021 Netflix special called, knowingly, *His Dark Material*, which opens with a disclaimer that there will be jokes in the show about 'terrible things' but that these are 'just jokes, they're not the terrible things'.

Carr prefaces the gag I want to look at with: 'This should be a career ender. Okay, strap in everyone. Are you ready?' Then he says, 'When people talk about the Holocaust' and throws a knowing look to the audience that implies, *Dare me*. He continues:

> When people talk about the Holocaust they talk about the tragedy and horror of six million Jewish lives being lost to the Nazi war machine, but they never mention the thousands of Gypsies that were killed by the Nazis. No one ever wants to talk about that, because no one ever wants to talk about the positives.

The audience laugh and many applaud.
He then explains:

> That's a very good joke for the following three reasons. Firstly, fucking funny. Well done, me. Secondly, edgy. Edgy as all hell. It's a joke about the worst thing that's ever happened in human history. People say 'never forget', well this is how I remember. I keep bringing it up. Third reason that's a good joke is that there is an educational quality to it.

He goes on to name other groups who were targeted and killed by the Nazis, which he says is not taught in schools, ending on a whimsical routine about my alma mater – the Jehovah's Witnesses – before talking about doing a gig in a hospice and being the only comedian to joke about cancer, which he says means that 'the dark ominous presence was being taken down and laughed at'.

Despite all the context Carr gave about the deliberate, provocative nature of his intentions, the joke was widely disparaged by both left- and right-wing pundits, by human rights groups, and even by many other comedians (a few spoke up for their friend Jimmy and the concept of free speech but essentially nobody defended the joke itself). And although the special is over two years old, at the time of writing, the first autocomplete suggestion that came up when I searched for 'Jimmy Carr' on X/Twitter was still 'Jimmy Carr Holocaust'.

Before commenting further on why this joke has been so badly received – even when presented in the context of 'the worst thing you can say' – I want to look at another example of this kind of humour and how it lands differently.

Long-running American sketch show *Saturday Night Live* contains a weekly segment called 'Weekend Update' featuring two comedians in suits behind a desk doing topical one-liners about current news stories. Since 2014, the hosts of this segment have been Colin Jost and Michael Che, and in 2018, 'as Christmas gifts to each other', Jost suggested they write jokes for each other which they read cold on live TV. Che explained in an interview that he assumed Jost was going to prank him so decided to reverse the prank by giving him, a white man, 'really racist things to say' but on air he discovered that the jokes Jost had written for him were 'kind of tame' while Che, a Black comedian, made Jost do material about Rosa Parks which naturally made him stutter in apologetic horror. Che said in the interview that his co-anchor 'goes bright red and Black people love that'.[14]

One of the Rosa Parks jokes that Michael Che wrote for Colin Jost went like this: 'Last week was National Rosa Parks Day, or as we call it in my house: Uppity Bus Passenger Day.' Jost reads the joke unwillingly and then raises his hands in horror. Other jokes in a similar vein leave Jost shouting 'Why?' while Che barracks, 'That's pretty racist, Colin!'

I've looked hard for complaints in the press or online. There is only one common major complaint about Joke Swap. It doesn't happen often enough. There are thousands of tweets asking why it didn't feature in the latest Christmas episode. Not one person that I can find has complained about the content of the jokes. It seems to be everyone's favourite segment.

What is the difference between Jimmy Carr – a wealthy privileged white man – and Colin Jost – a white man so privileged he's married to Scarlett Johansson – doing jokes that, when written down, both seem to be disparaging marginalised groups? The answer is the public (those same people who complain about everything now, according to edgy comedians) generally know the difference between the content of a joke and the context of a joke. They understand who the joke is on.

Let's think about who owns the joke in these two scenarios. Colin Jost appears unwilling to read the jokes. He's horrified by the content. The power dynamic is clear. His Black comedy co-anchor is in the power position. Jost says in an interview in *Collider*: 'I'm seeing all of [the jokes] for the first time on air. It's thrilling, in a way, but also terrifying . . . The worst moments are always the lead-up to that moment, where you're in a hallway and you hear one of the writers say, "You can't make him say that! Oh my God! His life will be over. They'll kill him!"' The article concludes with the interviewer remarking: 'Jost . . . doesn't mind being the butt of a good joke.'[15] What the audience are recognising here is that the joke's on Jost. Not Rosa Parks or marginalised Black Americans.

Now let's examine Jimmy Carr's joke in which he describes Roma Travellers being killed in the Holocaust as a 'positive'. Carr does not, I'm sure, desire to kill Roma people or rejoice in their historic deaths. It's simply the most shocking thing he thought he could get away with saying. His audience were no doubt mainly laughing at how bold Carr was being – at the taboos he was willing to bust like they were nothing. He does say things people in the audience wouldn't dare say (unless they're retelling his joke!) and that is a large part of the appeal to those who love him.

Canadian philosopher Marshall McLuhan once said, 'Art is anything you can get away with.'[16] Jimmy Carr didn't get away with it – and he understands the current context really well because he prefaces his gag by saying 'it's career ending'. It wasn't censored. He was paid loads for it, and it's still up on Netflix for anyone to see, but overall, probably more people talked about it in disgust than laughed at it, and it doesn't seem likely that the routine will come to be looked at as some edgy outsider piece that will be understood better in twenty years because Jimmy Carr is so ahead of his time. It just didn't work. So why do Weekend Update's jokes work? How are they different?

Well because Michael Che writes the jokes, and he is Black. Imagine two white comedians on live TV pushing each other to read racist jokes. It wouldn't matter how unwilling they were. They don't own the material. Imagine the anger that would fill their timelines and the complaints the network would get. Ownership of the material is key. Whose funeral is it? Who gets to make the joke? We understand that implicitly.

Secondly, Jost understands that if he read these jokes with the same certainty and newsreader-style straight bat with which he reads his own gags, he'd be perceived as cocky and heartless. The comedy simply wouldn't work because we don't want to hear racist jokes. We are laughing exclusively at his discomfort at being pushed into dangerous territory by Che. We are laughing at a Black man publicly lowering the status of a white man on live television.

Jimmy Carr, on the other hand, does not own the material about Roma Traveller people. In other words, he is not writing from a place of experience or personal connection. He is also deliberately cocky about telling the joke about the genocide of this extremely marginalised group and the butt of the joke is not the Nazis or Carr himself. It is the Roma people. Carr even goes on to unpack why he and the joke are both so clever. He's *attempting* to contextualise it and make 'your shock' out to be the real butt of the joke. None of this works and so he just comes off as brazenly hurtful and more than that – Roma groups and other human rights groups talk about the potential damaging impact of the joke.

What is that impact? Well, just because Jimmy Carr wouldn't physically attack Roma people, the same cannot be said for everybody listening. Now we are back to 'men who think everyone wants to hurt women' misunderstanding the laugh of shock as a laugh of endorsement. That joke is being told in a 1,600-seat theatre and will be watched by millions of people around the world on Netflix. There are, of course, some people who are laughing because they dislike Roma people and are racist about or even towards them. Some argue that it is 'just a joke', but a joke like this is a magic carpet for an idea to get around the world in record time. A vehicle for bigots to share their ideas without being accountable.

Some argue shock comedy 'just isn't funny', but if that were true, it wouldn't be worth debating. If a comedian isn't funny to a lot of people, you don't really need to worry about what they say. It won't have any power. Comedy only has power when it's funny. And with power comes responsibility. Jimmy Carr is a very popular comedian.

Let's look at the real-life, wider social context in which he told this joke. The 2022 British Police, Crime, Sentencing and Courts Act intentionally makes it easier for the police to arrest travelling populations and confiscate their homes.[17] In recent years, homicidal threats and slurs have been spray-painted on the Roma Holocaust memorials in Germany and a memorial in Glasgow was desecrated twice.[18] Hate messages were also left at the memorial in Lety, the concentration camp for Romani people in what is now the Czech Republic.[19] Amnesty International have declared Roma people the most criminalised, stigmatised, least defended group in the UK.[20] Amnesty also reports that in the Czech Republic, Romani children are automatically 'sent to schools for children with "mild mental disabilities". They're put in segregated classes and schools, and teachers and other pupils treat them badly just because they're Roma.'[21] Across central and Eastern Europe, 'millions of Roma live in isolated slums, often without any electricity or running water, and struggle to get the health care they need. Many live with the daily threat of forced evictions, police harassment and violent attacks.' On average, Roma people's life spans are ten years shorter than other people's in the same area. Amnesty's official report concludes: 'This situation is not the inevitable result of poverty. It's because of centuries of prejudice and discrimination from governments, institutions and individuals. Together, they have pushed the great majority of Roma to the margins of society – and kept them there.'[22]

The question is not 'Is the joke offensive?' Obviously, it's offensive. That's the point of the joke. But Carr and many edgy comedians would argue that offence doesn't cause any harm. I think the better question is 'Does Jimmy Carr's joke add to the existing, measurable stigma against the Roma Traveller population?' And it does, because now there is a new, memorable, popular, pithy verbal grenade in the form of a punchline to be used against an already criminalised, demoralised group. Jimmy Carr cannot be unaware that some of his viewers will have the attitude that 'it's funny because it's true'.

Will teens be likely to retell the joke verbatim in schools to/at/in front of Roma teens? Yes. Shocking humour is sticky. If famous, confident Jimmy Carr says it, they can repeat it. This is especially likely if it reinforces racist tropes and slurs they've already heard in their community. They've most likely seen the gag, devoid of its cushioning about how shocking it is, on TikTok, and this is how it will be repeated. It is a short journey from there to backing a Roma kid up against a wall in the locker room to watch them squirm for fun: 'No one ever wants to talk about the positives.' Structural violence can quickly turn into physical violence. If racism is called or a teacher hears, the attacker has the 'it's just a joke' defence. While Jimmy Carr is paid to tell that joke in a fancy suit, how can a child be punished for repeating the gag?

Why do you want to be 'saying the unsayable'?

Matt Lucas and David Walliams have apologised for the stereotypes they perpetuated in their 2000s sketch show *Little Britain*.[23] One of the characters David Walliams played was a trans woman who believed she passed for cisgender but was portrayed as a grotesque caricature as she went down the street shouting, 'I'm a lady!' This exact catchphrase has been shouted out of car windows and on public transport to humiliate and draw attention to trans women.[24] It made already difficult lives more difficult. Jeers usually get thrown before fists. This can be the real-life impact of shock gags.

The same show subverted the stereotype of the promiscuous, predatory, closeted gay man with Matt Lucas's 'only gay in the village', who wanted his identity known but avoided physical intimacy. Whereas the 'I'm a lady' sketches simply involved ridicule at the very idea of being a transgender woman, the 'only gay in the village' material invited the audience to see that some gay men were tentative about sexual contact.* This upended the stereotype of the oversexed gay man. Here's a character we can empathise with, as well as laugh at. This cannot be unrelated to the fact that Lucas is a gay man, whereas neither Walliams nor Lucas is trans. It appears to have seemed to them that trans people were ludicrous figures of fun. But Matt Lucas owned the jokes about being a young gay man and understood what was funny about subverting the cliché and introducing us to someone more truthful or at least new. The difference is clear to see in the writing.

It amazed me that when Walliams and Lucas had all the opportunity to make pretty much anything they wanted after the success of *Little Britain*, they chose to do another sketch

---

* Or even asexual, which doesn't invalidate their sexuality.

show that focused on marginalised stereotypes including a Jamaican woman called Precious Little, who was lazy. The joke? 'Precious' is a 'funny' Jamaican name and Jamaicans are work-shy people. It's impossible that this wasn't used towards and about Jamaican women in the service industry. 'Has Precious Little missed a spot? Arrived late? Forgotten something?' Your cheap laugh sure is expensive for somebody.

Are you my one and only?

In comedian Hari Kondabolu's 2017 documentary *The Problem with Apu* he points out that Apu, the Indian owner of the Kwik-E-Mart convenience store in *The Simpsons*, was the only Indian representation he regularly saw in his childhood. There were no other recurring Indian characters on TV and he was a big *Simpsons* fan, so it was particularly difficult that Apu sounded, as Kondabolu describes him, 'as a white guy doing an impression of a white guy making fun of my father'. The documentary features a clip of Kondabolu doing a set in a comedy club when a heckler shouts one of Apu's catchphrases at him in a cod Indian accent. The comedian replies: 'You're the reason I do comedy, sir. You're the reason I thought to myself, "Nobody like us exists, except this cartoon character".' I think it's difficult to realise if you see lots of people like you on TV – respected, reading the news, running the country, as well as comedic send-ups – what it's like to have 'I'm a lady' or Apu's 'Thank you; come again' be the sole way you get to see yourself, other people see you and, by extension, the thing strangers most often say to your face.

When Hank Azaria sat down with Hari Kondabolu on NPR in 2023, he admitted it had taken him a long time to come around to the idea that he shouldn't voice the character and that it had been damaging: 'It's important to point out that pre-Hari [doing a documentary about] Apu, I did not think about that stuff. I didn't even know it happened. I had to be told 54 times before it sunk in.' He added: 'I read a little news blurb where a guy was attacked. It was actually a Middle Eastern guy who was attacked in his store and was called Apu while he was being attacked. I think if I had any doubts at that point … there were certain key moments in that whole is-this-real question journey I was on, where I got the answer. You know, Apu had become a slur, in other words … a lot of times, I have conversations with my white friends and family or acquaintances or whoever, and that gets through.'

Kondabolu responds: 'I worked at the Queens District Attorney's Office Bureau of Hate Crimes after 9/11. I was a college student. You know, reading the accounts of hate crimes and seeing accounts that, "Thank you; come again" or Apu's being mentioned often enough where … it's heartbreaking, especially when it's Queens, the most diverse place in the world.' Azaria says that he will continue to explain to white people why the white stereotypes in the show are different so Hari, who is exhausted from talking about it, doesn't have to: 'It's my amends. I need to keep having the conversation. I owe it.' And Kondabolu replies, 'I appreciate that very much.' This is an excellent example of the repair, love and growth that can be found when comedians recognise that their work does have power and that how they wield it matters.

I often wonder what drives comedians to mock people with marginalised identities. Sure, you can tell any joke you want if you live in a country with free speech … But why do you want to? Why do you want to make the life of Black immigrant women more difficult? Especially the ones who are already in the most thankless jobs, cleaning up your dirty coffee cups or scrubbing your loo at an airport while you fly first class to Bermuda? It reinforces already iniquitous injustices. *You're* *going to Black up for that?* If your goal is simply to shock, then understand the price someone else might be paying for you to do that and ask if there's another way of you getting the same thrill without the structural violence. Punching someone in the face will shock them and, if it's done right, a lot of people will laugh when they see the footage. Comedians don't do it though. It's not just illegal – it's not how we want to get laughs. It's not the craft.*

Far from 'saying the unsayable', 'Precious Little' simply made more sayable what's always said snidely by people who've been trained to be suspicious of people who are different from them. What mocking observations do you think you can make about marginalised groups that they haven't already heard or couldn't find online – in the same places people castigate comedians? It's hard to argue you're 'saying the unsayable' at a time in history when we have hot and cold running internet and where armchair trolls are making the unsayable the constantly said. When iconoclastic legendary stand-up comic Lenny Bruce was being arrested for obscenity in comedy clubs in the 1960s, he was specifically protesting censorship on stage. It's unlikely he'd feel the need now after a cursory doom scroll and a little light googling. It's all being said, all the time. Who exactly are we shocking now?

Is *Anything* Unsayable Now in a World Where No One Shuts Up?

Highly paid comedians with huge platforms say outrageous or hurtful things all the time. But it is true that there are

* There is 'a new generation of YouTubers' who invade space or grab people in the street to film 'a prank' but I'd suggest they're doing something different and this isn't really to be conflated with the craft of a comedian. https://www.bbc.com/news/av/magazine-31972380/

some things that you can't say now without widespread public criticism and sometimes even (usually very temporary) loss of opportunity and career advancement. This is not really new. People always shouted at their televisions, but no one heard it. Sometimes they wrote a letter to the paper or complained to the network, but you had to find a stamp and walk to a post box. Now people shout online, and tag the comedians and network execs who can instantly read it. That is the result of free speech spreading to the masses. It is not full right of reply though. No Roma Traveller person has been offered a multi-million-pound Netflix deal to respond or even a seat on a panel to discuss it, to my knowledge.

In this landscape, controversial comedians can, in fact, thrive off vitriol (and the clicks that come with it), without actually having to share their platform with the groups they've made fun of or demoralised. When Ricky Gervais – who has made an excellent living courting controversy – deadnames* trans people and talks in crass terms about gender confirmation surgery, it feels colonial to me. In the same way Englishmen went to India and smashed up or mocked things they didn't understand and then brought back tea and pyjamas as a jolly good shout, I see Gervais entering a land he doesn't understand or have any feeling for. He points at things that look hilarious to him for others who don't belong there to laugh at too. His jokes about trans people sound like an Englishman during the Raj, pointing at a man in a turban and humiliating him out of ignorance and a lack of empathy. His material works like an advertising campaign for the anti-gender movement with whom he would share very few values, but who must be thrilled with his material doing their

---

* Deadnaming is the act of referring to a transgender or non-binary person by a name they used prior to transitioning, such as their birth name.

work. Rather than hearing Gervais's views on what makes people with AIDS or the trans community risible, I'd be far more interested in hearing him talk about how he sees men like himself evolving or resisting the changes of the modern world. It's an experience he owns. He has insights from the inside.

I'm sure transitioning or living the life of a Roma Traveller can be very funny at times. I'm sure there's comedy in living with HIV. Ask anyone who's living with cancer and they'll tell you if they don't laugh, they won't get through it. And I very much suspect the funniest, freshest, most insightful and truly shocking jokes (if shock is what floats your boat) are going to be from those who know these experiences first-hand. I'd much rather hear a routine about the experience of wearing a turban from someone who wears one than a British officer in colonised India. That's not to say that marginalised artists don't sometimes play into damaging tropes and repeat stereotypes they've internalised, or they know will sell in a world that doesn't offer them much social capital, but our best chance of seeing fresh, exciting work that adds to rather than reinforces those tropes is through proper representation.

This isn't to say everyone has to have experience of everything they speak about on stage – that would be dull and very limiting. But there are some experiences that are commonly misunderstood and yet we never hear about from the point of view of the very people who get it and know it and live it. And why not? Why do we pay Ricky Gervais fortunes to talk in a derisory manner about what he imagines transitioning might be like, but we rarely, if ever, pay transgender comedians to speak from their experience?

Eddie Izzard (also known as Suzy) is a notable exception, but it's important to recognise that her material has traditionally been imaginative whimsy and not personal revelation (and it's also true that she has been ridiculed, often viciously, in recent years). It is crucial that creatives are not compelled to speak about their identities and trauma, just because we are curious about their experience. As much as it pains me to agree with Ed Vaizey on anything, he was right to say (as we saw in the last conversation) that it is really important that trans people be allowed to just be and 'not be seen as exotic but completely mainstream'. There's a value in artists who represent marginalised groups and don't speak about their identity, just their humanity. However, especially when we are giving global platforms to public figures who mock the trans experience as a curiosity, we must find space for artists who can speak fully to their own experience as well.

To date, by platforming people from the dominant group over and over again, we have come to see one sort of person as neutral. We are not encouraged to see that every Black trans female experience is as different as every white cisgender male experience, for example. One is niche and particular, and the other has been socially constructed as standard. This is simply because of the hundreds of stories we've consumed through the eyes of the mainstream group.

We've seen white men as presidents, CEOs, scientists, artists, homeless people, doctors, lawyers, painters and serial killers. We see a white guy and, honestly, he's a blank canvas. We have to make assumptions about him based on how he's dressed and how he speaks and who he tells us he is. We project very little on to him because of his essential qualities, assuming we know or think he's heterosexual, gender conforming and not visibly disabled or neurodivergent. We see a white guy as able to speak for all of us because for generations he's been held up as the standard of human, qualified to represent us all in Parliament. Police us all in the streets. Judge us all in court. Teach us all in university. Stand in for us in medical studies.

Write all the novels and plays with multiple points of view. White men decided what went into the canon and directed almost all the films and dominated almost all the science labs and science fiction writing jobs and tech companies. We have been raised to think all this is normal, and we have seen little else modelled.

This doesn't mean all white men have an easy time. Many of the white men in the world have challenges and deep trauma I've never faced. It just means more of their stories will be told and I've been invited to empathise with them all my life. For generations men have gone to war, for example, some as teenage boys who were completely underprepared. This is tragic and toxic and deserves societal scrutiny. How has comedy helped me understand this? As a child and young person, I watched *M*A*S*H* (about a medical unit in the Korean War) and *Blackadder Goes Forth* (a period sitcom set in the First World War) and the film *Good Morning, Vietnam* (starring Robin Williams as an armed forces radio service DJ) and there were times between the jokes (and in many cases during), I was asked to empathise for their fear, trauma and loss of life and limb. These pieces made me consider the futility of war but also the (very largely) white male experience within it. There is, of course, an irony that it is usually done without much, if any, representation of the experience of those they fought. To quote Frankie Boyle (himself an often controversial voice in comedy): 'Not only will America come to your country and kill all your people . . . but they'll come back twenty years later and make a movie about how killing your people made their soldiers feel sad.'[25]

Because we've heard from one voice speaking on behalf of all the other voices for so long, people from other groups are angry. Some people from other identity groups have always been angry but many saw no other model and, while they may have felt disenfranchised, they didn't feel entitled to be vocal about it, or they simply weren't allowed to be. When the internet came into its own and social media took off, like a miracle we had the means to publish and broadcast.* We were able to speak to each other and find our audiences. With this new technology at our fingertips, we began to speak for ourselves, and it was intoxicating. We demonstrated we were good at it and we built big followings making little TV shows on social media, rough and ready radio shows known as podcasts, and journalism, activism and opinion pieces in blogs and on social media. And now that we've demonstrated our skill, talent and worth and are finally visible, we want the right to tell our own stories on mainstream platforms.

It is a natural consequence of having a new, fresh voice that has been silenced for generations that people from marginalised groups want to share in the social capital. It is also inevitable that people with a new voice will be critical of old voices and expect them to change and capitulate. If you keep people in the dark for generations, they will not be quiet when they find their own light. We are in a new and unpredictable time when gay men will advocate to play themselves in movies and Black women will lobby to write their own screenplays. Autistic people will demand proper representation in films about them and hashtag Nothing About Us Without Us. How can it be any other way, when people have been in the margins for generations and have fought their way to visibility? We have

* I use 'we' here because I was someone who was constantly and explicitly told (in writing) that the industry 'did not want women' and so comedy agents 'could not represent me' even if they saw the value in my work or admitted I was talented or I had managed to break through in some small way to a mainstream platform. It wasn't until podcasting that I could find and build my own audience. Gatekeepers decided what audiences wanted before the democratisation of the internet.

all seen ourselves reduced to a few clichés because we've been written and rewritten by writers who project expectations and prejudices onto us.

This is a good time to ask ourselves what our goal is. If our aim is to demand that individuals from every identity group are fully resourced, empowered human beings whose humanity comes ahead of our identities, then our short-term goal is to reclaim our voice and representation. Let's have the comedy specials from those marginalised groups, and let's hear the stories, attitudes and points of view which have been suppressed for so long.

I believe our long-term goal should be that we are all seen to be as potentially 'neutral' as white, straight, gender-conforming men while celebrating our vibrant rich differences, which make our society wonderful. The ideal future is one in which cis and trans people can play each other in movies and there is so much excellent, empathetic representation that all creatives can create a variety of truthful characters and stories. Black female artists, for example, who've been raised in a culture of mainstream stories, can already write the dominant experience without any trouble because they have so many reference points and have been schooled to have a deep cultural understanding. It is not that white men cannot write Black female characters – we hope they do as they often have the biggest budgets! But it's important to have relevant artists and consultants on their creative teams to make sure the actors themselves don't have the burden of speaking up when stereotypes are being reinforced. It is crucial that these creatives are well paid, encouraged to speak freely and really listened to.

If we decided to develop our collective culture in this way, eventually it would reflect such a wide range of human experiences it would be standard for artists to be truthful and elevating while being imaginative and free.

Are identity politics and freedom of speech opposites? Or the same thing?

I don't know if or when this paradise of equality for humanity could happen, but I do know that along the way we must protect our freedom of speech. We've had it for such a short time. Remember that plays were censored in the UK, and every word had to be approved by the Lord Chamberlain till 1968. This was the same year that the Hays Code was lifted. This was the list of what was and was not allowed in Hollywood films (which also affected how films intended for the US market were put together). While the Hays Code was in effect, British films were seen as potentially racy to the Americans, as was Broadway theatre to the Brits. Artists were constantly having to enquire as to whether they could say this or do that. It seems understandably bizarre to creatives who remember the 1960s that today's theatre and film communities seek to restrict what we ourselves can and can't say – alongside demands from our audience.

How do we reconcile this paradox? We want everyone to have the same freedom of speech as Jimmy Carr and Ricky Gervais, but we want to take note of the problems created in a world in which not everyone has access to the same platforms from where to enjoy that freedom. How can we protect the needs of the marginalised without policing expression? Censorship, whether self-imposed or by legislation, is surely not the answer. But I do think it's reasonable to ask artists and platforms to curate their work intentionally and not recklessly. Your freedom of speech can quickly encroach on someone else's freedom *from* structural violence. You've also got the freedom to drive a car, but it isn't absolute. You're used to understanding there are many caveats about having to drive responsibly, so you don't hurt, or even seriously inconvenience, anyone else. There's a fairness and etiquette to road rules as well as concern for the safety of others. Sometimes it seems strange to me that comedians expect total right of way with other people's identities and feelings without any manners, basic empathy or concern that their manoeuvres might make a contribution (whether large or small) to a less safe, more brutal world for others. Sometimes comedians are better people when they're driving to the gig than they are onstage.

I think a valid, responsible and genuinely artistic question for comedians to ask themselves is this: if what they're saying would be hate speech unless it were a joke, how does it differ from actual hate speech? Is there a significantly different context or point being made? If they have a huge global audience, do they trust all of those watching to share their value set and understand their use of rhetoric and irony when sharing ideas that in any other context would land as bigotry? If not, is their shock laugh worth it? If they think it is – then they should make that comedy. If they, or those they consult and trust, can see the mean jokes they are writing about marginalised people reinforce rather than subvert the power structures, then they should write something better. Something that punches up – or at least sideways. Perhaps something whimsical that punches no one at all.

That is what the speaker can do to protect the status of free speech. But what about the public? My question to audiences is this – if a comedian is trying to shock you, and you react by writing about how shocked you are, then are you pleasing them or punishing them? We live in an age where attention is the most valuable currency, and so people do and say whatever they can to get it. It's important to examine what outcome you are hoping for here. If you are trying to get a comedian's damaging jokes taken off a major streaming platform, ask yourself whether hashtagging about their show is likely to motivate that broadcaster to remove their content, or is likely to draw more eyes to their work? What's our goal here? When a line is crossed, the answer is rarely to censor. It can be far more valuable to drain power by disengaging. Pull the plug. Walk out. Turn off. Flood the timeline with something else.

Let's resource and amplify Roma and trans voices, for example, rather than creating neon signs flashing towards the content of men who've chosen to bait them. Do you know any comedians or writers from those groups, and if not, can you seek some out and find some whose work you enjoy and share it or even find a way to pay for it? Clicks make money and no one cares why people are clicking. So send the clicks away from the comedian or joke you find de-humanising and towards humanising and resourcing those who are its target.

Let's learn to spot – or at least question – the difference between a joke that's deliberately offensive but that will likely have no impact in the real world because it's also absurd – and a joke that will be weaponised against marginalised people. If you assess that it has no real-world structural power and is unlikely to change anything, ignore it. If you feel it has such power, then diverting attention to other things is key. Algorithms mean making it a *cause célèbre* will create a sorcerer's apprentice-style, never-ending flow of the same sort of content and worse.

Also, if we show our ire every time we are offended, then we dilute the power of our objections. We make martyrs out of creatives with amoral or immoral intentions and free speech pioneers out of cheap shooters. We have started a flame war we are unlikely to win, so let's stop fighting fire with fire and think about different plays.

Is there an edge to the edgy comedians?

There will always be comedians who exploit shock comedy, whose brand is contravening norms. But when these comedians say anything for a laugh is justified, they don't really mean it. We all have a line between what is acceptable and what isn't, and very few comedians have the same line as their colleagues working in clubs in the 1980s. The world has progressed, and all comedians (in some fashion) are a product of their world. One of the most powerful things we can do is to focus our efforts on changing the world *around* the artists. When society finds certain exclusionary ideas repugnant enough, those ideas get taken off the air because they are so out of step with the mainstream value set.

As edgy as Dave Chapelle is, and as much as he wants to 'say the unsayable', I notice that he doesn't use the slurs Richard Pryor used about gay people. Ricky Gervais wouldn't do a routine in the style of racist 1970s/'80s comedian Bernard Manning. Why not? It *would* shock. It *would actually be* 'unsayable'. These comedians are interested in operating *just outside* what they perceive to be the most progressive value set right now. When today's demands become an ordinary expectation of life, it won't be edgy to rattle that cage any more. They will always play on the edge of our widening circle of societal empathy. That doesn't feel very noble to me. It feels like holding the envelope back, rather than pushing it.

Perhaps we are all just baboons demonstrating, with the grooming ritual of laughter, who's in our stamm and who isn't. Deep down in our most primal place, we fear that if everyone's in, then no one's in because it's not special. Sometimes we need to have an in-joke with our nearest and dearest because it's 'our funeral'. But if the human race is to really progress in a way where we resource and endorse the humanity of all individuals, we need to raise the status of those we lower legally, fiscally and structurally, before we lower it in fun. If we cannot stop our wealthy, well-dressed jesters from mocking them, it is our job to raise them up so that they feel so central and resourced, that teasing and nicknames are a compliment. That might be silver-jumpsuit territory, given the history of the world, but it's worth working for.

In the interim, we need to examine what happens when we don't just attempt to exclude and banish powerful dehumanising jokes, but when we attempt to exclude human beings from society. We need to discuss the cousin of censorship – which often plays in the comedy space – cancel culture. What it means. What it does. And most mysteriously of all, whether it really exists.

Conversation Five

The Conversation about Cancel Culture

Is the court of public opinion now in session?

In 2014, a tweet parodying a news story was posted by the Twitter account of *The Colbert Report*. It read:

> I am willing to show the #Asian community I care by introducing the Ching-Chong Ding-Dong Foundation for Sensitivity to Orientals or Whatever.

Dan Snyder, owner of a Washington DC-based NFL football team which was at that time known as the Redskins, had just announced the creation of The Washington Redskins Original Americans Foundation which aimed to 'address the urgent challenges plaguing Indian country, based on what tribal leaders tell us they need most'.[1] Snyder did this while refusing to change the name of the team that Native American leaders and other human rights activists had told him was offensive. Stephen Colbert, whose television comedy show was known to satirise right-wing current affairs anchors, wanted to make the point that this was absurd, hypocritical, insulting and poorly thought out. Someone at the network who ran the social media accounts lifted a quote from his late night show out of context and published the tweet.

It was a hyperbolic parallel designed to satirise, but a Korean American social justice internet activist (who goes by her online name of Suey Park), felt the tweet perpetuated slurs against Asian people no matter its intent. In response, she started the Twitter hashtag #CancelColbert. When networks call time on TV shows they are said to be 'cancelled' and she felt this tweet was grounds to bring the show to an end – or at least reason to provoke, bring attention to her cause, get an apology and have the tweet taken down. Rather than apologising, Colbert responded in character, continuing to parody the football team's attitude – but also asked his fans not to harass Suey Park. He made it clear he didn't personally run the show's Twitter feed and deleted the whole account, live on TV. Suey Park received multiple rape and death threats from angry Colbert fans and ended up shaving her head and moving cities. She reported being 'stalked and hunted' for months afterwards.

That is the first recorded call for 'cancellation' in this colloquial sense of the word.*[2] The situation's complex kaleidoscope of intention, impact and repercussions is indicative of the myriad of issues in what is now known as 'cancel culture'. There couldn't be a more ironic origin story for cancellation, than those on the left holding others on the left to account for not being sensitive enough, causing an angry mob of progressives

* A similar usage and other possible origin might be a violent scene in the 1991 movie *New Jack City* when Wesley Snipes's character Nino Brown says, 'Cancel that bitch, I'll buy another one,' referring to ending his relationship with his girlfriend. However, the Suey Park/Colbert incident seems a far more direct line to today's cancellation campaigns. It was popularised on Black Twitter by 2015 so it is possible there are multiple roots to the term and its usage.

with virtual pitchforks to come for another progressive, asking for sensitivity, until she is literally run out of town.

Suey was suggesting they cancel the show – but given the show's name is also a man's name, this seems to be how we have come to a place where it is frequently suggested that human beings be cancelled. You can stop making a television show but how do you cancel a person? What does that mean? Why do we use this bleak language, and does it have an effect on our collective psyche? Should we be using other words when we make requests or demands for change from human beings, rather than TV shows? Is there any value in calls for cancellation?

'Cancel culture' has become a shorthand for the practice of the public holding individuals or companies to account for their actions and demanding change, but in reality it means a multitude of things. The experience can range from an individual having an uncomfortable afternoon on social media, to being forced to apologise publicly for a perceived error, to losing a job, to becoming unemployable for years, to being ostracised by certain communities, to living life as a social pariah, to being arrested for illegal activity they might have otherwise got away with. It is a collective attempt to excommunicate someone from their largest stamm.[3]

Is cancel culture a new idea?

While 'cancellation' may have been coined a decade or so ago, public outrage having ramifications for individuals is nothing new. Silent film actor Roscoe Arbuckle, better known as 'Fatty' Arbuckle (a name he hated!), was a famous Hollywood star in the early twentieth century. In 1921, a woman fell ill at a party that he and some friends were hosting. The actress Virginia Rappe was seen by a doctor who declared her intoxicated, and two days later she was admitted to hospital where she died of peritonitis caused by a ruptured bladder. She suffered from chronic urinary tract infections, which are known to be exacerbated by drinking alcohol. But her friend Bambina Maude Delmont said Arbuckle had raped her and he was charged with sexual assault and manslaughter. The doctor who examined her could find no evidence of rape – not that that rules anything out in a patriarchal system even today, much less in 1921 when medical technology was far less advanced.

We do not know what really happened, but we do know that the police and the newspapers unpleasantly used 'Fatty' Arbuckle's size against him, depicting him as a disgusting, lecherous man who used his weight to overpower women. This was not his reputation at all. He was known to be very shy, especially with women. We also know that William Randolph Hearst, the Murdoch of his day, said the story 'sold more newspapers than any event since the sinking of the *Lusitania*' (the catalyst for the US entering the First World War).[4] If the word 'clickbait' had existed then, Hearst would have been the one to coin it. We also know that Delmont, his accuser, tried to extort money from Arbuckle's lawyers.

None of this – including the fact Arbuckle had two mistrials due to hung juries, and a third in which he was found innocent and issued with an exoneration and an apology – gives us any information about what really happened. Convictions for rape are statistically insignificant even now, but that is not what is relevant to our discussion on cancel culture. On 18 April 1922, six days after Arbuckle's acquittal, Will Hays – of Hays Code fame, the head of Hollywood's brand-new censorship board – banned Arbuckle from ever working in American movies again. Hays did this after being encouraged by the moral outrage of various groups including the Federation of Women's Clubs, the Federal Trade Commission and the Catholic Church. He also recommended all screenings of Arbuckle's films be, you guessed it, cancelled.

Under push-back from a strong sector of the public that still pushes back in similar situations today, Hays eventually lifted the ban. No one wanted to employ Arbuckle, though, and he was publicly shunned. Much like most cancelled men today, he found ways back into the industry, but died twelve years later, on the same day he was commissioned by a studio to make his first feature film since the scandal. Often people on the right like to paint cancel culture as a uniquely modern phenomenon but in fact, what is modern is that it is often more progressive people bringing the pressure to bear.

The history of public pressure to censor content and have individuals removed from platforms tends to feature moralistic groups like those who supported Hays. The censorious, prudish Hays Code, which we briefly mentioned in the last conversation, sanitised Hollywood films for decades, famously insisting that kissing couples on screen always keep one foot on the floor. I am not conflating allegations of rape with puritanical measures like forbidding showing an on-screen married couple in a double bed, rather I am focusing on the direction of the outrage. The appeals for censorship came from conservative America, frequently from religious groups. Senator Joseph McCarthy rooted suspected communists out of Hollywood in the 1950s and garnered support from the American right. In Britain, Mary Whitehouse campaigned from the 1960s to the 1980s to censor swearing, sexual scenes and other perceived morally suspect content from our small and large screens, and she found an ally in Margaret Thatcher and many of those who loved her. Of course, the left have always fallen out of love with their own, and stars have risen and fallen, but it is difficult to find historical examples of public campaigns that target individuals or call for censorship from the left. It is very easy to find them from the right.

Does the fall of the gatekeepers mean the rise of the mob?

Today, entertainment has been substantially (although not completely) democratised. If you want to run your own television network, radio station, newspaper or publishing house, in a way you can. For hardly any outlay, you can start a YouTube channel, write a blog, sell your own eBooks, or launch a podcast. The internet 'long tail' means that many millions of people try these things and barely scrape together an audience of double figures, but a surprising number of people who make content in their bedrooms now command large and loyal followings.

Democratising content also means democratising debate. If I'm displeased about the latest offering from the grassroots or the gatekeepers, I don't have to find another gatekeeper who will let me have my say. I have instant access to the town squares of X (formerly known as Twitter), Facebook, Instagram, TikTok, Snapchat and YouTube. There I can respond in any way from a pithy one-liner to a four-hour video essay about whatever it is that I disapprove of or heartily endorse. When the establishment had the only megaphone in town, they usually amplified the voices of the public that chimed with their own. Today a variety of voices from the left, right and centre can rise – but those saying the most provocative things usually get the most attention and therefore tend to cut through the noise.

Right-wing voices will tell you that the trend for contemporary, moralising, puritanical outrage and the attendant harassment of individuals – especially for what people say or post rather than do – is a left-wing malaise. This evidently isn't true. There are many recent examples of the right shaming, punishing and ostracising people without any nefarious intentions for their perceived indiscretions, many of which predate the term 'cancel culture'. As Jon Ronson catalogued in his book *So You've Been Publicly Shamed*, an American called Lindsey Stone, who worked with adults with learning difficulties, posed for a jokingly disrespectful photo in front of a sign that read 'silence and respect' at a military cemetery in 2012. It was part of a running in-joke that her friend posted on Facebook. A veteran found it offensive and shared it, which escalated into an online hate campaign that meant Lindsey was fired and found herself unemployable. She was too scared to date and hardly left the house for a year. She repeatedly apologised but her mistake was deemed unforgivable.

Yassmin Abdel-Magied is a young engineer and journalist, who in 2015 was named an Australian of the Year. She wrote a respectful but controversial post on ANZAC Day 2017 (an annual war veterans' remembrance day) that extended the 'lest we forget' trope to other current horrors (outside the wars the veterans of Australia and New Zealand had fought). These horrors included the war in Syria and the offshore detention centres where the Australian government keeps refugees in inhumane conditions.[5] The fall-out from right-wing 'patriots' was so extreme, Yassmin found it was made impossible for her to return to her job as an oil-rig engineer and was let go from her job as a journalist with the ABC (Australian Broadcasting Corporation). Because her address and phone number were released (a practice known as doxxing), she felt she had no choice but to leave the country. Those who ostracised her online made no secret of their racist and Islamophobic motivations – the language they used was violent, misogynistic, threatening and clear. Yassmin was no longer welcome in Australia.

The left definitely doesn't have an exclusivity clause on cancellation (as much as the right might want to perpetuate that idea). But I don't think many angry, xenophobic 'patriots' are reading this book – so I'm going to examine why the left calls for cancellations while also suggesting that 'cancel culture' doesn't exist or that if it does, it doesn't really have much power. Those who deny its existence point to individuals like the disgraced comedian Louis CK, who won a Grammy after supposedly being cancelled.

That's a valid point, but proof that people continue to exist and work after a period of 'cancellation' isn't proof that shaming and shunning aren't happening. What's more, entire media ecosystems have sprung up to exist specifically outside the parameters of 'cancellable' content – which, by definition, end up attracting the most histrionic and extreme voices. Those who feel that they have fallen afoul of mainstream culture may take the opportunity to 'lean in' to a new, edgy, outsider status, delivering their work to a more extreme audience and radicalising themselves and others through a combination of frustration and cynical professional advancement – even if that wasn't their immediate intention.

I want to look at how we use it, what we are hoping to achieve and whether it is morally and pragmatically fit for purpose.

At its core, cancellation is an attempt to hold people accountable by society because they have not been held accountable by the power structures. I will examine its flaws and worst excesses later but for now, let's look at what it is attempting to accomplish at is best. Today, in addition to the moralising right having a megaphone, marginalised groups have their own system of amplification. Historically they had the option of silence or revolution. The internet has given them something in between. The ability to find each other quickly, boycott and pressure. One marginalised voice will waft into the void. Many together, it seems, have some power.

Once more, let's examine the case of the British suffragettes who began civil disobedience in 1905, the destruction of property in 1908, and bombing and arson in 1913. It wasn't their first response. It was their last. They only stopped due to the outbreak of war. The first petition calling for women's suffrage to the House of Lords was from the Sheffield Female Political Association in 1851. It was almost six decades later that British women got militant. They'd filled out every form, shaken every hand and attended every coffee morning, influencing the right people as best they could and doing everything they were told would win them the vote through a democratic process. The irony is, the democratic process isn't obliged to include you until you are included. So, they were kept in busywork by power structures that had no interest in doing more than supplying large quantities of red tape in which the women could entangle themselves.

In 1918 the British government gave *some* women the vote. They claimed it was in recognition of their war effort, and that the decision had nothing whatever to do with the women's civil disobedience. While it is certainly doubtful that it would have been achieved without the suffragists' patient and relentless lobbying of the government, politicians also knew that the suffragettes would go right back to militancy if they weren't given something. This was an opportunity to end the conflict without being seen to be 'giving in to terrorists'. Their militancy brought pressure to bear that no doubt helped seal the deal for those doing the more collegiate work.

This was obviously not cancel culture – it was organised civil disobedience and more akin to revolution. But it is a strong example of what happens if power is consistently misused, and the law claims to fight for justice but in fact protects the status quo. There has always been a power in people organising, boycotting and demanding change. Sometimes this has been as colossal and far-reaching as a decades-long campaign for universal suffrage. Sometimes it's as focused as wanting one individual to be brought to justice.

Take the way women have been treated in Hollywood, for example. For generations, actresses were abused and dismissed. Did they try reporting powerful men who had misused their power to intimidate and fire women who would not cooperate, sometimes even inflicting violence on them? Of course. They were dismissed, disbelieved and sidelined. Did they try taking men to court? Yes. They usually lost – or when they won, they were smeared as gold diggers. Did they try asking studios not to employ certain men? Of course. They found themselves unemployed. The reason there was a culture of silence was because women saw what happened to those who spoke out. They were usually branded as troublemakers and ousted from the community. Speaking out was an expensive luxury hardly anyone could afford.

The powerful have rarely if ever been interested in giving ground they didn't have to give. If relatively powerless people had been heard, they'd have had the conversation before now. This nuclear Armageddon-style, internet pile-on power is often the only option people feel they have. It seems like it's the marginalised who won't compromise but, in truth, it is the arrogant, famous, influential and dominant who've not given an inch in years. Much like the men in power who never intended to give women the vote, men in Hollywood were not going to give up abusing their power without a fight. Their first, second and third response was almost always, 'You can't tell me what to do, and it is not my problem if you don't like it, even if you suffer from my actions.'

A high-profile, landmark example of this is Bill Cosby. Sixty different women have an eerily similar story about Bill Cosby drugging them, sexually assaulting them (or attempting to), or corroborating testimony about him pressuring them to take a pill before they refused and escaped. Bill Cosby himself admitted under oath in 2005 to purchasing Quaaludes with the intention of giving them to young women he wished to have sex with. The first reports about Bill Cosby came in the 1990s. Women complained and took him to court in private lawsuits. Nothing was done to stop his never-ending abuse until women teamed up to provoke public opinion and force the judicial system to pay attention in 2014.[6]

Forty-five of the women came together so we could see all their faces on the front cover of *New York* magazine – and it was only then that Cosby lost his privileged place in society, was arrested and called to account. He is now out of prison on a legal loophole – but he will never again have the opportunities to do what he did with the same freedom. He will not be welcome in show business circles with all the perks that come with it. It's not impossible to find people who are so sentimental about the Huxtables that they're prepared to call between forty-five and sixty women lying gold-diggers – but enough people agreed that if the judicial system was failing all of these survivors, then the court of public opinion needed to step in. The front cover of a magazine is no one's first port of call.

Similarly, in 2017 the #MeToo movement brought to justice men who had engaged in long term, well-established criminal behaviour and it highlighted the systems that had enabled and hidden it – or even industry-wide open secrets – because our judiciary had failed us. The #MeToo movement is a response to a long practice of men in power sexually exploiting and abusing women and disrupting, or even effectively ending, their careers. It was a radical movement, but much like the case of the suffragettes, asking nicely, reporting men to the authorities and filling out the right paperwork wasn't working. The law is meant to be there to protect us and at least seek justice. When it fails, not in isolated ways, but as a trend, there is often a long-overdue uprising.

So – why don't we all pile on for justice?

Surround-sound power can force the hand of the authorities. What else can it do? Well, almost anything it wants. But there might be other examples of cancel culture or public justice that worry us, especially where the 'crime' is a perceived failure of morality, rather than a criminal offence. Without the authority of the statute books to refer to, in these cases, those calling for cancellation are not only casting themselves in the roles of guilt-deciding jury, prosecuting counsel and sentencing judge, they're actually deciding what is and is not worthy of being punished. The larger problem here is that the pillorying of individuals can upstage the structural problems themselves.

One interesting example to examine thoughtfully is that of comedic actress Ellie Kemper being made to apologise when photos of her as a nineteen-year-old debutante surfaced in 2021.

The photos were taken at a parade and ball in the American South, and the society which staged the event, the Veiled Prophet Organization (VPO) was founded in an environment of very serious white supremacy – thus Kemper was dubbed, for a while, a 'KKK Princess'.[7] Clearly, many Black Americans are rightly furious and disgusted at all sorts of organisations and power structures which have excluded, hurt and killed members of their community. In Ellie's response, which included a full and frank apology, she said, 'The century-old organization that hosted the debutante ball had an unquestionably racist, sexist, and elitist past. I was not aware of this history at the time, but ignorance is no excuse. I was old enough to have educated myself before getting involved.'

One question I want to examine is this – was Ellie, as a teenager in 1999, likely to have been better than her community and to some extent was she an unwilling or at least unwitting, sexually objectifed pawn in an unpleasant, larger game? The

VPO used some very disturbing imagery including 'the veiled prophet' himself, a ceremonial figure who originally appeared in white robes, a pointed hat and held two guns. Obviously very Klan-like. This imagery changed over time, but continued to be very creepy. More recent pictures show the prophet in sparkly, papal-style robes with a bridal-style veil and something like a kettle on his head (as he would've been dressed in 1999). The whole thing looked quite Monty Python.

However, this belies its sinister origins. The VPO itself was founded in 1878 in response to white and Black railroad and factory workers teaming up to go on strike to protest wage cuts, child labour and long hours. The founders established this legend and pageantry, which was paraded through the streets, to inspire fear in the workers and reassert their white, elitist power. At the ball, daughters of these rich men were presented, and this intimidating faceless 'prophet' would crown one of these teenagers his Queen of Love and Beauty.

Kemper says she didn't know the origins. We should consider whether that was possible. There had been lots of anti-racist protests about it in the 1960s and 1970s, but Kemper wasn't born till 1980. Many teenage girls in my hometown were Freemason* debutantes and it was just what you did if your parents signed you up and I honestly don't imagine any of them looked into the history of the society. All the buzz was about getting a long, white frock. It's important to remember that in 1999 the internet was still in its infancy and Google was not yet a verb. So, it is possible she didn't know and, although a

* I'm not suggesting Freemasons are akin to the VPO, but they are famously a society who hold secrets and sometimes influence and no one in my home town asked any questions. The Freemasons have recently been accused of blocking the career trajectory of women and men of colour in the police force in the UK, for example. https://www.theguardian.com/uk-news/2017/dec/31/freemasons-blocking-reform-police-federation-leader

freshman in college, was still a teen going along with what was expected. How did she feel when a masked, robed older man dubbed her his Queen of Love and Beauty and she had to sit next to him as a king-like figure? I'm not saying, let's feel sorry for the pretty, white, rich teen who got the crown. I am saying that her age and gender are also a factor here in this disturbing role play. In any other context, we'd be concerned for her, right?

If we are to hold her to account, my larger question is this – are we holding the lawyers, dentists, retail professionals, accountants and full-time parents equally responsible and pillorying them for attending the same ball? Or belonging to other clubs and societies that were founded in active white supremacy? If a dentist's career is not disrupted, why is an actor, (especially one not known for political activism), being made to apologise before she can continue to work? Are we making an example of one person, who has visibility, to be a warning to the others? Well, yes, to some extent, that's how cancel culture works. Sometimes the way the machine operates is by making examples of visible individuals as a morality tale for others. For a short time, if you have a profile, your life can become a parable.

In fact, Kemper is not the first celebrity to come unstuck for participating in the VPO. In 1968, the civil rights group ACTION threatened to stage protests against musician Count Basie (who was sixty-four at the time) unless he pulled out of performing at the Veiled Prophet parade.[8] He later withdrew 'for personal reasons'. This demonstrates that boycotts of the past were not always brought to bear by the right. The difference here is the historical nature of Kemper's participation. She was required to speak out against the organisation and its racist roots and you may well say, 'Good – so she should. She's benefited from being part of that elite, racist society that didn't allow Black people till the late 1970s, bar trying to use Count Basie and other Black musicians as a shield' but it's difficult to articulate why someone associated with comedy television programmes needs to do that, while the teachers educating our children, the social workers advising our families or the judges sentencing our community members do not. It seems extremely arbitrary.

I'm not suggesting we round up all the dentists and therapists to make them explain or justify their communities' histories or their teenage infractions and mistakes, but I do think there are people who have more of a direct hand in shaping our infrastructure and we do not seem to feel entitled to bring them out into the town square in the same way. Some of them were not debutantes being marshalled into a weird, sexualised crown. They were, quite literally, the men behind the mask. They were the adults keeping the tradition alive, knowing its origins only too well. So why are we going after a random comedy actor? What is the relevance?

Part of the issue is the parasocial relationship that many people have with the celebrities they see on their TV screens and in their social media accounts. We feel we know Kemper and that gives us an extra emotional stake in her past misdemeanours. But this relationship is strictly one-way and largely illusory. I imagine if Ellie's children had seen these pictures and learned about the VPO, they might have asked for and deserved an explanation. I absolutely would understand if Ellie's colleagues or friends asked her if she understood the implications of the history and her personal experience with it.

Ellie Kemper was in *The Office* – she wasn't running *for* office, or forming public policy, or standing for the school board. In those situations, it makes sense to background check someone's moral credentials that speak to their character, as long as we are not being puritanical or assuming that because they shoplifted at fourteen, they are likely to embezzle now. But who benefits from interrogating sitcom actors?

I am not suggesting that this kind of public scrutiny is too punitive a thing for a white person to go through. White people being uncomfortable isn't the worst thing for us. If you're white and you felt like you couldn't say anything right during the summer of 2020 and it left you feeling guilty, sometimes personally defensive and uneasy all at once, then may I suggest it was good for you. I think what we white people were experiencing during that time was the emotional power base not being with us. Now imagine living your whole life with the emotional, fiscal, legal and judicial and social power base being against you. It was an object lesson and we should take it as such and remember it viscerally.

I am not arguing 'Not fair!' for Kemper as much as I am saying that singling out someone on TV as 'the problem' provides a salve that feels like something is being done about racism, when it is not addressing the symptoms or the cause. A forty-two-year-old Hollywood actress apologising for participating in a weird, sexist ritual twenty-three years ago, that probably feels like something creepy and objectifying that happened to her, more than something she chose to do (even if she willingly volunteered for it at the time) is misdirection away from the real structural racist, classist problems. Maybe we need to ask, 'Who was in charge?' not 'Who's on network television?'

However, in 2021 the Veiled Prophet parade and ball was cancelled and it has not been held again. The media attention about Kemper was surely a large contributing factor in that. You could argue that's progress. But . . . it was replaced by a suspiciously similar 'good old boy' celebration called the 'Happy Birthday America' Parade, and the veiled prophet was switched out for Archibald the bald eagle as the emblem of the US. It's a win but a small one that's hard to swallow, underlining in red ink its reinforcement of old-fashioned values that silently endorse what came before. As journalist Devin Thomas O'Shea wrote in *The Nation* at the time, 'The question is, will the political and economic order that the veiled prophet represents be dismantled? Will justice be constructed in its place? I hope so, but the network of power which the veil represents is still there.'[9] That is the problem. It's a little like wanting to get rid of a monarch but instead getting rid of the stamps with his head on them and feeling like you've done it.

Emma Dabiri (again in her book *What White People Can Do Next*) in arguing for coalition over allyship writes:

> The theorist, poet and philosopher Fred Moten describes coalition as emerging out of your recognition that it's fucked up for you, in the same way that we've already recognized that it's fucked up for us.

She also points to Fred Hampton, the charismatic young leader of the Chicago chapter of the Black Panthers creating a Rainbow Coalition between the Black Panthers, the Puerto Rican Young Lords and the working-class Southern whites of the Young Patriots to organise collectively against racism, police brutality, inequality and injustice. She cites other examples like these and goes on to say,

> Today's allyship fails to build the necessary coalitions identified by Moten . . . it lacks the vision of Hampton. With its reliance on information rather than knowledge, its fetishizing of privilege without any clear means of transferral, as well as the ways in which it actively reinforces whiteness, allyship is not only not up to the task, it is in many ways counterproductive.

Dabiri argues that today's version of allyship offers charity rather than solidarity and focuses on individual microaggressions and interpersonal slights, which comes at the expense of challenging deeply ingrained structural inequality. She posits that teaming up with those who can see that they have interconnected oppressions, even in very different ways, is essential to make meaningful change.

With this in mind, I can't help feeling that it could have been more constructive to ask Kemper to join a protest against the VPO, as someone who was once a part of it, and use her high-profile influence to replace the parade with something actually anti-racist and anti-sexist that the community could really benefit from. Instead of making her an avatar and a satisfying head on a platter for a week, she could have been asked to team up and go after the structure, even being invited to speak about her experience as a young woman participating in it and how she might reframe it now. Of course, Kemper could have initiated this coalition too. Either way, making the VPO the focus of the campaign, rather than an individual, would have highlighted power structures.

Kemper, alongside a coalition of those affected within her home town, speaking to her former community about making real change, could have been really powerful. She could still have acknowledged her part in it as an invitation for her community to also offer amends, but what is most important is what is built from there and I am not sure a rebranded parade was the best outcome. If someone looks like they might be open to a coalition, making a first approach that assumes a positive outcome is always a good idea if you want change and progress, not just theatre. There's always a second chance to get angry. There's not always an easy second chance to make a powerful, active alliance.

This is not to say that holding individuals to public account fairly arbitrarily hasn't changed the culture a little. There have been many stories of men contacting women to apologise, changing their conduct on movie sets, and generally panicking their way towards better behaviour. There must be many men who behaved as badly if not worse than some of the men who aren't working any more. Presumably, they lie awake at night worrying that someone will come forward and something will come out. They abused their power when they could, and now anxiety is with them for life. You may think that's more than fair.

But where it comes to excluding people long term from their industry and livelihood, when nothing criminal has occurred, and there is no due process, we need to examine how we're going about things. Recently a disgraced comedian (who'd issued an apology) was coming to the UK to perform some shows. A message went around on WhatsApp groups saying that a certain venue had allowed him to hire the space and called for other comedians (including me) to petition the venue, saying they'd never perform there again if they went ahead with it. The venue in question reversed their decision and cancelled his booking because of that pressure.

I didn't really feel safe to have this conversation with other comedians on the thread for fear of being seen as un-feminist and risking exclusion myself. But this is the dialogue I had with myself:

- *Do we want to live in a society where a person is permanently blocked from working?*
- *He's already had far more opportunities than I have though. Am I being 'censored' by not being offered the TV specials, airtime and budget he's been given?*
- *Well sure, but in this case, he just wants to rent a room so people who want to pay to see him can pay to see him.*
- *But then he blocked opportunities for women and denied*

their stories were true when he could've acknowledged his power abuses years ago.

- *So are we going to do to him what he did to others? Will that make it right? Aren't progressives always arguing for rehabilitation rather than punishment? I don't believe in prison – or at least the way it's currently run and structured – because it is inhumane and just hardens people anyway. So why should I believe in this kind of exclusion?*
- *Yeah I don't believe in punishment for punishment's sake, but I also feel for the women he hurt. What if they see us embracing him like nothing happened?*
- *Do you have to embrace him to allow him to use a space you might also use? Couldn't you just not go to the show? If no one goes to the show, then he might realise he's got to find a new profession.*
- *Well good. He should. He's lost his right to speak.*
- *What if he runs out of money and goes to get a job in a coffee shop? Will people picket the coffee shop? He's a famous man. Won't some women who buy coffee there feel uncomfortable?*
- *Yeah, probably.*
- *So do we need this man to be out on the street? Will nothing do but that? He has children. Should they suffer and not be provided for?*
- *He's rich. He's fine.*
- *What if all the women he hurt sue him? What if his accountant defrauds him? What if he weren't rich? For the sake of the hypothetical, should this man be able to get a job anywhere? Or should he die in penury? Is that punishment greater than his crime? What kind of crime means someone should become homeless and not be supported by society? What kind of crime means that your*

friends should be ostracised if they don't ostracise you? Who is beyond rehabilitation? We don't believe in the death penalty. We don't believe in Victorian punishments of people dying of poverty.

- *But the truth is he will still be able to do comedy in certain places. We just don't have to make it easy for him.*
- *Oh, he just won an award! He's fine.*
- *So cancel culture isn't real?*
- *But he's still being shunned and shamed. You know what that's like – personally . . . He's still walking into green rooms and having people walk out without looking at him.*
- *Sure, but you can't make women look him in the eye and shake him warmly by the hand when they feel he's reneged on his apology.*
- *But if everyone ostracises someone, what does that do to a person?*

Please know that I know that a lot of these men made sure the women they hurt were socially and professionally ostracised to keep them away from their shared community, so they could continue their abuse streak! It is still important to know what we are doing when we participate in it. Abusive men doing it doesn't absolve us when we do it like we're entitled to make 'tit for tat' a public policy. I decided to find out what happens in our brain when we're ostracised.

Being socially excluded can be immensely stressful. It threatens four fundamental psychological needs: self-esteem, belonging, control and a sense of meaningful existence.[10] When we experience this kind of severe stress, our brain releases an enzyme that attacks the hippocampus, which is responsible for regulating synapses.[11] As a result, our brain does the following:

- Reduces the field of view and focuses only on a narrow span of what it must do to survive. Myelin sheathing increases on existing neural pathways, and we are less likely to consider or try new solutions.
- Shrinks its working memory, so that it is not distracted by other ideas, bits of information or stray thoughts. This means we can't problem-solve as well as usual. (Think of the panic from contestants on a TV game show: the information is there but they cannot access it.)
- Becomes less creative. With less grey matter and modified synapses, we experience fewer ideas, thoughts, and we are less able to make connections between bits of information, so our capacity to create is reduced.
- Increases cell density in the amygdala, making us more likely to be reactive rather than self-controlled.
- Becomes less likely to connect with others. Fight, flight, freeze or faint are not 'sharing' types of activities. When the synapses have been modified in this way, we appear grumpy and unsociable.
- Activates regions that are also associated with physical pain, which may help to explain why people report that they are 'hurt' when others devalue or reject them.[12] Psychology professor Kipling Williams describes social exclusion as 'a social agony that the brain registers as physical pain'.[13]

Neuroscientist Daniel Reisel also presents the case for connection and restorative justice over punitive justice. Instead of imprisoning criminals, an alternative is to help their brains 'rehabilitate'. If our brains can develop new neural pathways post-injury, perhaps we can develop new morality wiring too? Putting the brains of sociopathic killers (who agreed to be studied) under MRI machines, Reisel discovered that many of them had a deficient amygdala which likely led to an underdeveloped sense of empathy. But he also emphasises that brains are capable of changing. And so, rather than subjecting violent criminals to further stressful social isolation – which may very well exacerbate the neural condition which gave them sociopathic tendencies in the first place – Reisel's work shows that for some people at least, restorative justice programmes that bring a survivor (or loved ones of a victim) and a perpetrator together in a safe and controlled setting can really work to stimulate a deficient amygdala and create a sense of moral responsibility which wasn't there before.[14]

If you're addicted to abusing power, the worst thing society can do is isolate you with other embittered men who've also been excommunicated because they abused power. Leaving you alone will not rehabilitate you. It will make you worse. It will leave you in fight or flight, making false apologies in public at best, while exacerbating your bitterness with other excluded people in private.

Brené Brown, as you may know, is a research professor at the University of Houston who has spent the past two decades studying courage, vulnerability, shame and empathy, and is the author of six acclaimed books on these subjects. She defines guilt as our inner voice saying, 'I've done a bad thing' and shame as our inner voice saying, 'I'm a bad person'. In her book *Daring Greatly*, she uses the example of accidentally standing a friend up for lunch and says some people think that a little shame is no bad thing because it'll help us get our act together next time; she explains that that's not the case:

> When we feel shame, we are most likely to protect ourselves by blaming something or someone, rationalizing our lapse, offering a disingenuous apology, or hiding out. Rather than apologizing, we blame our friend and rationalize forgetting:

'I told you I was really busy. This wasn't a good day for me.' Or we apologize half-heartedly and think to ourselves, 'Whatever. If she knew how busy I am, she'd be apologizing.' Or we see who is calling and don't answer the phone at all, and then when we finally can't stop dodging our friend, we lie: 'Didn't you get my e-mail? I canceled in the morning. You should check your spam folder.'[15]

She looks at the impact of shame in the family unit and within big corporations and concludes that putting people in the emotional stocks is as barbaric as putting people in medieval stocks. It might modify their behaviour, but it absolutely will not make your family, company or society a positive place to be. It will have people hiding thoughts and behaviours from you and looking for exit strategies. It cannot and will not create a healthy, thriving, creative, collegiate place where individuals can grow, learn from their mistakes and form better, more empathetic bonds.

Shame breeds fear. It crushes our tolerance for vulnerability, thereby killing engagement, innovation, creativity, productivity, and trust. And worst of all, if we don't know what we're looking for, shame can ravage our organizations before we see one outward sign of a problem. Shame works like termites in a house. It's hidden in the dark behind the walls and constantly eating away at our infrastructure, until one day the stairs suddenly crumble. Only then do we realize that it's only a matter of time before the walls come tumbling down.[16]

She explains that the signs that shame has already permeated a culture include:

> Blaming, gossiping, favoritism, name-calling, and harassment ... A more obvious sign is when shame becomes an outright management tool. Is there evidence of people in leadership roles bullying others, criticizing subordinates in front of colleagues, delivering public reprimands, or setting up reward systems that intentionally belittle, shame, or humiliate people?[17]

These tactics feel like quick fixes, but Brown is clear that they will erode societal foundations rather than build strong new ones.

When famous, wealthy men who abused their power when they thought it could not be taken away, find their careers stalling because 'time's up', it's hard to feel that there isn't just cause, but we need to allow those men to keep some support networks around them – and if we don't, we can't be surprised when they become even more toxic than they were to begin with. While individuals are free to boycott or avoid, harassing others to abandon them is unhealthy and counterproductive. They will have friends, family and maybe even colleagues who wish to emotionally support them and they may well be processing how they came to abuse their power in conversation with those people. This is an important part of their process. I interviewed writer and activist Clementine Morrigan, who is best known for her deep analysis of cancel culture. She pointed out:

> The way that cancel culture works is that if a person has been accused of something, there is now a social campaign to isolate them from everything meaningful in life. And we act as if this is just self-evidently, obviously, a good thing, that people who have done seriously bad things should not be a part of society. We take them away from society so that

they can't hurt other people, and we punish them. And so my question is, do either of those strategies actually produce safety or justice? And my argument is no, they don't.

If you want someone who has done something seriously wrong to actually change their behaviour, what they need is help and resources in order to do that. If you strip away everything that they have in their life, their community, their support, their friends, and also their financial stability, how are they ever going to do the work that it takes to take responsibility for what they have done? Also, if you drive people out of your community, they go somewhere else – because people are social beings, and they will continue to try to seek out relationships. I don't think that it creates the incentive for actual accountability. It just moves the problem on somewhere else.

Morrigan also points out in her work that there is an assumption of guilt that cannot be interrogated in any way. The accused has to 'take accountability', whether there is any validity in the accusations or there are two complex sides to the story. She speaks about experiencing being spuriously ostracised by her former community for perceived minor infractions (not sufficiently posting on social media about specific social issues which Morrigan says she has clear evidence of doing). She is currently experiencing ongoing harassment, including, at times, physical violence and destruction of her property (including having coffee poured on her handmade zines by a masked man at a fair and having her tyres slashed) from those who claim to want social justice.

The problem is exacerbated if a vast gulf exists between the often high-profile target of the accusations and the partial or sometimes total anonymity of the accusers. Yomi Adegoke, journalist and author of critically acclaimed novel *The List*, a story of internet anonymity and accusations that result in ostracisation, joined our conversation. Adegoke said:

> Anonymity isn't inherently in and of itself a bad thing when we're dealing with allegations. I completely understand why it is often necessary, in order to protect survivors' privacy and mitigate the potential of further abuse. But where I think things start to fall apart a little bit is the fact that we're dealing with the internet. And especially coming from a journalistic background, as I do, internet anonymity and anonymity in other contexts aren't the same thing. The amount of checks and balances and fact-checking and everything that would have had to have been done for the allegations against various high-profile men to make it to the point of a documentary, to make it to the point of a credible newspaper article, those standards are not what we're holding anonymous tweets to.
>
> And I think what's frustrating is right now in the discourse, we're struggling to hold multiple ideas in our heads at once and understand that more than one thing can be true. For instance, it is true that many disenfranchised people (largely women), who have survived abuse have been able to use those channels to finally, after years of silence, be able to hold their abusers accountable. It's simultaneously true that the internet is the Wild West. The level of regulation is practically close to none. And any of the three of us in this conversation right now could say anything about one of the others anonymously. And the barrier to entry in order to do that is zero. And the only thing that is stopping us from doing that is sanity. And that is a really, really, really low barrier, essentially.

Wait . . . are we the bad guys?

While, as discussed, we don't tend to search out establishment professionals in our communities for historical offences, that isn't to say that 'regular people' without high-profile jobs in the entertainment industry aren't also the focus of cancel culture. What are the implications when someone without the protections of wealth and celebrity are targeted? For example, what about when tutors at universities or teachers at drama schools living pay cheque to pay cheque are fired at short notice without references? Perhaps they've been accused of holding views or using language that students find unacceptable. Sometimes their teaching methods seem insensitive to a younger generation. Perhaps some of it was historic or standards have changed and they've not moved with the times. Some teachers I know have been left on the breadline after a lifetime of service to an institution because they've been defensive and apologised badly or not at all until it was too late. Other teachers have delivered slick, fast apologies that have been accepted even though it's unlikely they've reflected much or had time to change a lifetime of thinking. Frankly, I think we are in danger of rewarding a performance, rather than giving a human being a reasonable amount of time to consider and digest how they might adapt to a fast-changing world after decades of practice and the assumption of status in the classroom.

There are also times when I fear that students don't always know what will build the resilience they need for their craft and teachers are sometimes correct to push back and encourage them to try things that make them uncomfortable. This is especially true in drama schools where students do not wish to engage with a text or an exercise and complain about teachers who push them to try. I have spoken to both students and teachers who have told me this. No one should be made to do anything without their consent but sometimes we need to be encouraged to go further than we want to, in the same way that physical exercise means tearing our muscles a little to make them stronger. We don't want to exercise so hard that we can't move the next day but if we don't move at all, we can't expect to build our strength.

There is much evidence that a little discomfort builds resilience.[18] The American Psychological Society's definition of resilience is a process of 'bouncing back' from difficult experiences and 'adapting well in the face of adversity, trauma, tragedy, threats or significant sources of stress'.[19] People who report a higher level of resilience often have lower levels of anxiety, psychological distress and mixed anxiety/depression.[20] It can even have a mitigating effect on depression caused by childhood or adult trauma.[21] Teachers at drama schools may be expanding a student's ability to dig deep and explore an exhausting array of emotions in a character or helping them learn to bounce back so they can survive in an industry fraught with rejection. It is hard to push yourself into places of discomfort and even more difficult if you won't approach a text which might trigger traumatic feelings.

This can put teachers who live with little financial security in an extremely difficult position. How do they do their job well and hold on to it, if students tell the academy they're paying tuition fees to, they won't work with a teacher who pushes them to do things they're uncomfortable with? This is not to say that some teachers in drama schools don't have unnecessarily harsh and emotionally abusive methods and should not be messing with the heads of nineteen-year-old students.

I've worked with teachers who have abused their power and humiliated students which has sometimes done irreversible damage. There are some drama schools where that kind of abuse has not just been overlooked, it's been encouraged. I am not excusing or condoning this. In fact, I've spoken out against it and tried to shield students from it. It is definitely not for teachers to provide the trauma or threats themselves – they should help students build resilience and greater emotional access in a craft that deals largely with emotions. However, every cancellation that has resulted in a job loss or 'early retirement' to avoid conflict with students has not been just or correct. Cancellation doesn't just happen to movie stars; it can leave people with ordinary jobs in dire financial straits.

There are many young people with marginalised identities who operate in communities run by those who identify as Social Justice Warriors. Their social circle is there. Their activism is there. Usually their accommodation is there, and sometimes even their livelihood is tied to their community of like-minded friends. Often people in these communities are living and working with or for stammily (chosen family) and have nowhere else to go and their cancellation can lead to homelessness and extremely poor mental health.

Sometimes those most vocal or influential in the group will hold the others to the highest possible standards. Certain academic language must be used. Tiny infractions are punished harshly: lapsing from veganism in minor ways, trans people associating with other trans people who have been found wanting or ideological doctrines not being followed to the letter. It is extremely common for criticism to escalate into enforced apologies and 'taking accountability'. Sometimes the apology is made but it is declared not sincere and only made for reasons of self-preservation. While the original impulse may come from a positive place – the desire to create an equal and equitable society – the upshot can be an environment of constantly shifting goalposts, and the barriers to navigating it safely becoming ever higher.

I am frequently contacted by those on the inside and outside of these circles, asking that I 'stop following' someone on social media or disassociate myself from someone who's been a guest on my podcast because of a perceived infraction. Sometimes I am informed that their name is circulating on a list of people who have been deemed to have views that are unacceptable or have not spoken out on a political issue in the way that the group finds acceptable. Recently I was sent 'the wrong name' as two artists with the same first name were confused. This feels almost identical to right-wing McCarthyism to me.

The rush to judgement can be extreme. I recently received a direct message from a stranger that read: 'Fuck you if you say you're a feminist and you haven't posted about [this issue].' I replied with all the content I'd made about the issue on my podcast and screenshot the posts I'd made on Instagram that she couldn't see because of shadow banning.* She apologised profusely and we had a lovely chat. She was actually an empathetic person but she had learned to operate in a culture that insists on compliance and shoots first and asks questions later, to extend Yomi Adegoke's Wild West metaphor. It is a world in which there is an assumed entitlement over when and how other people speak and the constant threat of shaming and shunning.

Not for the first time in this book, this all reminds me heavily of the way the Jehovah's Witnesses are run. Remember, we were told the spiritual food came from the Governing Body, directed by Jehovah's heavenly holy spirit. The key quality required from the brothers and sisters in the congregation was unquestioning obedience. Personal study was only to be done from Watchtower Society publications. You will be welcomed

---

* Shadow banning is the practice of social media platforms blocking or partially blocking a user's posts to their followers, usually due to the sharing of political content.

warmly at the beginning and for that period you can ask questions, but once you start to be accepted by the congregation, questions will be treated with suspicion. Answers to questions are final. Of course, in reality, as I explained in our first conversation, everyone had doubts about some things the Watchtower Society said, but we knew if we expressed those doubts we would be shunned – so we lied and said we didn't. Some of their doctrines had massive holes in logic but we all lied to ourselves and each other, pretending we couldn't see them.

It's a doomsday cult and there had been any number of 'soft launches' for Armageddon with the dates sailing by. We had all been taught to believe that the generation who witnessed the First World War would still be with us when Jehovah brought about Judgement Day, but as that prophecy became more and more implausible, they decided to change the meaning of the word generation to mean 'many generations'. Their explanation for that has been altered any number of times. Each time they present this 'New Light', the rank and file have to nod and smile like 'the proles' in George Orwell's novel *1984*, repeating 'We have always been at war with Eastasia' (despite our recollection to the contrary) or in our case: 'We've always believed "generation" has meant: contemporary people of a certain historical period, who share identifying characteristics without reference to any specific amount of time.'

I know that some active Jehovah's Witnesses find this risible. Sometimes behind closed doors or anonymously online, the rank and file admit this to each other. Many do not believe any of the Watchtower Society's doctrines, but have too much to lose and so cannot admit publicly that they know they are in a high control group. This is such a phenomenon that there is an underground movement of those who identify as PIMO, which stands for 'physically in, mentally out'. Some believe that as much as 30 per cent of the Jehovah's Witness community is

PIMO. Of course this is impossible to verify as it's an underground population, but the anonymous online discourse would suggest it's no small number. I think that many progressives in our society are effectively PIMO about various contemporary conversations including the practice of cancellation, and they're only discussing it in their smallest and most intimate stamms. They're pretending to believe doctrine. They're pretending that they endorse the punitive shunning of other liberals. They are pretending that they understand and agree with all the changes in the latest social movements without the ability to think or talk things through or ask important questions – because they cannot afford to lose their community.

This observation, based on my religious experience, is borne out by research. Pippa Norris writes in her 2021 academic paper 'Cancel Culture: Myth or Reality' that arguments against cancel culture 'can be dismissed as rhetorical dog whistles devoid of substantive meaning, myths designed to fire up the MAGA faithful, outrage progressives, and distract from urgent real-world problems.'

However, she finds in her research that something else may be at work. She explains: 'Within academia, scholars most likely to perceive "silencing" are mismatched or non-congruent cases, where they are "fish-out-of-water". Her findings are based on empirical survey evidence within the discipline of political science. Her data is derived from a global survey in 2019, involving almost 2500 scholars studying or working in over a hundred countries.

She finds that:

> As predicted, in post-industrial societies, characterized by predominantly liberal social cultures, like the US, Sweden, and UK, right-wing scholars were most likely to perceive that they faced an increasingly chilly climate. By contrast,

in developing societies characterized by more traditional moral cultures, like Nigeria, it was left-wing scholars who reported that a cancel culture had worsened.

She points out that this tracks with Noelle-Neumann's 1974 'spiral of silence' thesis, 'where mainstream values in any group gradually flourish to become the predominant culture, while, due to social pressures, dissenting minority voices become muted. The ratchet effect eventually muffles contrarians.'

Norris' study finds that cancel culture is not a myth but that 'scholars may be less willing to speak up to defend their moral beliefs if they believe that their views are not widely shared by colleagues or the wider society to which they belong.' In other words, when we normalise shaming and shunning for our own ends (whether we think it's justified or not) it will be weaponised against us and those like us.[22] Context is everything.

Who shall cancel the cancellers themselves?

Old-school left-wing politician Tony Benn, sadly no longer with us, once offered five essential questions to ask any powerful person, known as *The Five Essential Questions of Democracy*:

1. 'What power have you got?'
2. 'Where did you get it from?'
3. 'In whose interests do you use it?'
4. 'To whom are you accountable?'
5. 'How do we get rid of you?'[23]

Answering those questions on behalf of a social media mob racing to bring down a pop star who said something stupid into a live mic provides some pretty stomach-churning answers:

1. We can end careers and remove people from their social support system.*
2. We gave it to ourselves.
3. We use it to try to address imbalances in power structures but in doing so must be aware we are creating new, unfettered ones.
4. We are answerable to no one except the potential sea-change of the stamm.
5. We can't be got rid of.

This state of affairs is partly sustained because of what Dr Olúfẹ́mi O. Táíwò, associate professor of philosophy at Georgetown University, describes in his book *Elite Capture: How the Powerful Took Over Identity Politics (and Everything Else)* as the politics of deference. He explains:

> A prime example of deference politics is the call to 'listen to the most affected' or 'center the most marginalized,' now ubiquitous in many academic and activist circles. These calls have never sat well with me. In my experience as an academic and organizer, when people have said they needed to 'listen to the most affected,' it wasn't usually because they intended to set up Skype calls to refugee camps or to collaborate with houseless people.[24]

Taiwo goes on to argue that actually 'centering the most marginalized' would require a different approach entirely, in a world where 1.6 billion people live in slum-like housing and a further 100 million have no homes at all, and 2.2 billion do not

* In some cases the whole thing. When young queer people only have their stammily or older teachers find colleagues who love and agree with them withdrawing so as not to 'go down with the ship', they can be left entirely alone.

have safely managed drinking water. He writes that what people refer to as 'centering the most marginalized', in his experience

> has usually meant handing conversational authority and attentional goods to whoever is already in the room and appears to fit a social category associated with some form of oppression – regardless of what they have or have not actually experienced, or what they do or do not actually know about the matter at hand.[25]

This procedure of deferring to the closest person who can be dubbed a moral authority stops conversation and therefore stops action. Táíwò points out:

> For those who defer, the habit can supercharge moral cowardice, as the norms of deference provide social cover for the abdication of responsibility. It displaces onto individual heroes, a hero class, or a mythicized past the work that is ours to do in the present. Their perspective may be clearer on this or that specific matter, but their overall point of view isn't any less particular or constrained by history than ours.[26]

Deferring in this way makes select people accountable where we all should be. Furthermore, it projects 'a sanitized and thoroughly fictional caricature of them' and gives them a burden to carry. He argues that deferring to collectives or their culture works the same way. Táíwò is not arguing we go back to asking the poshest white guys and leaving relevant voices out of the conversation. He's arguing for critical thinking, debate, for a combination of lived experience and expertise (sometimes one and the same thing!) and for us to ask who is not in the room or on the thread.

If we do not hold ourselves to answer Tony Benn's questions

honestly, and instead consistently defer to the most elite members of marginalised groups, we are in danger of ending up in an intellectual high control group with people deferring, keeping doubts and questions to themselves, reciting the party line and then moving on.

Are they a narcissist or are you just breaking up with them?

Sometimes a romantic break-up is brought into the public sphere and arguments the couple had are used as evidence that one of them harmed the other. This leads to calls for cancellation and public pile-ons. Of course, there are times when real abuse has occurred (which we will explore soon) but there are other times when it seems like the first person to publicly say 'narcissist' wins. Clementine Morrigan points out that all romantic relationships involve boundaries that need to be respected and needs that people want met. Sometimes a relationship doesn't work out because someone's boundaries mean they cannot meet their partner's needs and a compromise can't be reached. While that can feel extremely painful and trigger very real attachment issues, she points out that it does not always mean harm has occurred and it is not the definition of abuse.[27]

Let's interrogate that idea further and think about the beginning of a romantic relationship. When you hugely fancy someone and/or are falling in love with them, your desire to meet your new lover's needs is often bountiful and your regular boundaries are usually lowered to some extent. You think about this new person all the time, want to plan or make special things for them and you might have to stop yourself from messaging them too much. You can spend hours on the phone and days in bed with them. You can feel elated, compelled and like nothing else matters.

When this first flush of excitement and attraction has worn off, you might find it harder to meet their needs. Cooking a meal might feel like a mid-week chore rather than a midsummer night's dream. You might also restore some of your more usual boundaries: 'Sorry – can't talk. At work. Text you later x'. That does not mean you've 'love bombed' someone and are now withholding affection and being abusive. It might mean that you inadvertently advertised a way of life that you cannot or do not wish to sustain and so, very probably, did your romantic partner. Many relationships end for these reasons. It is common for people to become defensive and communicate less, or less well, as they exit a relationship. It is wonderful to be able to end a relationship with kindness and appreciation, but it is usually messy and emotionally difficult to detach yourself. That's why Taylor Swift, Olivia Rodrigo and Adele are so wealthy.

Sometimes the 'three signs that someone is a narcissist' that are reductively shared in a square on Instagram along with naming and shaming an individual, could also be 'three signs that someone is going through a break-up and is putting up walls to protect themselves'. We can't allow simplistic online memes to shape our narratives when it comes to complicated human relationships. (We should also acknowledge that narcissistic personality disorder usually develops out of a childhood trauma-coping mechanism and the way we throw it around as an insult means it's hard for people to come forward and admit they're struggling with it – which doesn't help the dating pool or anyone in it!)[28]

It has become common to allow a therapist to hazard a diagnosis for an ex they've never met. Most likely the therapist is just helpfully offering possibilities about the dynamics in a given relationship, but I frequently see these diagnoses shared as pretty conclusive and often the person is named or made identifiable to their community in some way. It is important to remember that the therapist is only hearing one side of a very subjective story. It can be soothing to hear: 'It was not your fault. They were incapable of truly loving anyone', rather than examining what went wrong and what patterns you might have propped up or participated in or even just accept that this person wasn't right for you. These things are hard to do when you're at your lowest, feeling rejected and bereft.

When we are in a break-up, we are disbanding our most intimate stamm: our stamm of two.* The same things that we discussed that happen to our brain when we are socially ostracised are very likely happening in this situation – and that is why we experience so much pain. You feel like you're being cancelled by the person who knows you best and is meant to love you the most. It is easy to assume if we are in emotional agony, someone has caused it and that person must be the person who we are breaking up with. If they are making us feel like this, they must be an abuser – but that is not necessarily the case.

Not necessarily, but sometimes it very much is! Some people do love bomb, gaslight, manipulate and emotionally abuse, which is precisely why it's so important that we read deeply and widely and learn what these terms really mean.[29] It is also important that we examine what actually happened in our relationship and have some outside consultation and time to gain perspective. It is important that we do not minimise abuse by conflating it with bad behaviour, incompatibility or even, in most cases, infidelity.

In 2015, emotional and psychological abuse in a domestic setting became a criminal offence in the UK, precisely because it is so damaging.

---

* Even if you're polyamorous, the person you're breaking up with is usually part of a twosome. If you're in a throuple, I'm sure it's even more complex!

Specific examples of this kind of abuse include:

- humiliating a partner in front of others
- calling a partner insulting names, such as 'stupid', 'disgusting' or 'worthless'
- getting angry in a way that is frightening to a partner
- threatening to hurt a partner, people they care about, or pets
- the abuser threatening to harm themselves when upset with their partner
- saying things like, 'If I can't have you, then no one can'[30]

These are just some examples and of course there are many ways of degrading, humiliating or threatening someone (and some of them can be more subtle than this) but we must think critically about the differences between someone being a really bad boyfriend (for example), two people being highly incompatible, difficult dynamics at the end of a relationship and someone being abusive.

It's important to note that all of these things might be involved in any given dynamic. Some people in romantic relationships can replicate emotionally abusive patterns they saw modelled in their home or community without recognising that they're toxic, manipulative and harmful. You may not intend to be abusive and yet you may be harming your partner. Just as we have to analyse whether someone was truly being a perpetrator, we have to analyse whether we have, at times, been unintentionally but carelessly abusive.[31] It's possible that a relationship has such an unhealthy dynamic that both parties are being abusive to each other.

If someone actively intends to groom, isolate, humiliate, emotionally torture and control, this is sociopathic and deeply dangerous. This is also a gendered issue. If a man is being abusive to a woman (either consciously or because of what he has internalised as acceptable behaviour) there is the extra very real threat of physical violence, remembering one woman is killed every four days in the UK, by her current or former intimate partner. By contrast, in 2023, three men in the UK were killed by a current or former female partner.[32] Furthermore, in the majority of cases where a woman kills her former or current partner, it is in self-defence and/or the man has been the primary abuser.[33]

It is crucial we don't allow TikTok memes and armchair diagnoses to conflate bad relationships, big arguments and painful break-ups with abuse and allow that to cut individuals off from their communities when they are also grieving the end of their relationship. It is also important because real, dangerous, serial abusers get lost in the noise and that can have terrifying and even fatal consequences. Feminism absolutely needs us to think critically about this and have complex discussions with each other so that we are truly taking care of those who are suffering and in danger. It is also important that we think very carefully about our motives for going public – online and/or in our wider social circle – about what happened within our relationships if we decide to do that, because controlling a partner's reputation after a break-up is something that emotionally abusive people do when they can no longer control their partner. If you are thinking this through, try to talk to someone you trust and interrogate as honestly as you can about whether it is the right thing to do or if it's something you should consider and delay.

Please don't read this as me saying you personally weren't in an abusive relationship or that you need to prove to anyone else what you know inside. Every reader of this book will have their own story and their own experiences. This is an invitation to analyse a trend of quick and easy meme answers to complicated, difficult human dynamics and reconsider participation in naming and shaming social media campaigns which lash out reflexively and publicly, because it feels cathartic or looks like solidarity.

Which Way to the Stocks?

A word on human nature: human beings have a tendency to cast each other out when they are scared. When I worked in women's leadership in the corporate world, my colleague Fiona Thompson (an executive with many years' experience in politics, banking and consultancy) and I identified a practice we named 'jackal baiting'. If our ancient ancestors were in a stamm of thirty, with enough calories to sustain twenty-eight, and the jackals* started to circle, rather than letting them savage the whole group, it may have been expedient to allow one to be taken. In an emergency, there is no time to have a committee meeting about who is disliked or has not been pulling their weight.

Steven Pinker, psycholinguist, cognitive psychologist and popular science author, theorises that gossip is one of the main drivers of the evolution of language. He quotes psychologist Leda Cosmides on the importance of humans having: 'the ability to enforce social contracts of the form "If you take a benefit then you must pay a cost"', and adds: 'This alone puts a demand on the linguistic expression of rather subtle semantic distinctions.'[34]

Fiona Thompson and I posited in our work that for early humans, living with predators, this gossip needed to be

* Jackals rarely, in fact, attack humans. They go after birds, mice and plants. However, 'lion bait' didn't have the same ring and whenever we talked about it to each other or groups of women, 'jackal bait' was the term that stuck. The jackals are metaphorical and we apologise to them in the way we do to sharks!

ongoing because at any minute a group needed to be able to know who was 'on the out' and therefore was to be left behind. We have evolved to survive and that gossip is still a part of our survival instinct. The best way not to be 'jackal bait' is to be on the committee who decides who should be jackal bait.

Fiona and I both remembered this kind of role play being acted out as teenage girls. I had one strong memory of a school disco where a popular girl had locked herself in the loo crying because someone else had kissed her boyfriend. There was a thrill in the drama of it all. Girls were saying how terrible it all was with delighted smiles on their faces that they were unable to hide. 'Come quick!' they were saying to each other as they ran towards the heart of the action. This situation is probably familiar to you and you may have similar memories. I think the visceral thrill at play in this kind of situation is that 'the pack is being shuffled'. The safest members of the stamm may soon be relegated to being jackal bait. Perhaps there is room for someone formerly on the dangerous edge of the group to grab a higher position and become safer in the stamm.

Asking for accountability and amends where harm has been done is valid. But we have to remember we live in society and human nature can be cruel. Righting wrongs in public can become theatre and spectacle with a gladiatorial taste for blood in the mouths of the audience, some of whom have a more vested interest in witnessing fresh pain than healing old wounds.

It is important to acknowledge that not long ago human beings, like you and me, people from whom we are descended, took their children to see public hangings and made a day of it with a picnic. We are not better than them. We are made of the same stuff. We must beware of wanting spectacle and catharsis because we live in an unfair world and sometimes feel lost, trapped, downtrodden or disappointed. We must check these instincts for our humanity now and also for our future chances of real equality.

As Ligaya Mishan wrote in her 2020 *New York Times* article, 'The Long and Tortured History of Cancel Culture':

> cancel culture is rudderless, a series of spontaneous disruptions with no sequential logic, lacking any official apparatus to enact or enforce a policy or creed . . . What cancellations offer instead is a surrogate, warped-mirror version of the judicial process, at once chaotic yet ritualized. It's a paradox reminiscent of the mayhem in medieval Catholic traditions of carnival and misrule, wherein the church and governing bodies were lampooned and hierarchy upended – all without actually threatening the prevailing hegemony, and even reaffirming it.

Mishan references anthropologist Natalie Zemon Davis who suggests that such carnival misrule offered 'alternatives to the existing order'. From the church's point of view carnival was, as Mishan writes, a useful catharsis –'a brief hiatus from the moral strictures of daily life, when the populace was allowed to indulge their mutinous impulses and expend their restive energies, the better to return to compliance on the morrow.'

In other words, we must not mistake taking down individuals for actual real world change, like a social media video game using human beings instead of avatars – again like 'the proles' in Orwell's *1984*, distracted by the lottery they would never win – each outraged click playing into the hands and pockets of tech billionaires, while our world lurches further into disaster. So what can we do? Well, that is up to us and the subject of our last conversation.

Conversation Six

What Are We Going to Do about All This?

Have we made an ass out of you and me?

We've covered some serious (and some comedy!) ground in our first five conversations. How we approach conversing in the first place, our relationship to the past, gender nonconformity in an ever-changing world, free speech through the lens of comedy and the very concept of cancellation are all complex issues that need time and consideration and I hope this has allowed you space to engage with your own thoughts and ideas as much as it has with mine.

I cannot imagine you've agreed with everything I've said as we are different people with different experiences and ways of looking at the world, but you may have come to agree with me that we are currently trapped in patterns of disagreement that are severely limiting our progress. If you have, then you will see that change is urgently required, partly because the right is becoming more radical in its ambition and more pragmatic and tactical in its strategy, and partly because the left has become more divided in its views and entrenched in its positions. I believe we need to change how we're conversing and consequently acting (or not acting!) in order to move forward. It's why I've written this book.

You might consider yourself just a drop in the ocean, and think that nothing you do can really make a difference. But it's important to remember that a thousand drops can make a wave, and lots of waves make up an ocean. I wish there were someone else to do it for us but there is not. We are the only change that's coming.

You may be somebody who considers yourself to be politically active but worry that you spend most of your time sharing other people's content on social media, and want to reanalyse what else you could do and how you can rethink your practices and communications. You may be someone who is a hands-on protester, organiser and planner but feel frustrated that you are not getting anywhere. As my good friend, colleague and protest singer Grace Petrie sometimes jokes when performing at *The Guilty Feminist*, 'I've been singing protest songs since 2010 to try to make Britain a more left-wing place and if anything I've made things worse.' If so, you may want to refresh your tactics and rethink your strategy.

Wherever you're starting from, welcome to our last conversation, which we are going to divide into three sections. The first section is called Thinking it Through. If we've become practised in accepting the latest received wisdom, posting articles we've only skim read and sharing ideas without analysing them, then we need to get into the habit of questioning our assumptions and thinking through and round things. Even if we think we do that already, it's hard for any human being to question our norms, because what is familiar can feel like it holds some inherent truth by default. It's good for all of us to stop and take stock.

The second section is called Talking It Over. It is about how we are communicating with others and rethinking our skills when having divisive conversations with friends and strangers. This section is important because currently I believe almost all of us are deeply under-skilled; even if we're doing okay, we could be better. We should always want to improve these skills. Surely, we have to be *at least* as interested as capitalists trying to persuade in order to make a buck, when it comes to sharing our most precious ideas that we believe can make the world a fairer, more just, less violent place. Coca-Cola does not advertise by saying, 'Fuck you if you drink Pepsi, you asshole'. How dare we be less convincing than the marketeers of fizzy, sweet water with long overdue change that the world is truly thirsty for?

The final section is called Changing Our World and is about doing, organising and connecting. If you feel overwhelmed by the idea of taking on anything else, uninspired by the options for action you feel are available or generally unskilled and disconnected from the work you know you and your community are capable of, then this section contains some inspiration for ways forward. Having said that, I would be much more excited by you coming up with your own ideas alone, or with a team of like-minded human beings, to make change your way with creativity and the energy that comes with fresh invention and collaboration. Nothing in this chapter is an instruction. It's not a new high control group. This is not bestowed wisdom. It's a ball that is now in your court – and what you do with it is entirely up to you and those who engage you.

Thinking it Through

I believe the first thing we should do is rethink our models and assumptions. For everything. We need to practice asking why things are as they are. Let's start by questioning things that are not at all controversial and even playful, like first-year philosophy students. Let's take an example and break it down. Why do we have dessert last? Where did that practice originate? Is it the way it's done around the world? Do other cultures do it differently? Why do we assume that's the best and only way to do it? I've read that in some parts of India and China, sweet foods are put on the table with savoury items and there is traditionally no concept of 'dessert' (a word that derives from the French for 'clear the table' and is always at the end of the meal in Europe). Asking why things are as they are and whether we really like them that way, or whether we have just learned to norm and conform, is an important part of unpacking both our prejudgements and judgements of ourselves and those around us. We need to train our brains to make a practice of this to check we've not become rigid and unquestioning in our thinking.

We're not just flipping up the table here and shouting 'chaos!' Maybe, in exploring our pudding-course example, we can hypothesise a host of reasons. Let's exercise our brains instead of flipping open Wikipedia and 'finding out'. Sweet things used to be in short supply, so maybe they were seen as an occasional treat at the end of a meal. Perhaps because there's less nutritional value in dessert, it was traditionally served as an optional extra for those who could fit it in. Sometimes it's been (wrongly in my view) used as a reward to entice children into eating their vegetables. In cultures where this is standard, our palates have been trained to prefer sweet after savoury as opposed to savoury following sweet. Can we try a reverse dinner party and talk about how it feels to go sweet first? What kind of sweet/savoury things do we enjoy and why? Pineapple on pizza? Chutney on cheese? Can we train ourselves to enjoy something different or are our tastes fixed due to our upbringing?[1]

It's just a silly thought experiment with added chocolate (the best kind!) but asking these sorts of questions allows us to step out of our paradigm and consider, without a moment's hesitation, whether what we have seen and heard modelled as we've grown up is as we wish it to be or inherently 'best'.

Let's take a mildly more feminist or at least more personal example. Please be aware I'm modelling flipping our assumptions here. We can do this with anything and I'm recommending we do. In doing so, I'm revisiting themes from our third conversation so we can start to weave our topics and strategies for rethinking and conversing together. I'm not going over old ground so much as examining how we can create a practice of applying overthrowing our assumptions in our busy and distracted lives.

I grew up seeing images that were coded to me as 'attractive women', and they were almost always in high heels. I saw this frequently on the television and in my community. Women who were dressed up, going out on the town and visibly attractive to men, wore what someone from another time or culture might see as 'strange little stilts' on the backs of their feet. This made it difficult for most of them to walk fast or run. I saw that they were grateful to take them off at the end of the night, as they were often uncomfortable or even painful. It was clear they were not as easy to wear as the flat shoes men wore as a matter of course, no matter the occasion. When I tried on my mother's heels as a small child, I found it difficult to balance. I also noted that they elongated women's calves and reshaped their legs somewhat. Some women strutted powerfully in them, in a way they did not in flats.

When I was sixteen, my mother bought me my first pair of high heels for a school formal, and I was excited to have them because to me those shoes weren't just an accessory – they were an invitation into the world of womanhood. Somehow this uncomfortable footwear meant I had graduated into a different part of my life. Through osmosis, my taste had developed in a way that meant I genuinely liked them. It is difficult to unpick whether I like heels or not, because I am not a neutral being who exists in a vacuum – my nature has been nurtured.

For a long time, received wisdom among feminists was that high heels were a patriarchal imposition on women, to slow us down and please the male gaze.[2] Third- and fourth-wave feminism overturned this idea, by arguing that women should choose to do whatever makes them happy, and that owning their sexuality and enjoying being desired is a valid human response.[3] So how can I tell if wearing heels is feminist for me or not? Is it something I've been told to want and am just used to, or is it something that makes me feel sexy and powerful, and are the reasons irrelevant?

This time, after I'd theorised myself, I decided to do some research on the history of high heels. I discovered that these boots weren't made for walking. They were for Persian soldiers on horse-back, designed so the riders' feet didn't slip out of the stirrups when they were standing hands-free while using bows and arrows.[4] Persian soldiers were seen as the *crème de la crème* and incredibly virile and macho. One sixteenth-century diplomatic mission to Europe later, it was thought that Continental women wanted to see them, and men wanted to be them. Soon heels were all the rage for rich European men who mostly posed in them. They were especially loved by short kings (the old-school kind!) and aristocrats.

By 1630, the craze was for women to wear masculine clothes and accessories, including breeches, pipes and high heels. That's right – we co-opted heels to butch up and got stuck with them. The Great Masculine Renunciation, which began in the late eighteenth century, was a time of revolution and intellectual advancement in which fashion itself went out of fashion for men.* It became seen as more masculine to wear dark, serious clothing with little to no decorative purpose. The feeling was: 'We've got a government to overthrow! We've no time for cravats and we can't run in heels.' Men in wigs lost their heads. What do you know? We are back to gender signifiers being scrambled. There's nothing inherently femme about heels at all, so heels making me feel femme is a fiction I've trained my brain to believe, or a collective contemporary delusion I've tapped into.

I've upended my assumptions, but how could I upend my feelings? I'm a product of a late twentieth-century upbringing and if I like them, I like them. The only way to break this conundrum was to go for a period of three months not wearing heels in any situation, whether professional or social, no matter how formal. After that time, I decided the comfort of wearing flat shoes and the ability to stand firm and have longer conversations in most situations made me feel more powerful than wearing the shoes of an ancient Persian horseman. What a surprise! However, there are still times when my socially conditioned brain feels sexier in heels – and on those occasions, I still wear them. Overall, I have defaulted to flats, because I upended my assumption about heels. This is really the only way to 'make a choice' (as much as any stammal human being is making one when it comes to taste for fashion). Sometimes we need to ask questions we've never asked, or force ourselves to experiment with things outside our regular paradigm, to even know what our assumptions are – because (as Douglas

---

* Psychoanalyst John Flugel's theory of the Great Masculine Renunciation is challenged by cultural critic and fashion scholar Chloe Chapin, who sees the movement as more importantly being about assigning the concept of 'fashion' to women's dress. See Chloe Chapin, 'Masculine Renunciation or Rejection of the Feminine?: Revisiting J.C. Flugel's Psychology of Clothes', *Fashion Theory*, 26(7) (2021), 983–1008, https://doi.org/10.1080/1362704X.2021.1952919/

Adams observed) assumptions are things you don't know you're making.

There are times when a societal disruption forces us all to question our assumptions. The Covid pandemic caused a global lockdown, and some things we had long assumed we needed were no longer legal or available. During this time, we discovered there were, in fact, other ways of having our needs met. Although we had had access to video calling for years, we rarely used it, and it was seen as a poor substitute for face-to-face interaction, because we hadn't taken the time to get used to it.

People would travel to an office to write emails in a cubicle in isolation all day, even if they were unwell and likely to spread germs, because that was the norm, and they worried they would look like they were taking a sick day if they worked from home. For years before the lockdown, disability activists and some parents and carers had been requesting the option of video calling and live-streamed conferences, but the default assumption had always been that this wouldn't work or was too difficult to organise.

During the lockdowns we didn't just discover it was possible, we also learned the value of using these tools. We discovered that for much of the time they were perfectly adequate and, in addition, they had the advantage of allowing us to conserve both personal energy and fuel, and have more options in our work–life balance.

We also learned during this time the value of face-to-face communication, which we had previously taken for granted. Many of us missed the real connection that comes from an energising conversation in person. The consequence of having our assumptions challenged was the ability to assess and compare the value of remote working and in-room connection and make choices about both.

What is the consequence of us being forced to challenge our norms and create a new practice? Well, only 12 per cent of British people regularly worked from home before the lockdown.[5] Now, only 10 per cent of workers who have the option to work at home, never do so.[6] That is a huge cultural shift. On top of that, surveys show that both business leaders and office workers believe hybrid working has all sorts of other benefits, including improvements in mental health.[7]

All this because the highly unwelcome and distressing lockdown, amid a frightening and deadly pandemic, was a game-changer that helped us challenge our assumptions. It disrupted all our norms and forced us to think again and create new practices.

The good news is we don't have to wait for a global catastrophe to challenge our assumptions about how society works best. I once worked with a company that held hackathons for young software coders, many of whom were teens. A hackathon is a scrappy, high-octane, problem-solving, focused period where, in this case, teams would compete to hack together a quick-and-dirty solution to a dilemma. Pizzas were ordered, prizes were offered, community was built. But how did they make the problems themselves fun? Instead of presenting a dryly worded hypothetical reality like 'Our current fuel sources are unsustainable, what alternatives to electricity could we be using?', they would say: 'There's been a zombie apocalypse, and we're going to lose power on the national grid by this time tomorrow. You've got to find an alternative.' This gave the whole event the buzz of a gaming experience and, crucially, made the problem immediate.

Climate change is such a huge and complicated topic that it is outside the scope of this book, but it requires innovative thinking from a million stamms in coalition, and not indifference or overwhelm in the face of a seemingly insurmountable problem from the stamm of the whole human race, who may never team up to tackle it, even for our own survival.

It's really easy to make the assumption that by the time we get to the worst consequences of climate change, someone else will have figured out the solution. It's very difficult to imagine a time when things will be extremely different from how they are, even though scientists continue to assure us this is the case if we do not make serious change. (For absolute clarity, this doesn't remotely absolve corporations and governments of their responsibilities – they should of course be at the frontline of tackling this looming disaster.)

Our brains are wired for instant gratification and survival for the next five minutes, and as human beings we tend to prize convenience over long-term gains.[8] That's why it's easier to eat gummy bears in front of the TV than go to the gym, even though we understand we will have a longer, healthier lifespan if we do the latter rather than the former. Those who exercise every day are often the sort of people who enjoy the instant gratification of endorphins and other associated feel-goods more than others. Research shows that impulsive choices or preferences for short-term rewards result from the emotion-related parts of the brain winning out over the abstract-reasoning parts.[9]

This same very human interior force leads us to lazy assumptions that a problem that is not currently inconveniencing us personally and immediately is not our responsibility, and that there is little we can do about it. More than eight million people are currently displaced due to climate change and very few of us are truly doing all we can to stop it getting worse.[10] Hypothetical scenarios (that anticipate looming realities) in the hackathon style which create an immediate urgency can flip our brains into action mode and force them to upend our default assumptions.

What other strategies might we use to help us question our assumptions of powerlessness and our regular courses of action or inaction? We could ask ourselves a question like 'If I could have one hour with the Supreme Court to talk to them about the overturning of Roe v. Wade, what would I say to them – not to school them, but to influence them to change their minds?' This might allow us to rethink how we are campaigning, what arguments we are making, and whether or not we do have more access than we think to talk to the right people – who may in turn talk to more of the people in power. You might find you don't, but you won't know until you try.

These kinds of thought experiments can really open up a world of innovation for communication and activism that you're already walking around with inside your brain, that you're perhaps not currently activating. Helping other people to see the world as you do is a far more creative act than we think it is. It's what well-paid television writers thrash out in writers' rooms all day every day, and even with their highly trained brains, they find it challenging and often don't get it right. There's no reason to think communication is straightforward or that just telling people what you think they should already know will work. But it's not impossible either. You can learn the skills, but you have to know that there *are* skills. It's a lifelong learning process and as the world changes, attitudes change and tech changes, we have to be curious about how *we* need to change too. Anger is a great motivator, but, it's worth reiterating, it cannot be the only tool in our box.

If we wish others to be less fixed and rigid in their positions, this strategy of un-entrenching ourselves is the first step. Is there anything we're fighting for in principle that would, in practice, make little-to-no difference? Is there anything we believe because we've been told to believe it, but in reality it requires us to read more widely and think more deeply?

I recommend anybody who wants to make the world a better place organise regular meet-ups (in rooms or at least on Zooms – but ideally not just texting!) with fellow aspirational world changers, to unpack and question our assumptions. We could start with something fun, like the dessert exercise, or looking at the nature of queuing in different cultures: where and how and who stands in line, and what for, and what that tells us about society. This is just to warm up our brains and make them alert to rethink 'how things are done'.

After that mind-opening exercise, we could move on to something more relevant, for example asking 'What is an activist?' Does an activist have to act, and if so how often? How much of our activism is actually just talk? While there can be no action without talk, is there too much talk without action? Which activists do you most admire, and which activist campaigns have been most successful? Can you research and analyse why, and what strategies they used? How would we apply the principles of a successful campaign in the 1960s to a digital world? If you do your research, and make it a place for open and good-natured discovery and debate, you will begin to train yourself and your stamm to ask good questions, rethink your models and strike out anew, discovering both best practice and innovation.

At that same meet-up, can you create a practice of doing short, timed, warm-up exercises designed to stop you getting locked and blocked when talking about the important stuff? Train your brains – and each other – for empathetic critical thinking by formally debating low- or no-stakes issues: whether a popular TV show is great or terrible, say. Then can you move on to more hot-button topics? One of you could role-play someone you'd be fundamentally opposed to and, to prepare, research the most clever arguments you can find.[11] Just learning what arguments someone on the other side of the divide is using can develop your cognitive empathy for them. You're going to need to understand how they got there and what they're talking about to unpick their arguments and have real influence in a society that is perhaps co-opting their ideas. Make arbitrary rules as an exercise to train yourself to get better at influencing. Examples: whoever is debating 'the opposition' has to mount an argument while also getting them to laugh. Debaters can't deliver a fact without quoting a source they've read and fact-checked. Debaters have to imagine they're one of their role models (public or private) and argue in their style. Try getting people to let off some steam by allowing debaters to be as sweary or as ridiculous as possible. You'll learn from all of this. What works. What doesn't. What makes you feel defensive or wins you round. Most of all it will get you to rethink your default techniques and add to your toolbox. It'll give your brain a workout and make you loose and spontaneous, while forcing you to deep dive and not just quote stuff you've read on social media or in newspapers uncritically.

You might think you haven't got time for any of this but I'm going to suggest you don't have time *not* to do it. I often think I don't have time for exercise when I'm overworked but half an hour of yoga clears my head and I find it improves both the quantity and quality of work I'm able to do afterwards. Twenty minutes of cardio energises me, and I find the right ideas often just pop into my head when I'm moving. Sometimes my brain gets locked and so I go for a walk or talk to a friend and I free myself up. If you're feeling down about your activism or your group is uninspired, negative or not drawing new members in, you don't have time to keep doing things the way you've been doing them. You need to do ten to fifteen minutes of warm-up and turn an unproductive one-hour work session into an exciting, energised, creative forty-five minutes of fresh ideas from a group that's motivated to put them into action. If you're already cooking with gas and don't feel you need this, I bet, if you analyse it, you're intuitively creating an open, playful, dynamic space already.

Can you see a new view out of a familiar window?

Let us return to the issue of trans women in prisons, as I promised we would, to go deeper and see if we can model questioning our assumptions. Again, I'm not just revisiting old territory from our third conversation here. I'm zooming out on an issue we looked at closely to help us see what assumptions are inherent in the position that trans women in prisons are somehow out of place and cause a threat to the safety of other women. This is a test-case thought experiment. It is comprehensive and stand-alone so it can be saved and read as a separate essay about jurisprudence and the assumption of value in the prison system (and by extension cancel culture), if you prefer.

The assumption that a trans woman may be stronger than a cisgender woman, and therefore might cause her harm, holds implicitly within it not just the assumption that trans women are likely to be predators (which we took apart in our third conversation) but also the idea that prisons are violent places and that that is an acceptable norm. It assumes that we know prisoners are unsupervised or left alone in private places and frequently hurt each other and that that is acceptable and unstoppable.

We have already established in our third conversation that almost half the people staffing the prisons, who have power over and access to the women incarcerated, are men. There is much evidence that that power has at times been abused and there is little analysis about whether that abuse is commonplace – and yet that is not currently being challenged. Let's flip this whole thing on its head and question the assumption that prisons should exist at all, or at least in their current form. Let us ask how long prisons have been normal and what society thinks they are for.

Purpose-built state prisons, as we know them, were invented in the 1800s.[12] Orphanages, 'mental asylums', debtors' prisons and workhouses were also rife around this time. The Victorians loved taking people they didn't want around and warehousing them in unsanitary, dangerous and punitive conditions. Of all their inhumane inventions of this ilk, the prison industrial complex is the only such institution to remain.*

When we challenge our assumption on the idea of prisons existing, certainly as they are – bleak, unpleasant and designed to dispirit – we have to question how they have remained such an assumed model for punishment and (theoretical!) rehabilitation that we even continue to have 'correctional facilities' for children. These facilities do not seem to exist to discover the root of the problem, connect with and educate the child in question and to build their self-esteem and empathy. Why not? Some Nordic countries assume this is what troubled young people need and deserve, and their youth justice systems are built around the idea of trying to help the young person socialise and fix whatever is wrong. Those places tend to have very low rates of recidivism overall.[13] The assumption in most countries seems to be that borstals are there to make children suffer for their crimes. Loss of liberty is not considered a punishment in itself. They must wear a uniform to reduce their personal identity. They must eat unappetising meals and their contact with their parents and other loved ones must be very limited. It's easy to see with children that prison, certainly as it exists, is a deeply archaic model that

* The prison industrial complex (PIC) is a term used to describe the overlapping interests of government and industry that use surveillance, policing and imprisonment as solutions to economic, social and political problems. It was coined in 2009 by Professor Tanya Golash-Boza.

needs reform – and yet more than four hundred children are incarcerated in the UK at the time of writing.[14] In the US it's more like 60,000.[15]

Some may argue that there are violent teens who are a danger to others – and indeed, even the 'progressive' Scandinavian countries subject young people to confinement.[16] We've already explored in our fifth conversation why, neurologically, isolation and disconnection are destructive forces for the kind of person who is most likely to unempathetically hurt somebody else. You might be punishing a child with a different kind of brain or a personality disorder and overall you may well be making society less safe. It is also assumed if you are inside a borstal, you are not 'a part of society' that needs to be protected. We have already seen that care-experienced children are far more likely to be incarcerated, probably in part because they have no one to advocate for them and fight for them, along with losing their secure attachments (assuming they've ever had any!). What are we thinking putting the most vulnerable children in a cage with those most likely to be a danger to others? (Of course, some children can be in both of those categories.)

In addition, whereas 18 per cent of the UK population is Black or from another ethnic minority, over 50 per cent of children in prison are from these demographics.[17] We know children from these communities are over-policed and more likely to be criminalised. Why? If a white child with wealthy parents is violent or caught dealing drugs, they will have greater access to an expensive lawyer to talk them out of a custodial sentence. A white child of any demographic will probably be seen as inherently more innocent than a Black child because of culturally ingrained bigotry.[18]

Apart from anything else, prison (especially punitive warehouses) for children doesn't work, with over 30 per cent of those released reoffending in the first year, usually multiple times.[19]

I once spoke to a judge who said if he ever presided over a case in which the law effectively tied his hands and forced him to send a child to prison for even a short time his heart sank, because he was effectively sentencing them to a life of crime and incarceration. Prison gives children trauma, and it is the worst thing we can do for the young people in society's care and their communities.

If we can see pretty clearly that children should not be incarcerated because it is inhumane, unfairly targets disadvantaged youths, and makes the problem worse, let that lens allow us to flip our assumption and ask – then why is it the best thing for adults?

The Howard League for Penal Reform says:

> The prison system is like a river. The wider it gets, the faster it flows – and the harder it becomes to swim against the tide. Rather than being guided to safer shores, those in the middle are swept into deeper currents of crime, violence and despair. What began as a trickle turns into a torrent, with problems in prisons spilling into the towns and cities around them.[20]

Let us now consider women's prisons, as this is the focus of some feminists' concern and examine what might be the leading causes of harm to women inside them. According to the Prison Reform Trust, over half of the women in prison have suffered domestic violence prior to being incarcerated, and over half of the women in prison report having experienced emotional, physical or sexual abuse as a child.[21] This means many women in prison have been victims of much more serious crimes than they are accused of committing, and we are heaping trauma on trauma by incarcerating them.

Many female prisoners have dependent children – an

estimated 17,000 children are affected by maternal imprisonment every year – and both they and their mothers are deeply emotionally wounded by being separated from each other.[22] Women are much more likely to self-harm than men while they're in prison. In 2022, women comprised 29 per cent of all reported self-harm incidents, despite making up only 4 per cent of the prison population.[23] As we explored in our third conversation, women are hurting themselves because conditions and their state of mind are so bad.

The Howard League points out that prisons are not healthy environments.[24] They are unable to address the physical and mental health needs of women, and they exacerbate them – even more so with Black and ethnic minority women, for reasons already discussed. Furthermore, a 2017 study by the Advisory Panel on Deaths in Custody revealed that 30 per cent of women, prior to imprisonment, had had a previous psychiatric admission.[25]

A study the government itself published in 2022 said 'Women in prison are often even more affected and have disproportionately higher level of mental health, suicide, self-harm, drug dependence and other health needs compared to men in prison.'[26] It is clear, reading these depressing statistics, that the most marginalised women in society, who are already in most cases traumatised, are subjected to further trauma – and, because their children suffer, that hurt is likely to be inter-generational.

In 2022, 58 per cent of prison sentences given to women were for less than six months,[27] despite widespread recognition that short prison sentences are both harmful and ineffective, and in addition indicate that the offences are not likely to be serious in nature. Women are not being locked up because they are a danger to society, and would be much better off in programmes for work, education, intervention and rehabilitation while being able to stay in their own homes and communities.

If we genuinely care about women being abused and hurt by the prison industrial complex, we must ask why any campaign that's genuinely attempting to protect female prisoners from harm isn't focused on campaigning to ensure that almost all women (including trans women) never see the inside of a prison and instead get the mental, social and economic support they need not to offend in the first place (assuming they even have!). In other words, who exactly are we locking up and how can we possibly claim that we care about protecting women from any kind of potential harm when we are not even trying to address the issues that are clearly already hurting them?

As an interim measure, while we are campaigning to make sure the most disadvantaged women in our society are not simply shuffled off into incarceration that will exacerbate any problem they and society have as a matter of course, let us target right now the worst and most unfair practices in the prisons we have. This includes safeguarding from officers, but also must focus on healthcare (including mental healthcare), opportunities for education and a stable life beyond their sentence.

According to the Prison Reform Trust study, many women lose their homes while in custody, and 60 per cent of prisoners may not have homes to go to upon their release. In the UK, women are often imprisoned further from their homes, and they can have more difficulty retaining a 'local connection'. Ironically, this is a precondition for local authority housing. When Holloway Prison closed in London, women who were born and raised in the city, whose children and other family members were only a local bus ride away, were sent all over the country.[28] Often their family members couldn't visit them regularly, because of the time it would take and money it would cost. This is a huge, traumatic, emotional toll on women.

Part of the safeguarding required is privacy for all prisoners.

As we referenced in our third conversation, no one wants to shower in front of, or share a cell with, somebody they don't know (or usually even someone they do). If prisoners are unsupervised in these situations, they can feel unsafe – as we all would, having to shower or unwillingly sleep in proximity to strangers or people we don't trust: especially in an environment where everyone is deprived of connection, affection and protection. In a scarcity culture we feel more in danger. If women are to be imprisoned at all, affording everyone their own room and private time in the bathroom would immediately diminish anybody's concerns about reasonable safety measures.

Trans prisoners want privacy too. Instead of excluding a small number of trans prisoners (most of whom are not incarcerated for violent offences either) and throwing them into the male prison industrial complex (which also needs immediate reform and more privacy and protection for inmates) why not focus on giving all prisoners dignity, privacy and safety as a matter of urgency? If we throw off the assumption that we are stuck with prisons, and these prisons must be violent and degrading places with little to no hope on the other side, we open up a very different discussion.

I spoke to Jarryd Bartle, a lecturer and researcher in Criminology and Justice Studies at RMIT University in Melbourne. He explained that there is much evidence prison is ineffective as a rehabilitation measure and overall society would remain safe if the majority of people who've committed an offence stay in their community. It's important to say that this *doesn't* mean that someone who's committed a crime can go where they want and do what they want. Community orders mean people are monitored, sometimes closely with tech, that means the authorities know exactly where they are and, in some cases, even who they're with. Some people need to stay in their homes all the time, but most people do not and are better off interacting with their community.

In fact, most people are usually in compulsory programmes for community service and rehabilitation, which means they give back to the people who they may have wronged and that their empathy is developed, not diminished. Bartle is not an abolitionist and believes there are some violent offenders who are a danger to society, but that not all violent offenders are in this category. He says many have a problem with alcohol and drugs and if they're helped and monitored there's no reason they have to leave their communities to deal with it and it is far more likely, if they do, they'll be returned in a worse state and be violent again. He says there is strong evidence in Australia, especially with Indigenous communities, that community intervention is far more effective than state intervention.

Interestingly, Bartle said where it comes to evidence for all this, Covid, again, was a big disruptor:

> At that time a lot of people the government knew were not a danger to their communities were sent home [because of a fear of the virus spreading in prisons] and we didn't see an increase in crime rates because there were declines in prison populations. A lot of prisoners were placed on community-based orders. So I think that's a great real world example of how decarceration can work effectively.

We can learn from Black feminists to zoom out even further. Abolitionists, like Ruth Wilson Gilmore, have long campaigned that prisons per se are not the crux of the issue. Instead it is the wider context. She says: 'Abolition is about abolishing the conditions under which prison became the solution to problems, rather than abolishing the buildings we call prisons.'[29] This is what requires our urgent critical thinking and collaborative organisation.

So if the downsides are so clear, why haven't we done away with prisons entirely for those who are not violent offenders (or those who have been violent but would do better with community intervention and state monitoring) and created environments for those who are a genuine danger to society where they might stand a chance of developing empathy and genuinely begin rehabilitation? Well, because we've continued the Victorian assumption that people need to be humiliated and degraded, rather than pay a price that is actually valuable to them and their neighbourhood. Like dessert last or high heels, we've just got stuck with it, but unlike those things it's truly traumatising and extremely damaging.

As Bartle says, politicians want to be seen as 'tough on crime' and so a more compassionate effective policy is feared to 'not be a vote winner'. He says when talking to those who have the power to change the system, unfortunately the bottom line is the most convincing argument. In the UK, a study demonstrated that diverting adult offenders from standard prison sentences to alternative interventions saves the public sector between £19,000 and £88,000 per offender. When victim costs are considered, diverting offenders from standard prison sentences saves British society between £17,500 and £203,000 per offender.[30] The British study concluded the same thing that Bartle's work in Australia is demonstrating – standard prison sentences are not an economically efficient means of reducing reoffending. Prisons are not effective for rehabilitation, and they do not make financial sense for our society.

Now let's take this piece of critical thinking and reapply it. Reflect back on our conversation on 'cancel culture'. Consider the principle that community alienation is counterproductive, but *community intervention* is effective. If we know someone has caused harm in a community, a call for cancellation is a request for alienation. Instead we could ask 'Who in this stamm feels fit and safe to intervene and engage with this person?', or, 'How can we intervene and create a new, safer architecture, rather than socially ostracising individuals the way prisons do to everyone's cost?' There is a whole book to be written about alternative and productive ways forward with public calls for accountability but it is a useful exercise to start here. When we get stuck, we can look at successful models elsewhere and see how we might apply them.

Even in the face of all this evidence, at the time of writing there are no plans to change the current incarceration system significantly. Why not? The answer is perceived fairness and justice in society. Human beings are often angered by the idea of unfairness, and although there is little evidence that prison is a deterrent, the idea that someone can 'cheat the system' and not have a punitive experience rankles a large section of society.

So for any campaign to be successful, we would have to overturn our societal assumptions of what fairness and justice looks like. How would we do that? Well, let's do a compare and contrast. Data published by the Ministry of Justice shows that 57 per cent of adults in prison in the UK have a reading age below that of the average eleven-year-old.[31] A lack of basic skills such as reading and numeracy has been linked to higher rates of reoffending, and the likelihood of any given person turning to crime in the first place. There are campaigns to help prisoners learn to read while in prison[32] – but we should instead be asking why people who have been failed by the system in the first place are disproportionally sent there.

By comparison, a friend told me an anecdote recently, in which they were involved in a scuffle in the street which meant they had to appear in court. The barrister asked them if they were, by any chance, university educated. They replied that they had gone to university, but had dropped out during their first year. The barrister was delighted and said, 'Well, I can definitely get you off then – it doesn't really matter if you dropped out after a week. I can still say that you were university educated.'

In 2017 a medical student and aspiring surgeon attacked her ex-boyfriend in the leg with a knife, as well as other items which she used as weapons in a drug-fuelled rage, at her university accommodation at Oxford. The judge declared that a jail sentence would be too severe for her, as it could ruin her medical career. He also added that the actions of 'the extraordinarily able young lady' appeared to be 'a complete one-off'.[33]

If you have money, influence, and you look like the kind of person the judge might be friends with, it's pretty irrefutable that you have a much higher chance of walking away without a prison sentence. I'm not arguing we should advocate for prison sentences for medical students. But those who are from communities that have been under-resourced, under-funded and over-policed (Black people being significantly more likely to be both stopped and searched and arrested[34]), and therefore have slipped through the cracks of our society, should be afforded the same compassion, and more support, than those who have had access to education, support and capital – both social and fiscal – all their lives.

Some people of extraordinary ability from seriously disenfranchised communities are able to fight their way into opportunity because of talent, smarts and very hard work. But to use them as an example against others who don't have the same kind of aptitude, or brand of intelligence that is arbitrarily prized by society, takes us right back into the kind of thinking spawned by eugenicists, in which your genetic predisposition determines what you deserve in society and ultimately your lifespan. A worthwhile campaign is one in which we undermine the fundamental assumption that incarceration is about fairness and justice, when it is about anything but.[35]

Let us look at another aspect of justice: in 2022, the council that owned Grenfell Tower was found liable for the deaths of four of the seventy-two people who died in the fire. To date, nobody has gone to prison.[36] The British Post Office scandal was a large-scale miscarriage of justice in which around 900 people were convicted and around 230 people were imprisoned – all accused of theft and fraud due to faulty computer software developed by Fujitsu. Many have been left bankrupt. This has lasted two decades, and at the time of writing no individuals working for the Post Office or Fujitsu have been held accountable in any meaningful way.[37]

Any campaign about fairness and justice, and the prison system, could make clear that many of our assumptions are misplaced – and work towards truly protecting all citizens and strengthening society as a whole, with a focus on women and children, by creating an environment that is safe, rehabilitative and conducive to human dignity. (Once again, the activism and labour of Black feminists has, and continues to be, at the forefront of these ideas.[38]) If anybody at that point was still focused on the small number of trans women in women's prisons being a significant danger to female prisoners, then I think we would have to question whether the safety and wellbeing of convicted women was really their major concern.

Though the argument for moving towards a system that doesn't rely on carceral justice may feel challenging, think back to our second conversation – if future generations are to look with horror at various aspects of today's society (and they will), what elements might we be able to look on now, with fresh eyes, and reform? The prison industrial complex feels like a prime example of an unnecessarily cruel and inefficient system that's ripe for rethinking, given that, in the main, community interventions could serve our collective needs so much better. For that matter, the practice of socially alienating people with whom we disagree – or even those who have been destructive or harmful in our communities – may by future generations be deemed equally archaic and unwise. We cannot allow our righteous fury to allow us to model the mistakes made by the patriarchy.

Using this process of zooming out and reconsidering our frameworks and assumptions in many areas of progress will help us reconsider anything that may have become an orthodoxy to us or that we may be approaching in an unstrategic or unholistic way. After these conversations with ourselves, we need to be able to think about how to talk to people who disagree with us – firstly, those on our side of the political divide.

Talking it Over

You are already using lots of strategies to fit in and have your ideas heard. You may not be consciously aware of what those strategies are, but you have them all the same. When I deliver seminars and keynotes in corporate settings, and speak to women who work in male-dominated environments who are in some kind of 'diversity and inclusion' programme, I often ask them: what are you already doing when you feel out of place to convince other people, and yourself, that you're not? Often women analyse how they use warmth, charm, playfulness, heightened professionalism or authority so they can be hired and promoted. You may think women shouldn't have to do this. I agree. I talked to a group of women who work in construction once and we discussed their experiences and realised there were a hell of a lot of women who were talented engineers, architects and skilled overseers, carpenters and plumbers but they'd left the industry because the part of the job they were not good at was the elusive part that they were offered no training for: fitting in where they felt like an oddity or even unwanted. There were a few men in the room who were gobsmacked. It had never occurred to them to 'fit in'. I asked one guy who mostly worked in an office if he felt like a white-collar pen-pusher when he walked on a building site. He said something that made all the women in the room gasp and groan – 'I've never thought about it'.

So here's something – the more marginalised you are, the more skills you'll have at persuasion and self-inclusion, because you'll have been developing them all your life. Think of the skills you need when you go to your partner's school reunion. Are you included there? Sure. On entry, you're given half a glass of warm white wine and a name badge. Do you belong? Hell no. A reunion is exclusively about a set of shared experiences and memories, and you don't share any of them. A school reunion is about *belonging*. Furthermore, many people were enrolled at that school but would never show up at the reunion because they did not feel like they belonged at the school. In other words, you're with all the ones who really felt like they belonged, reminiscing about that belonging. You're only there so when your partner walks through the door, they can show the rest that they must be winning at life because someone agreed to come to this with them. They want to talk to their friends. Not you! At this event, you'd instinctively use everything in your arsenal to find the other plus ones and bond, even if you had very little in common with them. Probably you'd intuitively do this by making other people feel like they belong.

When arguing with people on our side of the political divide, we often shed those strategies in order to fight for the idea. The argument becomes king, and all our strategies for building community and empathy are abandoned – often closing the door on the idea being shared. Why do we intuitively know that we need to use strategies to include ourselves, but not to include our ideas? If our ideas don't automatically belong to somebody, our instinct is either to say 'They must!' or 'If my ideas don't belong to you, then I will not include you as a human being.' But we are much more intuitively strategic than that at a party, meeting a new client, or on a date.

You might argue that when it comes to political ideals, the stakes are higher than when making small talk with strangers. I'd agree with you. So why are we being more careful and protective with our social selves than with our big idea that might change the world? We should take more time to build empathy and be more persuasive and invite more thought – *because* the stakes are so high. If you figure out what you already do, and analyse what other people do who you admire, you may realise you've already got an amazing toolkit, which you can use in situations where you find it hard to connect with someone: you just have to put into manual those techniques you use automatically in other areas of your life.

Here are some things I do. If I'm having a conversation with someone and I'm advocating for a group I feel should have more rights, I tell personal stories, ask people to think anecdotally about their experiences, and ask them to imagine scenarios in which someone from that group might move through the world. I really try to focus on asking questions rather than giving my conclusions. I do not always do this! This is my best practice. Not my only practice.

When I feel frustrated, I remind myself that the position I'm holding is usually not one I've held all my life – especially if it relates to a marginalised group I'm not in. In that case, I sometimes say, 'I used to think that, but then I looked at this evidence, which changed my mind.' This has the impact of communicating that a reasonable person like you and like me had no way of knowing this until seeing the facts, and allows them to change their mind without losing status.

I also remind myself that very few people will completely change their mind in one conversation, and nor do I expect them to. In fact, I would rather they thought it through, did wider reading, had conversations with more people, and came to a slow, thoughtful conclusion that was authentic to them and well-considered. I'm not really interested in doing 'Road to Damascus'-style conversions, because then they're taking my word for it and can easily be convinced by the next person they talk to who makes a persuasive argument to think the opposite. Building a bridge so someone can take even one step onto it is better than pushing them into the river, if we truly want to change society.

Of course, if you feel your identity or humanity is in question, you have every right to withdraw from a conversation and avoid any human being who makes you feel this way. But you don't have to. There are many artists and communicators who share their experience in beautiful ways, both in person and online, who are persuasive and compelling and who change lives in the process. Those I know who work in this way are, of course, careful with their energy, and know how to self-protect. One such creative is Travis Alabanza, whose show *Burgerz* is a masterclass in igniting people's cognitive and affective empathy for the trans-femme experience of walking through the world.

The story starts with Travis telling us that they were walking across a bridge in London when a man, incensed by Travis's femme gender expression, threw a burger at them; no bystanders intervened or helped. Travis does some crowd work and asks a male audience member to join them onstage. They then ask the man how traditions of masculinity have impacted him while they cook and eat a burger together. This traditionally masculine bonding ritual of effectively barbecuing together, and the patience and time Travis takes for the man to become comfortable in front of the audience, is an extraordinary thing to witness. Night after night, audiences saw men (usually straight and gender conforming) become open and often vulnerable, sometimes weeping talking about their own experiences of the impositions and expectations of masculinity from their families, schools and society at large. It is an exercise in understanding why a man might have thrown the burger (which Travis, who is a comic genius, points out must've cost around ten quid in central London) and what the violence might have said about his internal feelings about gender.

The last turn is Travis cleverly asking the audience to imagine themselves as those on the bridge who saw and looked away. We find ourselves very much looking in the mirror right at the moment when we might be tempted to feel somehow better equipped to judge someone else. The empathy and understanding they are able to raise in a theatre is breathtaking. This is the power of skilled storytelling and strategic emotional thinking. There is no lecture in the world that can do this. No one can shame or scold you into the elevated levels of intellectual and visceral understanding you have when you leave *Burgerz*. Not everyone has the skill to do what Travis is doing and nor does everyone need or want to be an artist with an important social message sharing their personal trauma.

But we can all watch artists, storytellers and communicators who are doing this and analyse what they're doing, how and why. Deconstruct persuasive speeches from history. The language used. The tone of voice. The impact it had. What liberties do you hold dear? Who fought for them? How did they fight? Who did they speak to and how did they speak? What else did they do? If we really want to change the world, we have to skill up.

If you see someone on your side of the political divide who makes you want to weed-kill, ask yourself – how would Travis Alabanza do this? Or someone else you admire. That's not to say Travis never gets angry and never shows that anger. But a one-note, angry rant which didn't make the audience laugh, cry, think and feel wouldn't be as powerful as their nuanced, funny, intelligent, impassioned show.

Travis's audience is likely to be people who fundamentally agree with them on most things, but many of them will have questions and an incomplete understanding of Travis's experience. So while they're playing to a 'home crowd', not everyone in that crowd is necessarily fully informed or emotionally activated. And of course, some of Travis's audience might know nothing about Travis at all, and might come with an entirely different world-view. Which brings us to the next part of this topic.

How do we travel in time and space (without leaving home)?

It is really easy to get angry with those we love the most and are closest to in our family or community, and it's often easier to be more patient and polite with a stranger – at least offline! Is it possible that somehow we think that our nuclear and extended family, and our closest community ties, reflect on us? It is certainly really easy to become active, angry weed-killers at family celebrations, or when visiting parents or grandparents. Perhaps because we have a tendency to regress to adolescent behaviours anyway when we go to our childhood home: we find it easy to roll our eyes, snap at them, scold them or even storm out of the room. There is an assumed resilience to the texture and fabric of these relationships – we storm out because we presume we'll be allowed to storm back in again.

As the political divide widens, we are often asked to 'do the work' by having difficult conversations with people who would otherwise never hear these points of view, so we should examine whether we are wasting these opportunities. It's possible we have real influence to change ingrained ways of thinking that, in some cases, have not changed for generations, until we have started to think differently. This is all very well in theory, but how do we find the strength of will and emotional control to do it? This is a model for thinking about it that can challenge our assumptions.

If we have a neighbour who comes from a different culture, and we get to know them and we find a connection with them, we may notice disparities in our value sets as well as similarities. Getting to know somebody from another country, especially one with a culture very different from our own, is like getting to travel without having to leave home. We can taste their food, listen to their music, hear their stories and learn idioms and ways of thinking that give us a window into other lives lived. If your neighbour said or did something that you felt clashed with your feminist values, for example, it is unlikely that you would immediately impose your ideas about equality for women onto them wholesale. If you felt you knew them well enough, you might introduce a conversation that was subtle, nuanced and gentle, and you would no doubt begin by asking questions. Your first response would very probably be curiosity as to why your neighbour thought a certain way. Do the origins lie in their culture? In their upbringing? In ideas that they stand behind? Is it just their norms? Are they open to questioning it? In doing so, you will probably find that their lens on your world sees some of what you see as female empowerment as questionable.

This exchange of ideas will allow both of you to build cognitive and affective empathy, may make you upend some of your assumptions, and will very likely allow them to upend some of theirs. It's very unlikely that you will just say, 'You're wrong, this thinking is bad, and unless you change it we cannot be friends.' You understand that they've come to their ideas from different parts of the world, with different traditions, and while you may genuinely feel that some of their outlooks are not feminist, you would not demand that they change. You certainly would not expect some kind of instant conversion. In talking over a long period of time in your friendship, you may see them shifting their position, and if the friendship is vibrant and engaging, you will no doubt shift your position on other things. Most progressive people will inherently feel this is true, and will have had experiences akin to this. We understand that being brutal and demanding about cultural divides feels inherently colonial.

Many of our most challenging conversations with family members occur with those of an older generation. Often, when I am at a gathering and somebody very elderly whom I don't know well is there, I make a beeline for them, because I think that talking to older people can be like travelling in time. I sat next to a woman at a dinner party once who had served as a Wren in the Second World War. She told me all her stories about the outbreak of the war, joining up, meeting her husband, his proposal on D-Day, and it felt like getting to be there. Through *The Guilty Feminist* I have been able to interview a number of older people who have shared extraordinary stories of the past – from fighting nuclear disarmament on Greenham Common, to being codebreakers in the Second World War, to the sexual harassment they put up with in the workplace of the 1970s. These fascinating memories keep the past alive, but also give an incredible insight as to what those women battled and what everyday life was like sometimes before we were even born.

While some elderly people have adopted progressive value sets and others have been the changemakers themselves who have allowed us to live in a world where (for example) women can get bank loans and credit cards without them being co-signed by a man, others effectively continue to embrace the cultural values of a previous age. Can we reframe that cultural divide between an older family member, to replicate the way we would talk to a neighbour from another country? We share a connection with them, but we do not share all their values. When they make a statement that contains an assumption that we find objectionable or even shocking, can we begin with curiosity and see communication as a longer-term exchange of views, that will take time to progress? Can we replicate the idea that it's not our place to convert them or scold them, but that there is a value in helping them to question their assumptions and by extension some of ours?

In other words, when it comes to immigration, the best form of integration is a two-way street. Every conversation should be one in which you learn as well as share, understand as well as seek to be understood. When generations integrate, although we should be unwavering in our commitment to neither dehumanise or prejudge anybody, it is a poor strategy to uncompassionately demand compassion, to punitively argue for abolition, or to police those who deny the need for police reform.

One personal experience of this was when I talked to an elderly Australian relative about Aboriginal rights, engaging with something he'd seen on the television about how many Indigenous people in Australia were incarcerated. I explained that the Indigenous population was over-policed, over-criminalised and far more likely to go to jail than a white person who had committed the same offence – if indeed any offence had been committed at all.[39] We talked about how the community was suffering from generational trauma due to the genocide and deeply cruel treatment of Indigenous Australians. His response was that surely if they hadn't done anything wrong, they wouldn't be in jail. In other words, he hadn't really heard me. Facts and stats weren't working. It would've been easy to get angry and say that he was being bigoted, and every instinct in me wanted to explode, but that doesn't make his neighbourhood a better place for Indigenous people to walk around him.

So I squashed that instinct down and used a personal point of contact to build empathy. I pointed out that if I walked down the street with marijuana in my pocket, it is almost impossible that I would be stopped and searched, and that if I were stopped it would be very likely I would be able to lie and cry my way out of it because the police and a judge and/or jury (if it came to that) would project innocence onto me. I could see he intuitively understood that was true. In fact, I believe middle- and upper-class white women are the least criminalised people in the world, especially those who have had access to education and have a strong support network – but I left that part out because I felt it might make him feel defensive as a white person, and I needed his armour off, not more on.

So I got even more personal. I pointed out that if our family had adopted an Indigenous child instead of me, while she would have had exactly the same upbringing and opportunities and our family's love and even probably my name, she would be far more likely to have been on the end of racist tactics, limiting her opportunities, and would be far more likely to be stopped and searched, and to have to live with projections of criminality. In other words, if I were Indigenous, it's much more likely I'd end up on the unjust end of the 'justice' system. My elderly family member's empathy was really activated by this thought experiment, and not only did he take the point, he thanked me for taking the time to explain it to him. The news story was no longer a report about 'others'. It had been humanised for him. Later, I heard him talking about it to another family member and I felt like this conversation was spreading and worth having.

Some of my readers might respond that white people should not need to imagine that Indigenous people or people of colour are their family members, that they shouldn't need a self-centring illustration to see humanity in the people in their community. But, if they have been raised in a deeply prejudiced society at a different time in recent history, they might need to – and then I would far rather that I took the time to challenge their assumptions and build their affective empathy (if their cognitive empathy is hardened) than to write them off as a relic, further entrench their position, and leave them still operating in the community, actively exercising their prejudgement. Never once have I scolded a family member into a different way of thinking (though by god, I've tried!). I have no interest in making the world a little bit worse for Indigenous people, when with one story or thought experiment I might have the chance to make it a little bit better. Should white people be better than this? Yes. But often we are not, so let's fix it, however we can.

Sometimes critics of empathetic engagement and hand-holding are also fond of telling other people when they get things wrong that 'impact is more important than intention'. I would argue that the impact of compassionate, long-term engagement with those who we have the opportunity to talk to, is far more important than our most progressive intentions.

Are you the giant whose shoulders we're standing on?

A word to fourth-wave feminists.* To build on what I said in the conversation about gender nonconformity, we cannot even imagine how polarised the divide was between the genders

* Or however you identify. Some people prefer fifth or sixth wave!

when second-wave feminists were fighting for our rights before most of us were even born. They put up with so much and struggled so hard for us. That deserves respect. I often sense a suspicion among young feminists who want to write older feminists off because they suspect they won't share all of their values. Firstly, many second-wave feminists have caught every wave since. Secondly, some of them haven't but still deserve our respect, our patience, our curiosity and at least an attempt at empathetic communication.

This is also true for the divide between older and younger queer activists. Rolling your eyes at people who suffered from constant police brutality, structural violence and went through the AIDS crisis because they don't share your framework or use the same language as you isn't fair, wise or respectful. Patience. Understanding. Humility. You owe it to them.

Older feminists and queer activists – please remember that you were once radical and, no doubt, if you were young now, you'd be fighting for what your generation passionately believed were the new frontiers for human rights.

Protest singer Grace Petrie performed a stand-up storytelling show called *Butch Ado About Nothing* in which she explored her feelings as a millennial butch lesbian engaging with genderqueer Gen Zs. In it she poignantly says:

> The kids are alright ... I found butch space when I was looking for a refuge from my loneliness, because I was lonely in my bones for thirty years. I found these things because they were built by other butches who were looking for a refuge from their loneliness. And if kids today aren't lonely in that same way then I guess those things won't need to exist, right? ... I feel like I spent my whole life looking for this party and I just got here and they're packing it away. But you know what else? That is okay. That is progress. That

is the world we fought for. I don't want butch identity to be defined by misery just because mine was.

Did you see the Martin/Midler model?

In July 2022, Bette Midler posted something she thought was about abortion rights but referenced trans rights in a way that upset a lot of young people who predictably shouted at her.[40] Comedian Mae Martin, who is non-binary, posted a very compassionate response in which they said:

> These figure heads, like Bette Midler, fought hard for women's rights and they're upset when, in the context of reproductive rights, they read phrases like 'people with uteruses'. They feel reduced and negated and confused. I would say to them: Nobody is negating the fact that people assigned female at birth have a unique struggle against an oppressive patriarchy. Nobody is denying the power and magic of cis women. But, for instance: I was born female, grew up with all the struggles that entails, but I am trans/non-binary, not a woman.

Breaking down the crux of their point, Martin continued to explain:

> Woman is not an accurate word to use when describing me. The use of inclusive language when talking about abortion rights means that I – with all my shared experience and shared threat of pregnancy as I also sleep with cis men – can participate and be acknowledged in the conversation and fight alongside women. Nobody is denying that people have biological differences but [trans women, trans men and non-binary people] have a parallel struggle with cis women.

'We need each other. We need cis women as allies,' Martin concluded. 'We all have the same goal and common enemy.' Then they modelled empathy, writing, 'One day there will be things that I struggle to understand and operate and I hope that people are patient with me and explain it and teach me.'

I don't know if Midler saw Martin's post, but she certainly saw an avalanche of less empathetic posts that imputed the worst possible motives on her. She wrote: 'There was no intention of anything exclusionary or transphobic in what I said; it wasn't about that,' and added, 'I've fought for marginalized people for as long as I can remember. Still, if you want to dismiss my 60 years of proven love and concern over a tweet that accidentally angered the very people I have always supported and adored, so be it.'

She was hurt and retreated. There was no need for this. She's right. She has fought for rights for a long time and if more people had posted what Martin posted, it would have been a lovely community moment. Young people, please try to project the most generous explanation of why someone might have posted something first and don't be surprised if it builds empathy all around. Lots of people read social media and never comment on it. They see how you treat the older generation and honestly, it doesn't model the compassionate society you claim to be fighting for.

What would Mae Martin do? It's a good question to ask yourself because they're right – one day, you'll very probably need a young person to explain what the hell everyone's talking about.

Changing our world

Are you a radical pragmatist, or a pragmatic radical?

Assuming we have learned to question our own models

of thinking, and shift the assumptions of our nearest and dearest (and our nearest and most-annoying) it might be time to turn our attention to the wider world – those who form policy, and can really rethink the architecture of our power-structures.

Those who seek to change the world often fall into two camps: radicals and pragmatists. Radicals say, 'What do we want? Major reform! When do we want it? Now!', whereas pragmatists opt for, 'What do we want? What we can have! When do we want it? What seems like a reasonable timeline of compromises to you?' It's not as pithy, but the truth is – as we've seen in previous conversations – we need both pragmatists and radicals. Every major movement of social progress has had some people making angry demands, creating noise and disruption, and refusing compromises of any sort as an insult to the human rights of the group they are advocating for. It has also needed those who are patient, and both willing to work with those with whom they vociferously disagree, and to accept temporary measures to get where they wish to go, little by little.

The fear that radicals have about pragmatists is that those compromises will soon become the endgame. Sometimes pragmatists get to base camp and, because they are quite comfortable there, they do not attempt to climb to the pinnacle where the most vulnerable in the community they represent need to go for full rights and belonging. An example of this is a movement that is often referred to as white feminism, in which the goal seems to be 'influential white women having as much share of the capital and proximity to power as influential white men'. This allows a few who already have some access to have much more, and could reasonably be argued to exacerbate overall social inequality rather than doing anything to meaningfully close the largest gaps. The same has been argued about gay rights, inasmuch as when the most influential, usually white, gay men can marry and operate in the upper echelons of society with ease and belonging, the job can be seen to be done. It is often said that the first person to throw a brick at Stonewall was a Black trans woman. Unjustly, that brick built a house she never got to live in.*

Perhaps this is why contemporary movements for social progress have an 'all of us or none of us' policy. The dilemma is this – an all-or-nothing approach usually ends in nothing. For these reasons I believe that pragmatists need to get more radical, and radicals need to get more pragmatic. More than that, they need to get better at speaking one another's languages and collaborating, for fast accessible gains that mean we are on the path up the mountain, but also able to stay focused on reaching the pinnacle.

In our first conversation we looked at the wild disagreements and yet sometime collaboration between the pragmatic suffragists and the radical suffragettes in order to get the first step of women getting the vote. If they had said no to the legislation of giving moneyed or university-educated women over thirty the vote, they never would have got the vote for all women regardless of income or age ten years later. But had they decided that, as *they* were influential women over thirty, the job was done, and not continued to fight – most women would have continued to have no voice and few rights.

Some people think that what radicals are demanding seems impossible, and therefore not worth asking for, or even so unreasonable as to curtail the practical wins we might get if

---

* In fact, no one can agree who threw the first brick or even if it was a brick or a bottle, but certainly Black trans women like Marsha P. Johnson were at the forefront of the movement, so even if the brick is metaphorical there's a reason it's become a sticky idea. https://www.nytimes.com/2019/05/31/us/first-brick-at-stonewall-lgbtq.html

we asked for less. However, we need to realise that generally what radicals were demanding twenty years ago, pragmatists are getting over the line now. Equal marriage was demanded decades before it happened, and at the time it seemed like an impossible dream. To the children I know growing up today, it seems curious that this was ever in question – they wonder why any two people in love would ever have been barred from the public ceremony and legal protections afforded others. It seems completely arbitrary to them. It doesn't seem like a radical idea to children now at all, and if radicals had not introduced it into the public consciousness, however resistant society and its governors were three decades ago, it would never have been legalised in 2014 in England, Scotland and Wales.

This journey from radical to normal took a pit-stop in pragmatist town in 2004, with the introduction of civil partnerships. At the time this was exclusively for same-sex couples.* Many people felt, understandably at the time, that civil partnerships simply reinforced the difference in human rights afforded heterosexual and same-sex couples. As comedian and writer Hannah Gadsby said to me, 'It may give me some legal rights, but it's still an invitation to drink out of a different water fountain.'† Society caught up with this view so much so that it was a right-wing Conservative prime minister, David Cameron, who introduced full rights to same-sex couples to marry. Had Cameron felt that it would lose him rather than gain him votes, it's safe to assume that he would not have

---

* It wasn't an option for heterosexual couples until December 2019.

† Civil partnerships are now open to heterosexual couples too. If you want to be married as a trans person in your gender, then you need to jump through a lot of administrative hoops. If you're non-binary, your gender will not be legally recognised, so you can't get married or civilly partnered without being misgendered.

done so. The fact that he thought it would be a popular move means that same-sex couples being effectively married in civil partnerships had paved the way for the full human rights they should have been afforded in the first place.*

None of us enjoy settling for half-measures, and sometimes feel dispirited at having to celebrate diminished gains for basic human rights for ourselves or those we love. However, as long as we don't allow our movement to stop moving when we have something we need rather than everything we want, it is often the most accessible and fastest – if not the only – way up.

Coalitions are key. AIDS Coalition to Unleash Power, known as ACT UP, is an international, grassroots political group working to end the AIDS pandemic. They were formed in 1987, at the Lesbian and Gay Community Services Center in New York City in response to the way their community was being absolutely ravaged by HIV AIDS, which was cruel, swift and deadly. ACT UP brought pressure to bear across many political and influential fronts who were ignoring the crisis because it was mostly happening to members of society and stamms they did not care about. The activists pressured, perhaps most crucially, the Food and Drug Administration (known as the FDA) to allow experimental and trial drugs to be used.

What is interesting about this coalition is that it worked across many fronts. Artist David Wojnarowicz, who was himself HIV-positive, famously protested wearing a painted jean jacket emblazoned with the slogan: 'If I die of AIDS—forget burial—just drop my body on the steps of the F.D.A.' This was one head-turning tactic. But what is important for us, when thinking about it as a successful model of a movement

* The fact that the Conservative Party won the next election indicates that he was correct in his assessment.

in which thousands of people saved millions of lives, is this: there were also members of the coalition who had a deep, analytical understanding of the FDA drug approval process. ACT UP knew what their demands were and how they could realistically be implemented. In turn, government agencies dealing with the AIDS pandemic, especially the FDA and the National Institutes of Health, recognised this and started to consult with ACT UP and ask for their expertise and advice. They started working in coalition with some of those who they had seen as their enemies because their lives were at stake.[41]

It is important to know that members of ACT UP were from multiple stamms. They were the people shouting outside government buildings with signs and they were the people inside the buildings with briefcases and inside influence. People played to their strengths and worked in coalition, understanding everyone had a role. Although they were largely gay men, they advocated for intravenous drug users, also dying in great numbers, who were seen by the establishment to be entirely expendable and unimportant. They did not leave anyone behind. They worked together. They were not perfect. They were human beings under enormous pressure. Many of them were sick themselves or worried they would be – living in great fear. Naturally they sometimes bickered and even, at times, seriously fell out. But they did not let it divide the movement. They did not focus on the problems in interpersonal relationships or allow it to split ACT UP into less effective factions publicising their infighting in a way that would lose them credibility and power. They kept going and gained ground and didn't give up – and what they did worked.

We need to examine movements like this in detail and ask our elders how they did what they did while we still have them. We need to understand the principles and learn from them but also understand we are in a unique and unknown landscape and we must invent for ourselves the way others did before us. The reason movements are called 'grass roots' is because they spring from the ground they are on. Our land right now is rocky and arid, because of many of the factors we have analysed in this book, but there are green shoots and we can water them with coalitions, organisation and a willing spirit to move forward together. We have to understand that the work begins today, but the gains will not be delivered overnight. Our work is urgent and because of that it must not be rushed.

Whether or not we agree to small wins and interim measures, we have to remember that this is the strategy of the alt-right, and they are employing it to some success. The anti-gender movement is driving hard to roll back queer rights and abortion rights,[42] and they are making small incremental gains that will turn into large strides forward if we refuse to get organised because we cannot agree on best practice. At the time of writing there are three anti-abortion bills being read in British Parliament, and the UN warned in August 2022 that the rights of LGBTQ+ people are being deliberately undermined by some state governments in the US. Trans rights are already being rolled back in the UK, Europe and the US,[43] and this is emboldening the distrust and persecution of other queer people.[44]

Rarely are we transported to the top of the mountain in a private helicopter. Influential individuals might be – but whole community groups? Seemingly never. Do exhausted, demoralised stamms deserve a first-class ticket to the top? Undoubtedly. But those with the most energy, the most access, or those in coalition with people who are vulnerable and angry, must take the lead when no such transport is offered in the exhausting climb, carrying those who can no longer walk.

The only thing we must do is make sure if anyone gets left behind, we go back for them – and don't ask them to start another fight all on their own. If you feel you are more on the pragmatic side, it may be that you have access to many of the things you need to survive, and even some of the things that make life fun and easy. I've often said that I started *The Guilty Feminist* to wallow in my own oppression, and I learned more than anything how much access I already had. We usually only notice the doors closed to us. The doors open to us look like corridors, which we can pass through with ease.

Over years of listening to and engaging with communities to whom access is so frequently denied, and visiting refugee camps where people often hold relentless dignity in enforced degradation, I have become angrier about the state of the world and more active in my response to it. Feeling a keen sense of furious injustice doesn't seem like a radical response when you're up close, seeing human rights being trampled – it seems like an empathetic human response.

For this reason, if I am in rooms with influential people who can actually change policy, it is my job to exercise my 'privilege of civility', to try and activate their empathy as mine has been activated by those who have taken the time to educate me.* It is my role to influence, influence, influence, and never alienate further. This doesn't mean there is no time for demands and bluntness, but you need to assess your audience. Angry citizens taking to the streets in noisy protests are key, in collaboration with influence – because governments need to know that a chunky percentage of their voters are really angry,

* By 'privilege of civility' I mean that I am often able to be polite because my emotions are not as inflamed as those who are personally affected by some of these issues. I am not incarcerated and nor are any of my loved ones, but I bet I'd find it harder not to lose it if it were personal. As it is, I can calmly make the persuasive fiscal arguments.

and this really matters in terms of who they will support and elect. Letting our anger and demands be known in numbers, and persuading one-on-one, are both important tools. In other words, shouting at governments can work, but rarely individuals.

In 2017, İdil Eser, the former director of Amnesty International Turkey, was jailed for some time along with other human rights defenders. In the lead up to her arrest, she had been warning others that the government was becoming increasingly authoritarian, and many of her contemporaries told her not to put that negative energy out there, and that everything would be fine. It is a common human response to think 'It wouldn't happen here', because we can't imagine our world shifting so dramatically. We can disassociate from our fears even when there is evidence of them becoming a reality. In conversation with her, I asked what we needed to be on guard for in the UK, where there has for years been what Amnesty International refers to as a 'human rights raid', as draconian bills are passed into law with an alarming frequency. İdil said you need three things:

1. You need to publicly resist all injustice. The government is always looking out of the window to see how many of us resist which injustices and how much of their agenda they can push over the line without us noticing. They are studying this because they want to know how long they can stay in power. There are more of us than there are of them, and they do take notice of what we object to. Even if they don't roll back current policy, they discuss how much further they can push the envelope before there's a serious uprising.
2. Resilience. If 500,000 people turn up to the first march, 200,000 to the second march, and 5,000 people to the

third march, they see they can tire you, and soon you will become exhausted and look away.

3. Joy. Many protest movements leave this important element out. They become puritanical and judgemental, which dispirits their membership and chases people away. Joy is a magnet, and more than that – it builds resilience and gives people energy for the fight. Joy is sometimes said to be an act of resistance.

One of the great advantages of economic inequality for the powerful is that struggling to survive diminishes joy – it eats into our resilience for resistance, and keeps us distracted with survival. If you have capacity for joy, because you have access to the basics in life and even some of the luxuries and conveniences, then bring that joy to bear every day. Share it, encourage others in your community, and take pleasure in building bridges where difficult conversations need to be had. If we turn on each other, and on those who have not engaged politically at all because they are too comfortable or too disenfranchised, we play into the hands of those who would seek to exhaust and cause chaos between us.

Our joyful, resilient resistance, in the form of cooperation, organisation and constant meaningful forward-looking conversation that responds to our changing world, is not just desirable, but urgent and the only way forward. We must throw off the fear that has been engendered in our communities through a scarcity culture and competition for rights and access. We must come to the conversational table with curiosity, openness, a practised ability to analyse our models and assumptions, and a willingness to collaborate in meaningful coalitions with those whose advancement is inextricably linked to ours. However radical or pragmatic we might be, however difficult it might be to muster joy in a seemingly ever more unjust society, we must not forget to inject or at least allow joy in our movements.

What if we don't win?

Honestly, this is something I think about a lot in this violent, angry world. What if we don't win these huge social battles? And when I do, I think of this. A colleague of mine at Amnesty International called Lucy Macnamara, (who now runs her own philanthropy consultancy called Do Good Well) told me the origin of her work was that when she was a child she found an Amnesty flier and started writing to a political prisoner who needed encouragement. She said that when he was released, after about twenty years, he said that what kept him going and made him feel like his imprisonment served a purpose was that he was receiving letters and knew that his government was also receiving letters about him, which was shining a light on their human rights violations. The letters meant that every day he could get up and carry on, with pride and resilience. The public pressure was a factor in his release and therefore was said to be successful. My question is this – if the man had died in prison, would the letter writing campaign have been a failure? I don't think it would have. Because the man described the meaning that the letters brought him. All of those moments of hope and connection and understanding were his regardless of his release. They were worth doing in and of themselves. Life is only lived in moments. I do not know if we will win the larger battle, but I do know that offering someone else who may be suffering greatly a moment of being seen and understood and connected with and fought for, is worth having on its own. In addition to that, one of the young letter writers grew up to work in human rights and many of the others will have been involved in acts of bravery, connection and kindness in the same way. Stamms are energetic.

My recommendation is that if you're tiring of raging against the machine, you find a way to connect with human beings. Go and volunteer at your local community centre or refuge. Find a neighbour who needs a friend. Look for a place in your community that facilitates connections to refugees, locally or abroad, so you can support them the way you might a close friend or family member. This is not an act of charity but of coalition.

I have ended up with family-style relationships, close friendships or connections with various displaced individuals and families I've met over the years – some local and some overseas – and it has given me far more than I have given. I act like a godmother to the children in a family or just a friend to talk to on bad days. The most moving thing is that often someone who is displaced and has lost family just needs someone who cares enough about them to genuinely celebrate with for a moment when there is good news. A visa restoring some of their human rights after years without a square foot of land to legally stand on. Good exam results. Charity can't high five you and say, 'Yes! You did it!' – that has to come from a human being who knows you.

There are godparent-style programmes for children in care who move from foster family to foster family. You could be a constant in a child's life to listen to them and spoil them the way you might a family friend or niece or nephew.

These are just examples. There are many ways you can connect with all sorts of people in your stamms and see the results of coalition for those who have been unjustly marginalised by society. Every moment engaged that way is a win for empathy and a hope that that connection will turn into another and another, paid forward in our, often otherwise, bleak world. The human race will not survive forever but every moment is its own battle for the best humanity can be. Every time we connect with kindness, we win that battle.

There is another reason to connect with human beings in your activism or support work. Intimacy softens you and reminds you that your stamm is just made up of lots of imperfect human beings who are, mostly, doing their best. It reminds you what all of this is for. It's to make the lives of other human beings better. And we can't do that with only the tools of ruthless efficiency and accountability. It will take love, patience and a sense of humour. One-on-one connection will affect any larger, more structural effort by igniting your humanity.

I hypocritically caution against trying to do too much. I had to sideline other things I see as important and even urgent to write this book, which I gambled was my most important contribution right now. Everything comes at an opportunity cost. As someone with ADHD I have to be reminded of that often. Do one local thing. Choose one organisation to champion. Connect with one cause deeply. Do what you can, when you can. You can support or post about many things but don't let that become your job or obligation or you won't have time to properly invest in something that could really change things.

What now?

In this book, I have chosen six conversations that I wanted to have with good faith, with an open heart, and without fear. I won't have got everything right – partly because there rarely is an absolute 'right'. There are mostly points of view. I hope you have enjoyed challenging some of your assumptions, or even arguing vociferously with me in your head. I'm sure I will change my view about some things I have written in the coming years, as I discuss these points with my readers and listeners, colleagues and friends. I hope I do. I hope I need to write a revised version of this book in some years' time, because my thoughts have moved on – and so has the world and the conversation in it. I hope neither I nor the world are in the same fixed position in five years' time, and I hope society has progressed and I have listened and learned, and that you have too.

Change is essential for life, and it is the only constant on this planet we call home. Let us not get stuck in our 'rightness', or we will be left behind. Let us learn to change minds, starting with our own, because then we have at least a chance of changing our world. To end back where we began, there can be no productive action without conversation – conversation is life, conversation is human. Let's begin.

Notes

Introduction

1. https://thehill.com/opinion/4845492-gen-z-voter-polarization/
2. For example: Rafia Zakaria, *Against White Feminism* (Hamish Hamilton, 2021), and Ruby Hamad's *White Tears/Brown Scars*' (Trapeze, 2020).
3. Alexis Shotwell, *Against Purity: Living Ethically in Compromised Times* (Reprint), (University of Minnesota Press, 2021).
4. Among a great deal of research into cults and their control tactics, readers may be interested in what Dr Anastasia Somerville-Wong, researcher, educator, specialist in pastoral and spiritual care and Humanist Chaplain at the University of Exeter writes on her blog. https://secularliturgies.wordpress.com/2020/02/24/the-25-signs-youre-in-a-high-control-group-or-cult-by-anastasia-somerville-wong/
5. Margaret Thaler Singer, *Cults in Our Midst: The Continuing Fight Against Their Hidden Menace* (Rev. ed), (Jossey-Bass, 2003).
6. https://www.nuffieldtrust.org.uk/news-item/the-brexit-referendum-five-years-on-what-has-it-meant-for-the-nhs – 'This [claim] was indisputably wrong.'
7. According to the Pew Research Center in America, members of both parties who have unfavourable opinions of the opposing party have doubled since 1994, while those who have very unfavourable opinions of the opposing party are at record highs as of 2022. For a global view of the same phenomenon, see *Democracies Divided: The Global Challenge of Political Polarization* edited by Thomas Carothers and Andrew O'Donohue. Also see Mitja Sardoč and Vladimir Prebilič, 'Governing by slogans', *Policy Futures in Education* 21(7) (2023), 765–775. https://doi.org/10.1177/14782103221136186
8. Dorothy A. Yen and Bidit Dey, 'Acculturation in the social media: Myth or reality? Analysing social- media led integration and polarisation', *Technological Forecasting & Social Change*, 145 (2019), 425–426.

Toolkit

1. https://www.medicalnewstoday.com/articles/touch-starved/; https://www.pnas.org/doi/pdf/10.1073/pnas.1519231112/ Ruth C. Vortherms, 'Clinically Improving Communication Through Touch', *Journal of Gerontological Nursing*, 17(5) (1991), 6–9. https://doi.org/10.3928/0098-9134-19910501-04; Stephen Thayer, 'History and strategies of research on social touch', *Journal of Nonverbal Behavior*, 10(1) (1986), 12–28. https://doi.org/10.1007/BF00987202
2. https://www.ohchr.org/en/press-releases/2020/02/united-states-prolonged-solitary-confinement-amounts-psychological-torture? 'These findings point to the important role of interpersonal and particularly intimate touch in times of distress and uncertainty.' (p. 1)
3. Mariana Von Mohr, Louise P. Kirsch and Aikaterini Fotopoulou, 'Social Touch Deprivation during Covid-19: Effects on Psychological Wellbeing and Craving Interpersonal Touch', Royal Society open science 8.9 (2021), 210287–210287. Open Access available on: https://royalsocietypublishing.org/doi/full/10.1098/rsos.210287#d17882159e1
4. https://ourworldindata.org/urbanization
5. Among those who spent money on massages, the average spend per year on massage in 2023 in the UK was £560: https://www.statista.com/statistics/1457515/massage-average-spend-uk/
6. https://www.etymonline.com/word/tribe; https://www.learningforjustice.org/magazine/spring-2001/the-trouble-with-tribe. Robert J. Gregory writes about how tribes are often defined by the colonial powers that subjugate them and are therefore inextricable from colonial thinking: Robert Gregory, 'Tribes and Tribal: Origin, Use, and Future of the Concept', *Studies of Tribes and Tribals*, *1* (2003). https://doi.org/10.1080/0972639X.2003.11886479
7. Portnoy, Gary and Judy Hart-Angelo. 'Theme From *Cheers* (Where Everybody Knows Your Name)/Jenny'. *(7", 45 RPM, Single)*, Applause Records, 1982.

The Conversation about Why We Can't Have Conversations Any More

1. Jim Jacobs and Warren Casey, 'We Go Together', *Grease,* Edwin H. Morris & Co. Inc, 1971.
2. Jay N. Giedd, 'The amazing teen brain', *Scientific American*, 312(6) (2015), 32–37. https://www.scientificamerican.com/article/the-amazing-teen-brain; Suparna Choudhury and William Wannyn, 'Politics of Plasticity: Implications of the New Science of the "Teen Brain" for Education', *Culture, Medicine, and Psychiatry*, 46(1) (2022), 31–58. https://doi.org/10.1007/s11013-021-09731-8

3. William Damon and Richard M. Lerner (eds.), *Child and Adolescent Development: An Advanced Course* (Wiley, 2008).
4. https://www.jw.org/en/library/magazines/watchtower-study-february-2021/The-Head-of-a-Woman-Is-the-Man/
5. https://www.dnainfo.com/new-york/20161222/dumbo/jehovahs-witnesses-sell-85-jay-street-jared-kushner/; https://medium.com/@matthewcwoodruff/church-sex-scandal-led-to-the-sale-of-the-brooklyn-watchtower-building-to-jared-kushner-63ecff43b29b
6. The language that cults use to describe themselves is frequently filled with family words like this and some scholars believe them to be a tactic – 'in these confusing social settings, children may not even understand the concept of family nor even know who their biological parents are.' (p. 493) Doni Whitsett and Stephen Kent, 'Cults and Families', *Families in Society: The Journal of Contemporary Social Services*, 84 (2003), 491–502, 493. https://doi.org/10.1606/1044-3894.147. It is *not* this extreme in the Watchtower Society, but it does blur family lines and means you're more likely to be persuaded by elders to behave as you're asked to.
7. https://www.childabuseroyalcommission.gov.au/case-studies/case-study-29-jehovahs-witnesses/
8. https://www.theguardian.com/commentisfree/2024/jan/25/the-shockingly-high-rates-of-violence-against-indigenous-women-demonstrates-the-long-tail-of-colonisation/; https://www.independent.co.uk/news/uk/home-news/uk-cult-groups-sexual-abuse-b2121100.html; 'An estimated 2,000 cult groups are operating across the country, but ministers have not acted to stop them because of fears that they cannot legally distinguish between religion and semi-criminal cults, a charity leader said.' Hamad, *White Tears/Brown Scars*.
9. Donna Hart and Robert W. Sussman, *Man the Hunted* (Routledge, 2008)
10. https://www.jw.org/en/library/books/gods-love/disfellowshipped-person/
11. https://avoidjw.org/news/norway-jehovahs-witnesses-denied-state-subsidy/
12. https://www.openmindsfoundation.org/blog/coercion-at-its-worst-religious-mandated-shunning/
13. This is described in the study as 'empathic concern' which refers to other-oriented emotions – such as tenderness, sympathy and compassion – elicited by, and congruent with the perceived welfare of, someone in need. https://journals.sagepub.com/doi/abs/10.1177/1088868310377395/
14. https://medium.com/the-no%C3%B6sphere/the-scary-truth-about-human-empathys-decline-no-one-talks-about-dd894e820235/
15. https://www.pattivalkenburg.nl/images/artikelen_pdf/2016_Vossen__Valkenburg_Do_Social_Media_Foster_Empathy.pdf
16. If you wish to go deeper into this, there is evidence that autistic individuals showed increased affective empathy for negative emotions but reduced affective empathy for positive emotions compared to non-autistic

individuals. Monica Mazza, Maria C. Pino, Melania Mariano, Daniela Tempesta, Michele Ferrara, Domenico De Berardis, Francesco Masedu, and Marco Valenti, 'Affective and cognitive empathy in adolescents with autism spectrum disorder', *Frontiers in Human Neuroscience*, 8 (2014). https://doi.org/10.3389/fnhum.2014.00791

17. *Social Justice and Autism: Links to Personality and Advocacy [UCLA].* https://escholarship.org/uc/item/6fm925m3
18. To unpack this further it is 'the ability of the nervous system to change its activity in response to intrinsic or extrinsic stimuli by reorganizing its structure, functions, or connections.' Matt Puderbaugh and Prabhu Emmady, 'Neuroplasticity', in *StatPearls* (StatPearls Publishing, 2024). http://www.ncbi.nlm.nih.gov/books/NBK557811/
19. Kamila Jankowiak-Siuda, Krystyna Rymarczyk, Anna Grabowska, 'How we empathize with others: a neurobiological perspective', *Med Sci Monit.* 17(1) (2011).
20. Neuroimaging data has shown that people's brains can unconsciously classify unhoused people as objects, not people: https://journals.sagepub.com/doi/abs/10.1111/j.1467-9280.2006.01793.
21. Emma Dabiri, *What White People Can Do Next: From Allyship to Coalition* (Penguin UK, 2021).
22. https://www.parliament.uk/about/living-heritage/transformingsociety/electionsvoting/womenvote/overview/startsuffragette-/
23. https://www.visitheritage.co.uk/discover/womens-history/suffragists-and-suffragettes/
24. https://blog.nationalarchives.gov.uk/millicent-fawcett-statue-unveiled-in-parliament-square/
25. June Purvis and Sandra Stanley Holton (eds.), *Votes for Women* (Psychology Press, 2000).
26. June Purvis, *Emmeline Pankhurst: A Biography* (Routledge, 2003), p. 165.
27. https://academic.oup.com/hwj/article/71/1/98/641667/
28. Other protests around the same time numbered from 300 to 500,000 women. Katherine E. Kelly, 'Seeing through Spectacles: The Woman Suffrage Movement and London Newspapers, 1906–13'. *European Journal of Women's Studies.* 11 (3) (2004), 327–353; Leslie Hume, *The National Union of Women's Suffrage Societies 1897–1914* (Routledge, 2016 [1982]).
29. https://blog.nationalarchives.gov.uk/millicent-fawcett-statue-unveiled-in-parliament-square/; *Emmeline Pankhurst: A Biography.*
30. Jennifer Earl and Katrina Kimport, *Digitally Enabled Social Change: Activism in the Internet Age* (MIT Press, 2011).
31. Blake Richards and Timothy Lillicrap, *The Brain-Computer Metaphor Debate Is Useless: A Matter of Semantics* 4 (2022).
32. https://adami.natsci.msu.edu/blog/2013/04/the-evolution-of-circle-of-empathy.html; Jennie M. Warmouth, 'Widening the Circle of Empathy through Humane Education: A Qualitative Study with Diverse and

At-Risk Children', in *ProQuest LLC* (ProQuest LLC, 2017); Erika Weisz and Jamil Zaki, 'Empathy-building interventions: A review of existing work and suggestions for future directions', in *The Oxford Handbook of Compassion Science* (Oxford University Press, 2017), pp. 205–17, https://doi.org/10.1093/oxfordhb/9780190464684.001.0001

33. https://adami.natsci.msu.edu/blog/2013/04/the-evolution-of-circle-of-empathy.html
34. https://www.ncbi.nlm.nih.gov/pmc/articles/PMC3233761/
35. https://www.thetimes.com/uk/politics/article/censorship-on-campus-universities-scrap-challenging-books-to-protect-students-dp50d9fsd/
36. Victoria Bridgland, Payton Jones, and Benjamin Bellet, 'A Meta-Analysis of the Efficacy of Trigger Warnings, Content Warnings, and Content Notes', *Clinical Psychological Science* (2023), https://doi.org/10.1177/21677026231186625/
37. 'We found substantial evidence that trigger warnings counter-therapeutically reinforce survivors' view of their trauma as central to their identity . . . we found that trigger warnings are not helpful for trauma survivors.' Payton Jones, Benjamin Bellet, and Richard McNally, 'Helping or Harming? The Effect of Trigger Warnings on Individuals with Trauma Histories', *Clinical Psychological Science*, 8 (2020), p. 1, https://doi.org/10.1177/2167702620921341. And for further exploration of the pros and cons of trigger warnings: F. Laguardia, Venezia Michalsen, and Holly Rider-Milkovich, 'Trigger Warnings: From Panic to Data', *Journal of Legal Education*, 66(4) (2017), 882–903. https://www.newyorker.com/news/our-columnists/what-if-trigger-warnings-dont-work/
38. Rebecca Lewis, *Alternative Influence: Broadcasting the Reactionary Right on YouTube. Data & Society Research Institute* (2018), https://datasociety.net/wp-content/uploads/2018/09/DS_Alternative_Influence.pdf
39. https://www.nytimes.com/column/rabbit-hole/
40. https://www.pnas.org/doi/10.1073/pnas.2213020120/
41. https://www.statista.com/forecasts/1144088/youtube-users-in-the-world
42. https://www.statista.com/statistics/1347599/rumble-quarterly-mau/
43. https://www.independent.co.uk/news/world/americas/us-election-2020/qanon-capitol-congress-riot-trump-b1784460.html; https://www.salon.com/2023/05/06/rumble-a-haven-for-qanon-supporters-gains-traction-among-conservatives/
44. Ciarán O'Connor, 'Hatescape: An In-Depth Analysis of Extremism and Hate Speech on TikTok' (ISD, 2021), https://www.isdglobal.org/wp-content/uploads/2021/08/HateScape_v5.pdf
45. https://www.businessofapps.com/data/tik-tok-statistics/
46. https://www.nytimes.com/2020/06/04/podcasts/rabbit-hole-qanon-youtube-tiktok-virus.html?showTranscript=1/

47. https://www.brennancenter.org/our-work/research-reports/roe-v-wade-and-supreme-court-abortion-cases /
48. https://www.bbc.co.uk/news/uk-68305991/
49. https://www.theguardian.com/world/2023/nov/10/the-women-being-prosecuted-in-great-britain-for-abortions-her-confidentiality-was-completely-destroyed/
50. https://humanists.uk/2023/11/29/anti-choice-christians-in-parliament-launch-triple-attack-on-abortion-rights/
51. https://abortionrights.org.uk/history-of-abortion-law-in-the-uk/; https://hansard.parliament.uk/lords/2024-03-22/debates/6F125DEE-55F1-4337-B0EB-508CAA578B6B/FoetalSentienceCommitteeBill(HL)/
52. https://www.independent.co.uk/news/uk/home-news/police-testing-abortion-drugs-miscarriage-b2439733.html
53. https://www.france24.com/en/europe/20240304-france-to-enshrine-abortion-rights-in-country-s-constitution/

Does History Have a Right Side?

1. https://www.telegraph.co.uk/news/2020/09/12/students-call-george-bernard-shaws-name-removed-rada-theatre/
2. https://theworld.org/stories/2014/07/06/pygmalion/
3. https://core.ac.uk/reader/222830540
4. Kerry Powell, *The Cambridge Companion to Victorian and Edwardian Theatre* (Cambridge University Press, 2004), p. 229.
5. https://www.econlib.org/library/Columns/y2017/SchwartzShaw.html.
6. https://www.ivu.org/history/shaw/vivisection.html
7. https://scholarlypublishingcollective.org/psup/shaw/article-abstract/41/1/6/264336/Racism-and-Shaw?redirectedFrom=fulltext/
8. C. P. Blacker, 'Eugenics in Relation to the Maintenance of Health and the Avoidance of Disease', *The Journal of State Medicine*, 41(4) (1933), 226–239.
9. The speech can be watched here: https://www.youtube.com/watch?v=Ymi3umIo-sM/
10. https://www.cato.org/speeches/risk-policy-ethics/
11. https://www.theguardian.com/global-development/2020/nov/17/marie-stopes-charity-changes-name-in-break-with-founders-view-on-eugenics/
12. https://bylinetimes.com/2020/02/17/eugenics-and-the-intellectuals/
13. http://www.cambridge.org/core/services/aop-cambridge-core/content/view/94158269859ADC577FA74AC0271CF444/S0020859010000209a.pdf/brave_new_world_the_left_social_engineering_and_eugenics_in_twentiethcentury_europe.pdf; https://www.theguardian.com/politics/from-the-archive-blog/2019/may/01/eugenics-founding-fathers-british-socialism-archive-1997/

14. Fae Brauer, '"L'Art eugénique": Biopower and the Biocultures of Neo-Lamarckian Eugenics', *L'Esprit Créateur*, 52(2) (2012), 42–58.
15. https://via.library.depaul.edu/cgi/viewcontent.cgi?article=1270&context=law-review
16. Marie Skodak, 'The Mental Development of Adopted Children Whose True Mothers Are Feeble-Minded', *Child Development*, 9(3) (1938), 3. https://doi.org/10.2307/1125442/
17. Brookwood, M. *The orphans of Davenport: Eugenics, the Great Depression, and the war over children's intelligence (First edition).* (Liveright Publishing Corporation, 2021.).
18. Frank Burchill, 'Collective Bargaining' in F. Burchill (ed.), *Labour Relations* (Macmillan Education UK, 1997), 91–101, https://doi.org/10.1007/978-1-349-14497-6_6
19. https://www.theguardian.com/politics/from-the-archive-blog/2019/may/01/eugenics-founding-fathers-british-socialism-archive-1997/
20. Kelly Miller, 'Eugenics of the Negro Race', *The Scientific Monthly*, 5(1) (1917), 57–59, p. 57.
21. https://socialsci.libretexts.org/Bookshelves/Anthropology/Cultural_Anthropology/Cultural_Anthropology_(Evans)/06%3A_Deconstructing_Race/6.06%3A_Eugenics_in_the_United_States/
22. Marilyn M. Singleton, 'The "Science" of Eugenics: America's Moral Detour', *Journal of American Physicians and Surgeons*, 19(4) (2014).
23. Angela Saini, *Superior: The Return of Race Science* (4th Estate, 2019).
24. Bernard F. Dukore, 'Racism and Shaw', *Shaw*, 41(1) (2021), 6–34, https://doi.org/10.5325/shaw.41.1.0006
25. Colin Murphy, 'Judging Shaw – A Play Extract: Sketches on the Life (and Afterlife) of George Bernard Shaw', *Shaw*, 40(2) (2021), 323–331, https://doi.org/10.5325/shaw.40.2.0323
26. https://www.latimes.com/archives/la-xpm-1993-07-20-vw-14996-story.html
27. Brian Doherty, Graeme Hayes, and Steven Cammiss, 'We attended the trial of the Colston four: Here's why their acquittal should be celebrated', *The Conversation*, 7 January 2022, http://theconversation.com/we-attended-the-trial-of-the-colston-four-heres-why-their-acquittal-should-be-celebrated-174481/
28. Tim Cole, and Joanna Burch-Brown, *The Colston Statue: What Next? 'We are Bristol' History Commission Full Report* (2022), https://www.bristol.gov.uk/files/documents/1825-history-commission-full-report-final/file/
29. Ibid., p. 6
30. https://www.bristolmuseums.org.uk/m-shed/whats-on/historical-walk-bristol-abolition/
31. Formally known as the Mental Deficiency Act, and backed by Shaw: https://www5.open.ac.uk/health-and-social-care/research/shld/sites/; www.open.ac.uk.health-and-social-care.research.shld/files/files/ecms/

web-content/shld-web-content/education-resources-home-a-history-of-institutions-jan-walmsley.pdf

32. Sharks are killed for shark-fin soup, shark oil and fertiliser. Some are accidentally killed as a by-catch during over-fishing. There has been a 70 per cent decline in the shark population in the last fifty years which is a huge problem for the ecosystem. https://www.greenpeace.org/international/story/46967/100-million-dead-sharks-its-not-all-about-shark-fin-soup/
33. https://www.ucl.ac.uk/news/2020/jun/ucl-dename-spaces-named-after-prominent-eugenicists/
34. Ella Karev, 'Ancient Egyptian Slavery'. In Damian A. Pargas and Juliane Schiel (eds.), *The Palgrave Handbook of Global Slavery throughout History* (Springer International Publishing, 2023), pp. 41–66.
35. G. K. Chesterton and Michael Perry (ed.), *Eugenics and Other Evils: An Argument Against the Scientifically Organized State*, (Inkling Books, 2001).
36. https://mercyforanimals.org/blog/greta-thunberg-animals-environment/
37. https://9to5mac.com/2021/05/10/seven-apple-suppliers-allegedly-using-forced-labor/
38. https://www.theverge.com/2021/5/10/22428899/apple-suppliers-china-uyghur-forced-labor-report/
39. https://www.apple.com/speaking-up-on-racism/
40. https://www.washingtontimes.com/news/2021/may/11/apple-continues-use-china-slave-labor-report-shows/
41. https://personal.lse.ac.uk/robert49/teaching/mm/articles/Singer_1972Famine.pdf
42. https://apnews.com/article/ap-top-news-international-news-weekend-reads-china-health-269b3de1af34e17c1941a514f78d764c/
43. https://www.ilo.org/wcmsp5/groups/public/@ed_norm/@ipec/documents/publication/wcms_797515.pdf
44. https://www.ohchr.org/sites/default/files/documents/hrbodies/hrcouncil/wgtranscorp/session8/igwg-8th-compilation-general-statements.pdf
45. Conversation between Gloria Steinem and Diane von Furstenberg, https://www.youtube.com/watch?v=yIge8IBxNjo/
46. https://rapecrisis.org.uk/get-informed/statistics-sexual-violence/
47. https://www.cps.gov.uk/sites/default/files/documents/publications/perverting_course_of_justice_march_2013.pdf
48. https://www.openaccessgovernment.org/anti-black-bias/97383/
49. https://www.bmj.com/company/newsroom/fatal-police-shootings-of-unarmed-black-people-in-us-more-than-3-times-as-high-as-in-whites/

The Conversation about Gender Nonconformity

1. https://www.spokesman.com/stories/1997/nov/19/the-fear-trigger-the-trusty-little-amygdala-helps/

2. https://www.hollywoodreporter.com/tv/tv-news/joe-biden-cites-will-grace-320724-0-320724/
3. https://www.politico.com/news/magazine/2022/05/06/joe-biden-gay-marriage-00030367
4. Kathleen Battles and Wendy Hilton-Morrow, 'Gay characters in conventional spaces: *Will and Grace* and the situation comedy genre', *Critical Studies in Media Communication*, 19(1) (2002), 87–105, https://doi.org/10.1080/07393180216553; Rodger Streitmatter, *From 'Perverts' to 'Fab Five': The Media's Changing Depiction of Gay Men and Lesbians* (Routledge, 2008); Diane Raymond, 'Popular Culture and Queer Representation: A Critical Perspective', in Gail Dines and Jean M. Humez (eds.), *Gender, Race and Class in the Media* (Sage, 2003), 98–110.
5. This perspective is supported by all kinds of data and research, most obviously the British Social Attitudes Survey over the course of the 1980s–2010s, and specifically in the USA, Amy Stone's research: Amy Stone, 'Frame Variation in Child Protectionist Claims: Constructions of Gay Men and Transgender Women as Strangers', *Social Forces*, 97(3) (2019), 1155–1176.
6. https://www.nbcnews.com/nbc-out/out-news/percentage-lgbtq-adults-us-doubled-decade-gallup-finds-rcna16556/. Comparative UK data is here: https://www.ons.gov.uk/peoplepopulationandcommunity/culturalidentity/sexuality/bulletins/sexualidentityuk/2021and2022/; https://www.statista.com/statistics/317651/homosexuality-in-the-united-kingdom-by-age/
7. https://news.gallup.com/poll/1651/gay-lesbian-rights.aspx/
8. https://news.gallup.com/poll/147662/first-time-majority-americans-favor-legal-gay-marriage.aspx/
9. As documented in *The Case Against 8*, an American documentary that first aired at Sundance in 2014
10. https://www.statista.com/statistics/741849/modern-family-viewership-usa-by-age/
11. https://eugenicsarchive.ca/discover/connections/535eee2d7095aa0000000258/
12. And was standard practice for trans people in many countries across Europe, until it was made illegal by the European Court of Human Rights in 2017: https://lgbti-era.org/no-more-forced-sterilization-for-trans-people-in-europe-but-trans-pathologisation-remains/
13. Eimear McLoughlin, '#SaveBenjy: Sexuality, Queer Animals and Ireland', *Humanimalia: a journal of human/animal interface studies*, 7(1) (2015), 109–22.
14. https://www.dw.com/en/10-animal-species-that-show-how-being-gay-is-natural/g-39934832/
15. https://www.humandignitytrust.org/lgbt-the-law/map-of-criminalisation/
16. https://www.stonewall.org.uk/about-us/news/african-sexuality-and-legacy-imported-homophobia/
17. Ruth Benedict, *Patterns of Culture* (Houghton Mifflin Harcourt, 1934).

18. https://onlinelibrary.wiley.com/doi/full/10.1002/jad.12013/
19. https://www.ncbi.nlm.nih.gov/pmc/articles/PMC4160347/
20. https://cerebral-sexuality.com/2018/04/09/consensual-kinks-arent-unethical/
21. https://www.latimes.com/archives/la-xpm-2005-nov-27-me-then27-story.html
22. https://fakehistoryhunter.net/2021/07/31/not-marlene-dietrich-being-detained-for-wearing-trousers/
23. https://www.vanityfair.com/hollywood/2017/01/mary-tyler-moore-pants/
24. https://www.vintag.es/2022/03/lois-rabinowitz.html
25. https://michael-antony.com/page2.html
26. https://www.davidbowienews.com/2014/02/aged-17
27. Peter Conn, *Adoption: A Brief Social and Cultural History* (Palgrave Pivot, 2013).
28. Leo K. Killsback, 'A nation of families: Traditional indigenous kinship, the foundation for Cheyenne sovereignty', *AlterNative: An International Journal of Indigenous Peoples*, 15(1) (2019), 34–43, p. 38, https://doi.org/10.1177/1177180118822833/
29. https://cspm.csyw.qld.gov.au/practice-kits/safe-care-and-connection/working-with-aboriginal-and-torres-strait-islander/seeing-and-understanding/the-meaning-of-family-in-aboriginal-and-torres-str/
30. Conn, *Adoption*.
31. https://www.brunel.ac.uk/news-and-events/news/articles/Childbirth-and-the-Victorian-Workhouse/
32. https://www.theguardian.com/society/2009/nov/24/save-the-children-orphans-report/
33. https://www.education.ox.ac.uk/wp-content/uploads/2020/03/Bright-Spots-Insight-Paper-ChallengingStigma-web_Mar2020.pdf
34. https://homeforgood.org.uk/statistics/care-leavers
35. https://merrynallingham.com/19th-20th-century/the-rise-of-the-orphanage/
36. https://www.ons.gov.uk/peoplepopulationandcommunity/culturalidentity/genderidentity/articles/qualityofcensus2021genderidentitydata/2023-11-13/
37. https://www.healthline.com/health/transgender/how-common-is-transgender/
38. https://www.jstor.org/stable/1409033/
39. https://www.vic.gov.au/pride-our-future-victorias-lgbtiqa-strategy-2022-32/definitions-and-key-terms/
40. https://www.theguardian.com/world/2022/mar/14/cis-people-still-suffer-under-the-gender-binary-six-lessons-from-all-about-women/
41. https://www.crosslandsolicitors.com/site/hr-hub/transgender-discrimination-in-UK-workplaces/
42. https://www.totaljobs.com/advice/wp-content/uploads/Trans-employee-experiences-survey-2016-by-Totaljobs.pdf
43. https://www.lgbthealth.org.uk/wp-content/uploads/2021/08/Trans-People-and-Work-Survey-Report-LGBT-Health-Aug-2021-FINAL.pdf

44. https://transactual.org.uk/wp-content/uploads/TransLivesSurvey2021.pdf
45. https://williamsinstitute.law.ucla.edu/press/ncvs-trans-press-release/
46. https://pubmed.ncbi.nlm.nih.gov/32345113/
47. https://afsp.org/suicide-statistics/
48. https://www.stophateuk.org/about-hate-crime/transgender-hate/
49. https://www.ons.gov.uk/aboutus/transparencyandgovernance/freedomofinformationfoi/hatecrimesagainsttransgenderandnonbinaryindividuals/
50. https://www.ipso.co.uk/news-press-releases/press-releases/new-research-on-reporting-of-trans-issues-shows-400-increase-in-coverage-and varying-perceptions-on-broader-editorial-standards/
51. https://novaramedia.com/2023/02/20/welcome-to-terf-island-how-anti-trans-hate-skyrocketed-156-in-four-years/
52. https://www.ipso.co.uk/media/1986/mediatique-report-on-coverage-of-transgender-issues.pdf
53. Juliet Jacques writes beautifully about Nadia's win, and her own transition, here: https://aeon.co/essays/there-was-no-before-and-after-in-my-transsexual-journey/
54. https://www.dailymail.co.uk/news/article-12792257/doctor-60th-anniversary-david-tennant-transgender-rose-yasmin-finney.html
55. https://metro.co.uk/2023/12/08/doctor-transgender-character-sparked-bbc-complaints-19948307/
56. https://www.telegraph.co.uk/news/2023/12/25/bbc-hides-gender-critical-tweets-doctor-who-trans-character/
57. https://www.dailymail.co.uk/tvshowbiz/article-3110297/Laverne-Cox-Orange-New-Black-stars-let-day-release-glam-beach-shoot-Essence-Magazine.html
58. https://www.dailymail.co.uk/news/article-3123845/Remember-transgender-beautiful-Moment-Laverne-Cox-gives-trans-7-year-old-heartwarming-advice.html
59. https://www.telegraph.co.uk/culture/tvandradio/11972831/Offer-big-TV-roles-to-transgender-actors-broadcasters-told.html
60. https://www.theguardian.com/society/2017/oct/18/theresa-may-plans-to-let-people-change-gender-without-medical-checks/
61. https://time.com/135480/transgender-tipping-point/
62. https://www.stonewall.org.uk/about-us/news/new-data-rise-hate-crime-against-lgbtq-people-continues-stonewall-slams-uk-gov-/
63. https://www.gov.uk/government/statistics/hate-crime-england-and-wales-2022-to-2023/
64. https://medium.com/women-and-hollywood/today-in-metoo-times-up-legal-fund-raises-20m-berlinale-joins-movement-f3d84c282973/
65. https://www.hrw.org/news/2023/03/07/global-backlash-against-womens-rights/

66. https://www.scientificamerican.com/article/evidence-undermines-rapid-onset-gender-dysphoria-claims/
67. For more on the presentation/performance of abusive behaviour online, see John Suler, 'The online disinhibition effect', *CyberPsychology & Behavior*, 7(3) (2004), 321–6.
68. Academic researcher Aleardo Zanghellini's paper further explores the unhelpful dynamics for discussing trans rights on Twitter: https://journals.sagepub.com/doi/pdf/10.1177/2158244020927029/
69. https://www.historyandpolicy.org/opinion-articles/articles/a-policy-widely-abused/
70. Evan Smith, *No Platform: A History of Anti-Fascism, Universities and the Limits of Free Speech*. (Routledge, 2020).
71. https://www.newyorker.com/magazine/2023/09/18/the-women-of-now-how-feminists-built-an-organization-that-transformed-america-katherine-turk-book-review-betty-friedan-magnificent-disrupter-rachel-shteir
72. https://www.advocate.com/history/betty-friedan-anti-lesbian/
73. https://www.thefp.com/witchtrials/
74. https://www.youtube.com/watch?v=EmToioxG6zg/
75. https://www.youtube.com/watch?v=Ou_xvXJJk7k/
76. Charlotte Galpin, Gina Gwenffrewi and Ash Stokoe, 'Transfeminist perspectives: Beyond cisnormative understandings of the digital public sphere', *European Journal of Women's Studies*, 30(4) (2023), 502–15, https://doi.org/10.1177/13505068231209544
77. https://www.washingtonpost.com/religion/2018/10/05/hairstylist-fired-roundhouse-kick-antiabortion-protesters-shoulder-toronto/
78. Robert D. Tobin, 'Kertbeny's "Homosexuality" and the Language of Nationalism' in *Genealogies of Identity* (Brill, 2005), pp. 3–18.
79. https://corambaaf.org.uk/resources/looked-after-children-statistics/
80. https://gh.bmj.com/content/8/3/e010556/
81. https://www.nbcnews.com/feature/nbc-out/pink-pussyhat-creator-addresses-criticism-over-name-n717886/
82. https://www.reuters.com/investigates/special-report/usa-transyouth-data/
83. https://www.scientificamerican.com/article/what-the-science-on-gender-affirming-care-for-transgender-kids-really-shows/
84. https://www.bbc.co.uk/news/uk-england-68588724/
85. https://cass.independent-review.uk/about-the-review/
86. https://epath.eu/wp-content/uploads/2019/04/Boof-of-abstracts-EPATH2019.pdf
87. https://jamanetwork.com/journals/jamasurgery/article-abstract/2813212/
88. https://www.ucsf.edu/news/2020/01/416421/five-years-after-abortion-nearly-all-women-say-it-was-right-decision-study/
89. https://www.dailymail.co.uk/news/article-13518499/trans-detainee-rape-women-inmates-women-California-psychologist.html

90. https://assets.publishing.service.gov.uk/media/61e804cbe90e07037668e2c0/HMPPS_Offender_Equalities_2020-21_FINAL_Revision.pdf
91. https://assets.publishing.service.gov.uk/media/637e38d0e90e0723389cbeb9/HMPPS_Offender_Equalities_2021-22_Report.pdf
92. https://www.gov.uk/government/statistics/hmpps-offender-equalities-annual-report-2022-to-2023/hmpps-offender-equalities-annual-report-2022-23#transgender-prisoners
93. https://inews.co.uk/opinion/prisons-never-safe-women-trans-people-2180097
94. https://cpb-us-e2.wpmucdn.com/sites.uci.edu/dist/0/1149/files/2013/06/BulletinVol2Issue2.pdf
95. https://insidetime.org/newsround/male-officer-jailed-over-sex-acts-with-female-prisoners/
96. https://www.theguardian.com/society/2023/oct/15/alarm-at-rise-in-use-of-mixed-sex-wards-in-nhs-england-hospitals/
97. https://www.met.police.uk/foi-ai/metropolitan-police/d/october-2022/recorded-rapes-sexual-assaults-hospitals-january2019-september2022/
98. https://www.womensaid.org.uk/what-we-do/i-work-with-survivors/no-woman-turned-away/
99. https://www.ncbi.nlm.nih.gov/pmc/articles/PMC8671347/
100. https://www.thetimes.co.uk/article/spare-us-the-horror-of-the-unisex-toilet-96rl2lpfq6p
101. Justin E. Lerner, 'Having to "Hold It": Factors That Influence the Avoidance of Using Public Bathrooms among Transgender People', *Health Soc Work*. 46(4) (2021), 260–7.
102. https://www.littleleague.org/news/1974-the-year-little-league-changed-forever/
103. https://www.englandnetball.co.uk/play-netball/mens-mixed-netball/
104. https://ideas.time.com/2011/12/12/transgender-the-next-frontier-in-human-rights/
105. https://www.ohchr.org/sites/default/files/documents/cfi-subm/2308/subm-colonialism-sexual-orientation-un-ios-unrisd-input-2.pdf
106. https://www.epfweb.org/sites/default/files/2020-05/rtno_epf_book_lores.pdf
107. https://www.aclu.org/project-2025-explained and https://www.heritage.org/
108. https://www.europarl.europa.eu/committees/en/joint-femm-inge-public-hearing-on-financ/product-details/20210315CHE08502/
109. https://www.unwomen.org/en/news-stories/news/2023/03/to-tackle-the-pushback-on-gender-equality-foster-and-fund-inclusive-feminist-movements/
110. https://www.lse.ac.uk/gender/news/2022/AHRC-launch
111. https://centreforfeministforeignpolicy.org/portfolio-item/understanding-and-countering-the-anti-gender-movement/

112. https://www.uib.no/en/skok/160065/how-global-anti-gender-movement-impacting-research-and-activism-norway/
113. https://www.pbs.org/newshour/show/why-anti-transgender-political-ads-are-dominating-the-airwaves-this-election

The Conversation about Comedy and Freedom of Speech

1. https://www.washingtonexaminer.com/news/2121821/bill-maher-political-correctness-is-a-cancer-on-progressivism/
2. https://www.wbur.org/npr/736594233/hannah-gadsby-if-political-correctness-can-kill-comedy-its-already-dead
3. https://www.indiewire.com/features/general/dave-chappelle-netflix-equanimity-the-bird-revelation-1201912192/
4. https://www.newyorker.com/culture/culture-desk/sarah-silvermans-comedy-is-changing-with-the-times
5. https://edition.cnn.com/2024/10/16/entertainment/jerry-seinfeld-extreme-left-comments-intl-scli/index.html
6. https://www.hollywoodreporter.com/tv/tv-features/patton-oswalt-interview-netflix-covid-cancel-culture-1235185708/
7. Guillaume Dezecache, and R. I. M. Dunbar, 'Sharing the joke: The size of natural laughter groups', *Evolution and Human Behavior*, 33(6) (2012), 775–9. https://doi.org/10.1016/j.evolhumbehav.2012.07.002
8. Michelle L. Bemiller and Rachel Z. Schneider, 'It's Not Just a Joke' *Sociological Spectrum*, 30(4) (2010), 459–79. https://doi.org/10.1080/02732171003641040
9. Though there are traditions across the world that stretch further back, as Beatrice K. Otto explains: 'China has undoubtedly the longest, richest, and most thoroughly documented history of court jesters.' Beatrice K. Otto, *Fools Are Everywhere: The Court Jester Around the World (New edition)* (University of Chicago Press, 2007)
10. https://www.todayifoundout.com/index.php/2019/10/what-was-it-actually-like-to-be-a-court-jester-in-medieval-times/
11. Katherine E. Smith, 'Review of Fools and Idiots: Intellectual Disability in the Middle Ages by Irina Metzler', *Disability Studies Quarterly*, 40(1) (2020), https://doi.org/10.18061/dsq.v40i1.7445/; https://web.archive.org/web/20210411235654/https://magdaromanska.com/opera-blog-the-history-of-the-court-jester-and-verdis-rigoletto-2/
12. https://www.historyextra.com/period/medieval/what-was-life-like-for-a-court-jester/
13. https://decider.com/2020/01/15/hugh-laurie-on-return-of-a-bit-of-fry-and-laurie/
14. https://www.youtube.com/watch?v=gnmiqqiBb8k/
15. https://collider.com/are-snl-weekend-update-joke-swaps-real-colin-jost-interview/

16. https://quoteinvestigator.com/2022/08/10/art-anything/
17. 'We are extremely concerned at the potential disastrous consequences of the new criminal trespass offence introduced by the Police Act 2022.' https://www.opendemocracy.net/en/romany-gypsy-woman-high-court-policing-act-judicial-review/ (p. 2); https://new.basw.co.uk/sites/default/files/resources/good_practice_guidance_understanding_the_welfare_impact_of_the_
pcsc_act_-_july_2022.pdf
18. https://www.dw.com/en/nazi-graffiti-mars-berlin-monument-to-roma/a-18814597; https://www.bbc.com/news/uk-scotland-glasgow-west-51272457/ https://www.glasgowtimes.co.uk/news/18519910.callous-ignorant-vandals-desecrate-roma-holocaust-memorial-second-time/
19. https://english.radio.cz/police-investigating-vandalism-lety-memorial-8159055
20. https://www.amnesty.org.uk/roma-rights/
21. https://www.amnesty.org/en/latest/campaigns/2015/04/roma-czech-discrimination/
22. https://www.amnesty.org/en/latest/campaigns/2015/04/roma-in-europe-11-things-you-always-wanted-to-know-but-were-afraid-to-ask/; other evidence includes this documentary: https://www.youtube.com/watch?v=ALdlphTYdi4/
23. https://www.theguardian.com/world/2020/jun/14/david-walliams-and-matt-lucas-apologise-for-little-britain-blackface/
24. https://www.theguardian.com/global/2015/sep/13/juliet-jacques-trapped-in-wrong-society-not-wrong-body-trans-extract-memoir/
25. https://www.youtube.com/watch?v=uZwuTI-V8SI/

The Conversation about Cancel Culture

1. https://www.thenation.com/article/archive/dan-snyders-open-letter-redskins-nation-presented-commentary/
2. See Meredith D. Clark, 'DRAG THEM: A brief etymology of so-called "cancel culture"', *Communication and the Public*, 5(3-4) (2020), 88–92. https://doi.org/10.1177/2057047320961562/
3. Noelle-Neumann's spiral of silence thesis explains that 'where mainstream values in any group gradually flourish to become the predominant culture, while, due to social pressures, dissenting minority voices become muted. The ratchet effect eventually muffles contrarians. The evidence suggests that the cancel culture is not simply a rhetorical myth; scholars may be less willing to speak up to defend their moral beliefs if they believe that their views are not widely shared by colleagues or the wider society to which they belong.' Pippa Norris, 'Cancel Culture: Myth or Reality?' *Political Studies*, 71(1) (2023), 145–74, p.145, https://doi.org/10.1177/00323217211037023

4. https://www.smithsonianmag.com/history/the-skinny-on-the-fatty-arbuckle-trial-131228859/
5. https://www.smh.com.au/lifestyle/yassmin-abdelmagied-on-becoming-australias-most-publicly-hated-muslim-20170816-gxxb7d.html
6. https://www.cbc.ca/documentaries/of-the-more-than-60-women-who-accused-bill-cosby-of-sexual-assault-only-one-got-a-conviction-1.6698830/
7. https://www.telegraph.co.uk/tv/2021/06/02/ellie-kemper-tvs-alleged-kkk-princess-does-not-owe-twitter-apology/
8. https://books.google.co.uk/books?id=9TcDAAAAMBAJ&lpg=PA1&pg=PA56
9. https://www.thenation.com/article/society/veiled-prophet-st-louis/
10. Kipling D. Williams, *Ostracism: The Power of Silence* (Guilford Press, 2002).
11. Michael A. van der Kooij, Martina Fantin, Emilia Rejmak, Jocelyn Grosse, Olivia Zanoletti, Celine Fournier, Krishnendu Ganguly, Katarzyna Kalita, Leszek Kaczmarek, and Carmen Sandi, 'Role for MMP-9 in stress-induced downregulation of nectin-3 in hippocampal CA1 and associated behavioural alterations', *Nature Communications*, 5(1) (2014), 4995. https://doi.org/10.1038/ncomms5995
12. Mark R. Leary, 'Emotional responses to interpersonal rejection', *Dialogues in Clinical Neuroscience*, 17(4) (2015), 435–41.
13. https://www.scientificamerican.com/article/the-pain-of-exclusion/
14. https://www.ted.com/talks/dan_reisel_the_neuroscience_of_restorative_justice/
15. Brené Brown, *Daring Greatly* (Penguin, 2015), p. 54.
16. Ibid., p. 134.
17. Ibid., p. 132.
18. https://www.psychologytoday.com/au/blog/resilient-leadership/201910/get-comfortable-discomfort/
19. https://www.uis.edu/sites/default/files/inline-images/the_road_to_resilience.pdf.
20. Caitlin E. Loprinzi, Kavita Prasad, Darrell R. Schroeder and Amit Sood, 'Stress Management and Resilience Training (SMART) program to decrease stress and enhance resilience among breast cancer survivors: a pilot randomized clinical trial', *Clinical Breast Cancer*, 11 (2011), 364–8. 8.
21. Vicki Bitsika, Christopher F. Sharpley and Ryan Bell, 'The buffering effect of resilience upon stress, anxiety and depression in parents of a child with an autism spectrum disorder', *Journal of Developmental and Physical Disabilities*, 25 (2013), 533–43. 5.
22. https://journals.sagepub.com/doi/10.1177/00323217211037023
23. https://www.thenation.com/article/archive/tony-benn-and-five-essential-questions-democracy/
24. Olúfẹ́mi O Táíwò, *Elite Capture: How the Powerful Took Over Identity Politics (and Everything Else)* (Haymarket Books, 2022).

25. Ibid.
26. Ibid.
27. https://www.clementinemorrigan.com/p/real-life-is-complicated-but-compassion/
28. https://headlight.health/reducing-the-stigma-behind-narcissistic-personality-disorder/
29. https://www.usatoday.com/story/life/health-wellness/2023/03/17/narcissist-narcissism-key-terms-defined/11412129002/
30. https://www.womenslaw.org/about-abuse/forms-abuse/emotional-and-psychological-abuse/
31. https://www.ananiasfoundation.org/definitions/?gad_source=1&gclid=CjoKCQjwxqayBhDFARIsAANWRnSGnNdWgBGpZRu3U3b-O94beang-NFr_ceoCSkFPLW9Hy84oojKudsaAlEZEALw_wcB/
32. https://www.femicidecensus.org/data-matters-every-woman-matters/; https://www.ons.gov.uk/peoplepopulationandcommunity/crimeandjustice/articles/homicideinenglandandwales/yearendingmarch2023/
33. https://www.womensaid.org.uk/women-who-kill/; https://www.aihw.gov.au/family-domestic-and-sexual-violence/responses-and-outcomes/domestic-homicide#data-tell-us/
34. Steven Pinker. *Language, Cognition, and Human Nature*. 2013. https://doi.org/10.1093/acprof:oso/9780199328741.001.0001

What Are We Going to Do about All This?

1. For a more in-depth detailed history of all things sweet, see Michael Krondl, *Sweet Invention: A History of Dessert* (Chicago Review Press, 2011).
2. We transform our bodies to perform gender: 'the body resources or fleshes out the social categories through which gender is naturalized'. Rachel Dilley, Jenny Hockey, Victoria Robinson, and Alexandra Sherlock, 'Occasions and non-occasions: Identity, femininity and high-heeled shoes', *European Journal of Women's Studies*, 22(2) (2015), 14358, p. 144. https://doi.org/10.1177/1350506814533952
3. For further feminist reading: R. Claire Snyder-Hall, 'Third-Wave Feminism and the Defense of "Choice"', *Perspectives on Politics*, 8(1) (2010), 255–61. For a critique of 'waves': Elizabeth Evans, *The Politics of Third Wave Feminisms* (Palgrave, 2015).
   For continuation of third- into fourth-wave: Nicola Rivers, 'Between "Postfeminism(s)": Announcing the Arrival of Fourth Wave', in *Postfeminism(s) and the Arrival of the Fourth Wave* (Palgrave, 2017), 7–28.
4. https://www.rct.uk/collection/exhibitions/charles-ii-art-power/the-queens-gallery-buckingham-palace/high-heels-fit-for-a-king

5. https://obr.uk/box/the-behavioural-legacy-of-the-pandemic/
6. https://www.finder.com/uk/savings-accounts/working-from-home-statistics/
7. https://thehomeofficelife.com/blog/work-from-home-statistics/
8. https://www.inc.com/melissa-chu/why-your-brain-prioritizes-instant-gratification-0.html
9. https://pr.princeton.edu/news/04/q4/1014-brain.htm
10. https://www.internal-displacement.org/focus-areas/Displacement-disasters-and-climate-change/
11. 'When the lecture started, we flipped a coin in front of the class to decide which position each of us would take in the debate. We did this deliberately, with the hope of demonstrating explicitly to the students that critical thinking skills are needed and helpful regardless of one's position in an academic argument or debate.' Yu Tao and Ed Griffith, 'Making Critical Thinking Skills Training Explicit, Engaging, and Effective through Live Debates on Current Political Issues: A Pilot Pedagogical Experiment', *PS: Political Science & Politics*, 53(1) (2020), 155–160, p. 156.
12. https://howardleague.org/history-of-the-penal-system/ Before this time there was a lot of shunning and shaming (cancel culture but with stocks in the town square) as well as corporal and capital punishment.
13. The Nordic model of youth justice emphasises a collaborative approach between justice and child welfare systems. There are significant differences between countries (including higher levels of penal confinement in Denmark and Norway) but overall Nordic countries rely far less on confinement of young offenders in comparison to England and Wales: 'We found no evidence of deterrence associated with first imprisonment in Finland, a nation characterized by an exceptionally restrained use of the prison sentence.' Reino Sirén and Jukka Savolainen, 'No Evidence of Specific Deterrence under Penal Moderation: Imprisonment and Recidivism in Finland', *Journal of Scandinavian Studies in Criminology and Crime Prevention*, 14(2) (2013), 80–97, https://doi.org/10.1080/14043858.2013.805048.
    'A tough on crime attitude is not working. With this attitude, more money in the United States is being spent on re-incarcerating these prisoners, over 70 per cent of whom return in a matter of years when money could be going towards rehabilitating these prisoners to keep them from returning. It is easy to see Scandinavia's system is doing it right, preparing their inmates for a life outside of prison.' Alexis Riep, 'The Effects of Culture and Punishment Philosophies on Recidivism: Comparing Prison Systems in the United States and Scandinavia', *Honors Theses* (2019), p. 37, https://encompass.eku.edu/honors_theses/700/
    See also: Denis Yukhnenko, Leen Farouki and Seena Fazel, 'Criminal recidivism rates globally: A 6-year systematic review update', *Journal of Criminal Justice*, 88 (2023), https://doi.org/10.1016/j.jcrimjus.2023.102115; https://www.fangelsi.is/media/almennt/

Nordic-Statistics-2016_2020_final.pdf; Tapio Lappi-Seppälä, 'Nordic Youth Justice' *Crime and Justice*, 40(1) (2011), 199–264, https://doi.org/10.1086/661113;

14. https://hmiprisons.justiceinspectorates.gov.uk/hmipris_reports/children-in-custody-2022-23/
15. https://www.aclu.org/issues/juvenile-justice/youth-incarceration/americas-addiction-juvenile-incarceration-state-state/
16. Sofia Enell, Maria Andersson Vogel, Ann K. E. Henriksen, Tarja Pösö, Paivi Honkatukia, Bård Mellin-Olsen and Ida M. Hydle, 'Confinement and restrictive measures against young people in the Nordic countries – a comparative analysis of Denmark, Finland, Norway, and Sweden', *Nordic Journal of Criminology*, 23(2) (2022), 174–191. https://doi.org/10.1080/2578983X.2022.2054536
17. https://publications.parliament.uk/pa/cm5801/cmselect/cmjust/306/30609.htm
18. Phillip A. Goff, Matthew C. Jackson, Brooke A. L. Di Leone, Carmen M. Culotta and Natalie A. DiTomasso, 'The essence of innocence: Consequences of dehumanizing Black children', *Journal of Personality and Social Psychology*, 106(4) (2014), 526–45. https://doi.org/10.1037/a0035663/
19. https://www.gov.uk/government/statistics/youth-justice-statistics-2021-to-2022/youth-justice-statistics-2021-to-2022-accessible-version#proven-reoffending-by-children/
20. https://www.law.ac.uk/resources/blog/is-prison-effective/
21. https://prisonreformtrust.org.uk/majority-of-women-in-prison-have-been-victims-of-domestic-abuse/
22. https://prisonreformtrust.org.uk/urgent-call-to-provide-better-support-for-kids-with-mums-in-prison/
23. https://prisonreformtrust.org.uk/women-on-remand-more-likely-to-self-harm/
24. https://prisonreformtrust.org.uk/project/women-the-criminal-justice-system/
25. https://howardleague.org/wp-content/uploads/2022/04/APPG-womens-health-and-well-being-FINAL.pdf
26. https://assets.publishing.service.gov.uk/media/5aa28e0ee5274a3e391e37c0/Gender_specific_standards_for_women_in_prison_to_improve_health_and_wellbeing.pdf
27. https://prisonreformtrust.org.uk/six-in-10-women-sent-to-prison-serve-sentences-of-less-than-six-months/
28. https://workingchance.org/latest/five-years-after-hmp-holloway-closed-whats-happened-to-western-europes-largest-womens-prison/; https://assets.publishing.service.gov.uk/media/5d078d37e5274a0b879394c7/farmer-review-women.PDF.
29. Gilmore, Ruth Wilson and Naomi Murakawa 'COVID 19, decarceration and abolition', Haymarket Books 16 (2020).

30. https://prisonreformtrust.org.uk/wp-content/uploads/2023/06/prison_the_facts_2023.pdf; https://link.springer.com/article/10.1007/s11292-008-9063-3
31. https://www.gov.uk/government/publications/prison-education-a-review-of-reading-education-in-prisons/
32. https://www.shannontrust.org.uk/
33. https://www.bbc.co.uk/news/uk-england-oxfordshire-41389520/
34. https://www.theguardian.com/uk-news/2020/oct/27/black-people-nine-times-more-likely-to-face-stop-and-search-than-white-people/
35. See the work of Abolition Futures for a contemporary campaign in Britain and Ireland: https://abolitionistfutures.com/
For a detailed history of UK abolitionist politics from an intersectional perspective, see: Aviah Sarah Day and Shanice Octavia McBean, *Abolition Revolution* (Pluto Press, 2022).
36. https://www.bbc.co.uk/news/uk-england-london-62354354/
37. https://www.forensicrisk.com/news-and-insights/uk-post-office-inquiry-a-cautionary-tale-in-internal-investigations/
38. Angela Y. Davis, Gina Dent, Erica Meiners and Beth Richie, *Abolition. Feminism. Now.* (Penguin, 2022.)
39. Ruth McCausland and Eileen Baldry, 'Who does Australia lock up? The social determinants of justice', *International Journal for Crime, Justice and Social Democracy*, 12(3) (2023), 37–53, https://doi.org/10.5204/ijcjsd.2504
40. https://www.vanityfair.com/style/2022/07/bette-midler-trans-inclusive-language-erases-women-twitter-transgender-rights-macy-gray-jk-rowling/; https://www.gaytimes.co.uk/life/mae-martin-responds-to-bette-midlers-tweets-we-have-the-same-goal-and-enemy/
41. Carroll, Tamar W., *Mobilizing New York: AIDS, Antipoverty, and Feminist Activism* (University of North Carolina Press, 2015) pp. 157–158.
42. Sian Norris, *Bodies Under Siege: How the Far–Right Attack on Reproductive Rights Went Global* (Verso, 2023).
43. https://www.dw.com/en/lgbtq-community-is-there-a-backlash-in-europe/a-66675016/
44. https://www.theguardian.com/commentisfree/2022/jul/05/lgbtq-womens-rights-abortion-unite/

Acknowledgements

First, I need to thank my amazing editor, Sarah Savitt. She has a laser insight, a deep love of writers, a forensic understanding of books and, most importantly in my case, the patience of an especially patient saint. I also want to thank her whole team at Virago, who design covers, copyedit, typeset, do things I don't quite understand and find ways of making sure people read the book. They all deserve far more glory and applause than they get.

Thank you also to the many co-pilots and guests of *The Guilty Feminist* podcast and to my listeners who come out and watch the show, write in kind and encouraging words and aren't afraid to have difficult conversations with me and each other. Without you all I'd never have had the impetus or understanding needed to write this book!

Wesley Taylor spent hours helping research, shape and refine this book and got me to the top of the mountain. Max Olesker did the same in getting me down the other side. I have ADHD and juggle many projects at once, and it is no exaggeration to say that without them helping me into hyperfocus, you would not be reading this book!

There were many academics who agreed to take time out of their own research and publishing projects to put their top-class minds on this book. I wish to make it clear that I paid them for their work, because this should be standard practice (wherever possible) and so often isn't. Having their commitment, intelligence and expertise was a great privilege and I owe a sincere debt of gratitude to all of them:

Emily Mann is a researcher and PhD student at the University of Edinburgh. She was invaluable herself and also assisted me in finding some of the other key academics who consulted on this book in important ways.

Lucy Rycroft-Smith is a researcher and DPhil student at the University of Cambridge who specialises in making research accessible and summarising research for communication, which is what every author needs!

Dr Rachana Acharya is a Marie Curie research fellow at the Department of Chemical Engineering and Biotechnology and a postdoctoral affiliate at Newnham College, Cambridge, and above my paygrade. Luckily, she is a *Guilty Feminist* listener and agreed to help me shape my thoughts and check my facts.

Gina Gwenffrewi PhD is a lecturer in trans studies and English literature at the University of Edinburgh, who researches media, digital societies and trans cultural production – a perfect fit for the book, who kindly agreed to an interview, as well as some consultancy.

Dr Reubs Walsh is a neuropsychologist working as a postdoctoral research fellow at the Einstein Lab of Cognitive Neuroscience, Gender and Health at the University of Toronto. One of the finest minds I've had the pleasure to have difficult conversations with and a great thinker and debater, as well a long-time friend.

Dami Folayan is a PhD student in the Faculty of Education at the University of Cambridge, specialising in the sociology of education, decoloniality and women's empowerment, who consulted and gave me so much confidence in my ideas.

Dr Bee Hughes is an interdisciplinary artist and practice-led researcher. They are also senior lecturer in media, culture &

communication at Liverpool John Moores University. Their insights were challenging and excellent.

Rowan Douglas is based in the School of Health & Psychological Sciences at the City University of London and is a Cambridge graduate and PhD student who researches transmasculine people's experiences of negotiating identity in interactions. He's a brilliant mind and heart.

Lara Bochmann is a very clever PhD student in sociology at the University of Edinburgh with expertise in queer and trans studies. Their research focuses on embodiment and creative as well as participatory methods.

Caroline Angenieux is an editorial research assistant and psychology graduate from Goldsmiths University who applied for data about prisons under the Freedom of Information Act from the British government and did other fact checking for me.

Dr Adam Rutherford is a distinguished academic and writer – and author of the brilliant book *Control: The Dark History and Troubling Present of Eugenics*. He kindly granted me his time and expertise and answered my many and various questions.

Thank you also to my other fascinating contributors Travis Alabanza, Yomi Adegoke, Clementine Morrigan, Jarryd Bartle, Neil Datta, Vanessa Kisuule and Fiona Thompson.

My readers include journalist Phoebe Davis and friends Kathy Lette, Renee McTavish, Alex MacLaren, Greg Wise, Ivan Sedgwick and I'm sure others who I am forgetting now but will thank in person. I thank them for their encouragement and insights.

Tom Salinsky, my husband, confidant, tech support, trusted reader and ideas tester – what would I do without him? We hope we never find out.

Gina Decio, my rock and right-hand woman who makes my world go round and, crucially, keeps life at bay when I need to write. Without her, no book could emerge.

All others at our lovely company the Spontaneity Shop who work on *The Guilty Feminist* and other projects, creating a warm and wonderful environment of creativity and camaraderie, including Alex, Ned, Rachel and Zeynab.

Victoria Hobbs, my agent at AM Heath, who is calm, insightful and wise. Zoe King, my former agent, who gave me an amazing start.

Olivia Garnham and her ace team at Premier Comms.

Carolyn Soper and the team at Locksmith Animation; Bec Cubitt and the team at Lingo Pictures; Abby Singer, my screenwriting agent, and her team at Casarotto Ramsay & Associates; and Bjorn Wentlandt, my comedy agent, and his team at United Talent Agency – all golden presences in my life who manage to make sure I have time to balance all my projects and make me feel talented and valued.

Special mention to the Snab Christmas gang and the women in my life who constantly root for me and have encouraged me to keep going over the years when I felt discouraged or defeated, including Susie, Yomi, Emma, Sarah, Phoebe, Bisha, Juliet, Kathy, Monica, Brona, Sadie, Grace, Hayley, Georgia, Jemima, Jess, Jen, Hannah, Olivia, the Badass Babes and many more.

Also thank you to my very special Chateau Shenanigans gang who were there at the finish line and inspire me to be more imaginative, collegiate and playful every day. Thank you all for being on my side, even when you can't be by my side.

Thank you to my family too and close friends. There are people here I haven't named who are important to me. I'm so sorry if ADHD has meant your name hasn't appeared. It is no reflection on you or your specialness. My brain thinks terribly well laterally but sometimes is deficient in the linear department.

Index